KITTY CAMPION'S
VEGETARIAN ENCYCLOPAEDIA

By the same author:

Kitty Little's Book of Herbal Beauty
Kitty Campion's Handbook of Herbal Health

KITTY CAMPION'S VEGETARIAN ENCYCLOPAEDIA

All you need to know about fruit, vegetables, grains, nuts and seeds

Kitty Campion

This edition published in 1995 by Leopard Books
Random House, 20 Vauxhall Bridge Road, London SW1V 2SA

First published in Great Britain in 1986

ISBN 0 7529 0013 7

Printed and bound in Great Britain by
Mackays of Chatham

To Metin Peköz in whose innocence, grace and love I shine.

Introduction

This is a book intended to help all those who have ever walked into a health-food or wholefood store full of good intentions only to retreat dazed by all the mysterious items on the shelves and disillusioned by the lack of information as to what to do with them. There was a time when I wouldn't have known what to do with a chick-pea if it had got up and bit me, let alone where it came from, what was in it or how it tasted.

The average vegetarian cookery book assumes you know a great deal to begin with, when you may still be at first base trying to work out how to make a first-class protein out of disparate second-class proteins. Many such books lean too heavily on dairy produce as a meat substitute or let things you know are bad for you – like sugar, salt and alcohol – creep in in large quantities. A few go the other way and are so full of self-denial it makes a bed of nails look positively inviting by comparison.

You may be worrying, as you wean yourself on to a new diet, that you're not getting the right nutrients. Or, overcome with enthusiasm, you may arrive home the proud owner of a sackful of kohlrabi and not know what to do with it, or worse still find a recipe which you follow slavishly only to be turned off by the unexpected taste because the writer forgot to describe it. You may have heard that wholefoods are helpful for certain illnesses but not know which ones. You may be ignorant of the best season to buy certain foods, or of how they should look at their best, or you may simply be curious as to where they were grown or about their historical background.

Kitty Campion's Vegetarian Encyclopaedia addresses itself to all these problems. Each food is introduced by its family, genus and species. Its historical background and any interesting anecdotes are described. If there is more than one type – as there often is – the different types are listed. Tastes, smells and textures are explained, as is the best time at which to buy the food, and any pitfalls attached are clearly outlined. The nutritional content (and calorie content and digestion time) is generally given in a detailed table which is easy to refer to, but the main points are also given in a brief summary in case you haven't got the time to study the tables. Any illnesses helped by a particular food are also listed on the sound Hippocratic principle of letting food be your medicine, and medicine your food. And just to show it doesn't all have to be hard work a reasonably simple recipe is also offered for most of the foods, each with my comment attached.

I was originally trained as a professional chef and spent some of my youth in private houses and hotels in Europe and America happily ladling on gallons of cream, seasoning and alcohol in true old-fashioned haute-cuisine style. My conversion to wholefoods and vegetarianism did not come as a Saul-on-the-road-to-Damascus experience. It began gently enough with my training as a medical herbalist and started to rage, full flood, when I was confronted by a burgeoning number of patients who were digging their own graves with their knives and forks, through sheer ignorance. Many of the illnesses they brought to me, the chronic degenerative conditions I call the 'diseases of civilization' – various cancers, sclerotic illnesses, diabetes, hypoglycemia, allergies and arthritic and rheumatic diseases – were induced by apathy about health care on a general level but especially by poor diet.

So the recipes in my *Vegetarian Encyclopaedia* stem from my own philosophy about preventative medicine. You'll see I use very little salt, no white refined products whatsoever, and very little out of tins, and that I'm not overenthused by dairy products. Alcohol is used with discretion. Sugar and cream are replaced wherever possible by lesser amounts of honey and by yoghurt. Some of my preferences may surprise you. I never use margarine, for example, preferring to use unsalted butter. I won't cook with aluminium foil. The reasons for this and many other personal choices are clearly explained in the first chapter of my last book *Kitty Campion's Book of Herbal Health* (Sphere, 1985), so I won't go into them here. But I don't expect my patients to don sackcloth and ashes and give up everything they have ever enjoyed. So you'll find the odd intriguing or 'naughty' recipe included, and I'd advise you use these for high days and holidays only.

An interesting thing I've discovered is that the more meticulous my diet becomes, and the healthier I grow, the less I long for forbidden fruit. I now find for example that salt added to foods is positively distasteful because my taste-buds have finally woken up to what the true flavours of unadulterated foods should be. There are still foods I love and occasionally indulge in which do me no good at all. I adore cream but it fills me with catarrh and blocks up my sinuses, lowering my resistance to infection. That doesn't stop me eating it but the respect I have for my body ensures I only eat ice-cream two or three times a year. When I do, I love it and don't feel the slightest bit guilty. A digestion disrupted by fear, guilt, worry or hurry will cause far more damage than the odd overindulgence. But I'm sensible enough to decongest my sinuses over the next few days by eating only raw fruit and vegetables.

So to paraphrase Lucan's *Pharsalia*, 'Observe moderation, keep the end in view, follow the laws of nature.' Buy your food wisely, cook simply, cook well. Take some trouble to learn about the nutrients different foods contain so you can protect your own and your family's health. Above all enjoy your new way of eating. If it is interesting and rewarding you'll stay with it, and a long-term commitment to a really good diet can only bring you the most precious commodity of all, superabundant health and vitality.

Note on the tables

The nutritional composition of the foods described in the tables has been compiled from various sources. The chief sources used have been *Composition and Facts about Foods* by Ford Heritage, *The Dictionary of Food and What's in It for You* by Barbara Levine Gelb, and *McCance & Widdowsons 'The Composition of Foods'* by A. A. Paul and D. A. T. Southgate. Where appropriate these have sometimes been used in combination.

Additional values have also been derived from *Laurel's Kitchen* by Laurel Robertson, Carol Flinders and Bronwen Godfrey, *Let's stay Healthy* by Adelle Davis, and *The Natural Food Catalogue* by Vicki Peterson.

A dash indicates that the author has not been able to establish the exact amount of the nutrient; a nought indicates that a zero amount of this nutrient was recorded; and 'tr' means that a trace was recorded.

Note on the recipes

Unless otherwise stated, all recipes are for four people. If there is a specially nice way to present a dish, or it complements another dish, I have mentioned this too.

ACKNOWLEDGEMENTS

I am indebted to Gail Rebuck for commissioning this book, to Isabella Forbes my editor who supported me gently and tactfully through difficult times and to Mary Byrne my copyeditor whose meticulous attention to detail shines through my text.

I would never have got off first base without the enthusiasm of my literary agent, June Hall.

Chris Fulford, Liz Osbourne, Julianne Griffiths and Martin Murphy all tolerated a great deal more than they had to on the domestic and business front to ensure I found time to write.

The relentless questioning of my patients ensures I'm constantly supplying the right answers to support their own enthusiastic commitment to their health care so my special thanks are due to them for keeping me on my toes.

ADZUKI BEAN

Family: *Leguminosae*
Genus: *Phaseolus*
Species: *Phaseolus angularis*

The adzuki (or aduki) bean is a native of Japan and comes from a bushy plant which grows to 30 inches in height. The seeds are oblong shaped and dark red or brown in colour. They are sold mainly in their dried state and need soaking, preferably overnight, before cooking.

See also: Pulses, Sprouted seeds.

Nutritional and medicinal properties

In macrobiotics these beans are used to help kidney complaints. Soak 2 tablespoons of the beans in water overnight. Drain them and boil them in 3½ pints (2 litres) of water until they are soft and at least half the liquid has evaporated. Drain the remaining liquid off and divide it into three equal parts, which should be drunk spaced out through the day.

Adzuki Bean Shepherd's Pie *(serves 4–6)*

I first cooked this for a friend with a very delicate digestion, and it suited him well. It comes from *The Vegan Diet* by David Scott and Claire Golding (Century Hutchinson, 1985). My only variation was that I used ordinary Cheddar cheese instead of vegan cheese.

2 tablespoons vegetable oil
1 large onion, chopped
1 clove garlic, crushed
4 oz (100 g) potatoes, scrubbed and chopped
2 oz (50 g) mushrooms, chopped
8 oz (225 g) tinned tomatoes, drained and chopped
12 oz (325 g) adzuki beans, soaked, cooked until tender and drained
1 tablespoon chopped parsley
1 teaspoon dried mixed herbs
2 tablespoons miso (soya)
sea salt to taste

topping
1½ lb (750 g) mashed potato
2 oz (50 g) cheese
parsley to garnish

Heat the oil in a saucepan and sauté the onion and garlic for 5 minutes. Add the potatoes, cover and cook over a low heat for a further 10 minutes. (Add a little stock or water if needed to stop burning.) Add the mushrooms and cook for 2 minutes.

Then add the tomatoes, beans, parsley and mixed herbs. Bring the mixture to the boil and simmer for 10 minutes. Dissolve the miso in a little of the hot juice and stir in. Add salt only if necessary. Put the mixture into an oven-proof dish, cover with a topping of mashed potato, and sprinkle the grated cheese and parsley on top. Bake for 35 minutes in an oven preheated to 400°F (200°C, gas mark 6).

ALMOND

Family: *Rosaceae*
Genus: *Prunus*
Species: *Prunus amygdalus*

These are the seeds of a tree closely related to the peach – in fact the fruits look rather like small green peaches. The tree is a native of the eastern Mediterranean and has been cultivated in southern Europe and the Middle East for many centuries. Today it grows in almost all warm climates. Spain and Italy are particularly large producers.

The fruit of the almond surrounding the nut is tough, fibrous and edible when it's ripe, but when it is still young and the stone is soft it has a pleasantly sour taste and is often eaten as a local delicacy.

There are two basic varieties of almond. **Sweet almonds** have an inimitable, delicate flavour. It is this type which is usually used in cooking. If using sweet almonds it is always far safer to grind one's own in a nut mill because ground almonds are often adulterated with cheap nut flour and occasionally spiked with a dash of bitter almond. And bear in mind that bitter almond will always spoil the taste of any dish in which only sweet almonds are intended. In order to take the skin off almonds, simply immerse them in boiling water for a few seconds, drain them, then squeeze them between thumb and forefinger. This way the nut will pop out of its skin effortlessly.

There is little similarity between **bitter almonds** and sweet almonds. The powerful taste of the bitter almond is similar to that of the kernels of plums, peaches, cherries and other related fruits. The particular flavour of bitter almonds is due to substances formed when the nut is mixed with water. It is then that an enzyme promotes a reaction between the water and the glucoside which kernels or leaves contain, and two new substances are formed – neither of which are present in the living plant. These are benzaldehyde (oil of bitter almonds) and hydrocyanic acid (prussic acid at a strength of about 2 per cent). Both taste of bitter almonds but hydrocyanic acid is a deadly poison. Happily it is very volatile and evaporates into the air when heated.

See also: Nuts.

Nutritional and medicinal properties

Almonds are extremely nourishing and have long been valued as a good muscle- and body-building substance. They are high in fat, carbohydrate and protein and their calcium content is particularly valuable for building children's teeth and bones. Almond meal contains almost twice the vitamin B content of the same weight of roasted almonds.

Salted almonds

The home-made version beats the shop-bought one hands down. Our 'pishi' (African chef) used to serve these with cocktails, and very more-ish they were too. Being barely ten, I had to content myself with Gymkhana Lime and Lemonade, but they even went well with that.

Blanch and skin as many large almonds as you'll need, depending on the number of people. Sprinkle 1 teaspoon sweet almond oil over each 8 oz (225 g) prepared almonds, and bake at 225°F (110°C, gas mark ¼) for 45 minutes until they turn pale gold. Have a large piece of greaseproof paper ready scattered with 1 tablespoon coarse rock-salt for every 8 oz (225 g) almonds, and turn the almonds out on to this. Mix them well, and leave for a few hours.

Before serving, shake off any excess salt and sprinkle just a little cayenne pepper over the nuts.

ANGELICA

Family: *Umbelliferae*
Genus: *Angelica*
Species: *Angelica archangelica*

This is considered a biennial but will continue to live for several years if the stems are clipped off before they come to blossom. The plant belongs to the same family as fennel and parsley, growing up to 6 feet high with green-yellow, white or purple flowers in umbrella-shaped bunches. It has large leaves which are indented and divided into three sections and the stem is round, hollow and branches near the top where it is tinged with blue. The roots are red-brown and have a spicy, agreeable odour and taste which is sweet at first and then becomes a little bitter and sharp. The plant is grown mainly for its seeds, and likes a shady position with quite rich, damp soil.

It is a native of either northern Europe, around the Baltic, or Syria. It is now naturalized to Europe and the United States and grows wild in the Alps, the Pyrenees and northern Europe. It is abundant in the Faroe Islands and Iceland where the whole plant above the ground is cooked and eaten as a vegetable. In Britain, the plant is not recorded earlier than the sixteenth century. Today, it is grown commercially mainly in Germany and Europe.

Angelica is connected with angels in almost every European language but nobody seems to know exactly why. It is said to have been blessed by the Archangel Michael. This story may have arisen because it blossomed near or on his day (8 May) in many parts of the world. By the fifteenth century, it had acquired a reputation as a plant which gave protection against evil and the plague and its Christianized name hints at its deep association with early Nordic magic.

Wild angelica grows in Britain and continental Europe in damp woods, flowering between July and

August. It does not have such a strong flavour as **garden angelica**. In America the wild species (*Angelica atropurpurea*) is sometimes called Alexander. **Japanese angelica** is another very strongly flavoured species.

The taste of angelica tends to be strong and penetrating – some would describe it as musky – and varies considerably depending on the climate. Angelica needs to be dried well and used with discretion as the flavour is so singular.

The whole plant is useful. The oil from the seeds and roots is used medicinally as well as in liqueurs, wine and perfumery. (Chartreuse and Bénédictine are two of the more well-known examples of liqueurs). The leaves will flavour stewed fruit especially rhubarb and make a brilliant and unusual addition to orange marmalade (see the recipe). The leaves, seeds and sometimes root make a good, quite pleasant tasting tea with a slightly celery taste. The leaf tea needs to have honey and lemon added in my opinion. Candied angelica made from the stems is well known and is used as a garnish on cakes. The stems make an interesting addition to marrow preserve, apricot pudding and some ice-creams.

Nutritional and medicinal properties

Angelica contains a volatile oil and derivatives of coumarin, which helps to stimulate gastric secretions, controls peristalsis and increases appetite. It also contains bitter principles, sugar, valeric and angelic acids and a resin called angelicin.

Angelica is used to improve the circulation and warm the body. It is one of the best herbs to use against the cold in winter, particularly during convalescence when the coldness one feels is subjective. Because of its warming properties, it will relieve spasms of the stomach and intestines and dispel gas. It is said that its prolonged and regular use will create a distaste for alcoholic drinks. However, it is a strong emmenagogue and should not be used by pregnant women. Neither should it be used by diabetics as it tends to increase the level of sugar in the blood. It can be used externally as a poultice for rheumatism. It is of great benefit in the treatment of colds, coughs, pleurisy and all lung diseases. It improves the mucous membrane of the bronchial tubes and tones up the heart muscle. The fresh leaves were used to heal wounds in the old days and athletes used to bathe in decoctions of the root to ease over-strained muscles.

However, be aware that angelica can irritate the skin, and should not come into contact with the eyes. If using the seeds, use only freshly harvested ones, since they lose their vitality very quickly. Medicinally, prepare a decoction of the root, using 1 oz (2.5 g) to 1 pint (600 ml) water and take 3 tablespoons three times a day.

Angelica orange marmalade

This will make three large jars of a most unusual, slightly tart marmalade. I give it away as Christmas presents, and have a lot of fun listening to the recipients trying to guess why it tastes subtly different from ordinary marmalade.

*1 lb (500 g) sweet oranges
    (generally 3)*
2 lemons
*3 oz (75 g) angelica stems and a
    few leaves*
1½ pints (900 ml) water
1½ lb (750 g) fruit sugar

Wash the fruit and angelica. Squeeze the juice from the fruit, take out the pips, and mince the shells remaining. Then put the minced skins back in a bowl with the juice and the water. Slice the angelica finely and crush the leaves, tying them all up in a muslin bag. Put this with the fruit. Cover and leave to macerate for 24 hours.

The next day boil the mixture for a little less than 2 hours, until the peel is soft. Fish out the angelica bag and give it a good squeeze over the mixture before removing. Add the sugar and stir continuously until the marmalade boils. Keep it boiling and test for setting. (When a little sets in a cold saucer, is is ready.)

Leave it to cool, stirring occasionally to distribute the peel evenly, then pour into clear, sterilized glass jars. Cover the jars with greaseproof paper when the marmalade is completely cold.

APPLE

Family: *Rosaceae*
Genus: *Malus*
Species: *Malus pumila*

Apples are the most widely grown of all tree-borne fruits, available everywhere except the hottest and coolest parts of the world. They are one of the oldest fruits known to man although there is some dispute as to whether it was the apple or banana that tempted Eve in the Garden of Eden. Golden apples were the cause of disputes between the gods and you will recall the Greek legend about the golden apple which led to the downfall of Troy. The Romans brought apples to many parts of Europe, including Britain, and apples have been cultivated in the temperate regions of the world for over 3000 years. In the past they were particularly valued for their property of long storage. Often they were the only fruit available during the long dark winter months. John Endicott was said to have brought the first trees to America in 1628 and they gradually spread westwards, distributed by Indians, trappers and such legendary figures as Jonathan Chapman and Johnnie Appleseed. Indeed we are now familiar with the phrase 'as American as apple pie'. New varieties of apple have been returned to Britain from the United States.

During the nineteenth century, professional apple-growers hybridized many new varieties of apple, including the most famous English dessert apple, the Cox's Orange Pippin, which was first produced, from the Ribstone variety, around 1850 by Mr Cox, a retired brewer. There are now over 7000 varieties of apple in the world and generally they fall into three categories – dessert, cooking and cider. They range in skin colour from red to golden and in taste from tart to sweet. Apple-trees flourish in temperate regions all over the world. The main producers are Britain, France, the United States, Canada, Australia, New Zealand and South Africa. In the northern hemisphere the season lasts from August to March, and in the southern from March to September. Thanks to new storage techniques, **Bramleys** in England which are picked in September, are now available as late as July. Other cooking varieties include **Grenadier, Lord Derby, Newton Wonder** and **Early Victory** – mostly natives to Britain. Dessert varieties include **Cox's Orange Pippin, Russet, Laxton's Superb, James Grieve, Ellaston's Orange, Golden Delicious, Granny Smith, Dunn's Seedling, Red Delicious** and **Jonathan's.**

Nutritional and medicinal properties

Apples contain vitamins, easily assimilable sugars, and enzymes that are indispensable for the digestion. They also contain essential acids, such as malic acid, and minerals like potassium, sodium, calcium, magnesium and phosphorus. The skin is richest in these but modern pesticides and insecticides sometimes contaminate apples, so they should be meticulously washed.

Traditionally, the apple is thought to be very healthy, hence the old adage 'An apple a day keeps the doctor away.' However, they actually have a relatively low vitamin C content and food value. The processing of apples further reduces their nutritional value. An apple loses half its vitamin C content when peeled, and frozen apples lose most of their vitamin A and potassium. Since apples are 84 per cent water and most of their goodness is found in their fruit sugar, dried apples naturally have a higher food value (weight for weight) than fresh apples.

Apples are said to stimulate body secretion and can be taken as a health tonic medicine and bowel regulator. The malic and tartaric acid in them prevents disturbances of the liver and actively aids digestion. Unsweetened apple cider is said to prevent the formation of kidney stones. The low acidity of apples stimulates saliva flow and removes debris from the teeth. However, cheese is probably better for this purpose because it is not so acid. Eating several apples daily is believed to help arthritis, and lung and asthma complaints, and there was a time when apples were said to prevent emotional upsets and tension headaches. The pectin in apple peel certainly helps to remove noxious substances from the body by supplying galacturonic acid. The pectin helps to prevent protein matter in the intestines from spoiling.

Apples are recommended for obesity, poor complexions, bladder inflammations, gonorrhoea, anaemia, TB, neuritis, insomnia, catarrh, worms and halitosis, and chewing unpeeled apples will strengthen bleeding gums.

Apple tea, which comes in easy-to-use powdered form, is said to cleanse the urinary tract and prevent diseases of the reproductive system. It is made from the peel, which is dried in ovens.

Processed apples and apple products have far less vitamin C and A than raw apples. Un-

100 g APPLE

	With peel	Peeled	Dried	Juice
Calories	56	53	275	47
Protein (g)	0.2	0.2	1	0.1
Carbohydrate (g)	14.1	13.9	71.8	11.9
Cholesterol (g)	0	–	–	–
Fat (g)	0.6	0.3	1.6	tr
Fibre (g)	1	0.6	3.1	0.1
Minerals				
calcium (mg)	7	6	31	6
phosphorus (mg)	10	10	52	9
iron (mg)	0.3	0.3	1.6	0.6
sodium (mg)	1	1	5	1
potassium (mg)	110	110	569	101
magnesium (mg)	8	5	22	4
zinc (mg)	0.1	–	–	–
iodine (mg)	0.009	–	–	–
chlorine (mg)	–	–	–	–
sulphur (mg)	201	–	–	–
silicon (mg)	142	–	–	–
bromine (mg)	0.15	–	–	–
Vitamins				
A(IU)	90	40	–	–
B_1 (mg)	0.03	0.03	0.06	0.01
B_2 (mg)	0.02	0.02	0.12	0.02
B_3 (mg)	0.1	0.1	0.5	0.1
B_5 (mg)	0.10	–	–	–
B_6 (mg)	0.03	–	–	–
B_{12} (mcg)	0	–	–	–
folic acid (mcg)	0.5	–	–	–
biotin (mcg)	0.3	–	–	–
C (mg)	7	4	10	1
D (mg)	0	–	–	–
E (mg)	0.7	–	–	–
Organic acids				
citric (%)	tr	–	–	–
malic (%)	0.71	–	–	–
oxalic (%)	0	–	–	–
Water (%)	84.8	85.3	24	87.8
Digestion time (hrs)	2¾	–	–	–

sweetened apple sauce and artificially sweetened apple sauce have fewer calories than apples of equivalent weight and less of the vitamins and minerals. Apple butter, not surprisingly, has three times the number of calories, as well as more carbohydrate and phosphorus and twice the calcium, iron, sodium and potassium, of its fresh cousin, but it has no vitamin A.

Rahkomenakakku
(Finnish apple cake)

This recipe was passed on to me by Susan Uttley who, like me, believes in healthy eating, so she has modified it appropriately.

3½ oz (90 g) unsalted butter
2½ oz (65 g) demerara sugar
1 egg, lightly beaten
½ cup wholemeal
    flour   ⎫ sieved
1 teaspoon baking ⎬ together
    powder   ⎭
2 cooking apples (or enough to cover base completely)

topping
5 oz (150 g) white low-fat soft
    cheese
1 egg
3½–4 oz (90–100 g) Greek
    yoghurt, stabilized with a little
    cornflour
1 oz (25 g) sugar (use vanilla
    sugar or add a little vanilla
    essence)

To make the base, cream the butter and sugar together. Gradually add the egg, then the flour and baking powder. Spread the mixture over an oiled baking dish 10 × 8 in (25 × 20 cm). Then slice the apples thinly and layer them over the base, overlapping the slices, so that they entirely cover it. To make the topping, mix the ingredients together in the order shown and pour the mixture over the apple layer, taking care to coat the fruit (though it isn't necessary for it to be 'submerged'). Bake at 370°F (190°C, gas mark 5) for approximately 45 minutes. Serve hot or cold (when cold, it firms up and can be cut into squares).

This cake keeps in the fridge for 2–3 days. It freezes well – to thaw quickly, heat in a slow oven and serve hot. It can be made with other fruit such as bilberries or rhubarb, but apple tastes best.

ASPARAGUS

Family: *Liliaceae*
Genus: *Asparagus*
Species: *Asparagus officinalis*

The asparagus comes from the lily family which includes 150 species. Edible asparagus was first grown around the eastern Mediterranean and was prized by the ancient Egyptians, Greeks and Romans as a food and medicine. It became an official medicinal herb due to its laxative and diuretic properties, and some herbalists claim even today that it increases the libido, although in the old days it was recommended for a range of ailments as varied as bee stings, heart trouble and toothache. It came to northern Europe in the sixteenth century and was especially prized in Britain, France, Italy and eventually America. Known as sperage, or sparrowgrass, in the sixteenth century, it was grown on a small scale by the Elizabethans and Samuel Pepys was said to have loved asparagus. In his day, as today, it was usually served with butter or a form of hollandaise sauce. In parts of Eastern Europe, asparagus grows wild and is eaten by cattle.

There are three types of asparagus which are marketed according to their colour. **Green spears**, the most popular variety in Britain, is allowed to grow to its full height above ground. It has an aromatic flavour. There is also a green variety with a white base. The **blanched white variety** is used for canning, and is often considered the best and most tender variety, with a mild flavour and creamy white stem. **French asparagus** is violet or bluish and is stronger, with a far more astringent positive flavour.

Fresh white asparagus is available from mid-May until the end of June, while French asparagus is available over a longer period of the summer. Italy and France export asparagus all the year round. The English season runs from early May to the end of June.

When you choose asparagus, check that the tips are closed because open tips show ageing asparagus. The stems should be firm and juicy. Avoid cracked or woody stems. Best-quality asparagus is graded to be uniform in length and thickness with a firm white tip. Choose this for only very special dishes. Spears with closed tips and white stalks are suitable for vegetable dishes and sauces. **Thin asparagus ('sprue')** is adequate for mixed vegetable dishes where the appearance is not so important and for soups.

Nutritional and medicinal properties

Boiled, drained asparagus offers good amounts of protein, fat and vitamins A, B_2, C and E. Minerals include calcium, copper, magnesium, iron, phosphorus, sulphur and traces of sodium. Canned asparagus is very salty although diet canned asparagus has very little salt. Otherwise it has the same food value as cooked fresh asparagus except that it has less vitamin B_6. Frozen asparagus has the same nutritional value as fresh cooked, except that it has slightly less vitamin A and less B_6 than fresh cooked asparagus.

Asparagus is an excellent diuretic and I often put patients who enjoy it on bladder cleanses at the beginning of the summer. The urine they produce as the result of a fast on asparagus smells like motor oil, and looks about the same colour, but it is a wonderful kidney cleanser. Asparagus is also a good diaphoretic, and a laxative (due to its high fibre content). It is said to calm people under stress and it contains an amino-acid essential for the growth, division and regeneration of the body's cells. The juice of asparagus helps to break up oxalic acid and crystals in the kidneys and throughout the muscular system, so relieving rheumatism, uritis and arthritis.

100 g ASPARAGUS (boiled)	
Calories	26
Protein (g)	2.5
Carbohydrate (g)	5
Cholesterol (g)	0
Fat (g)	0.2
Fibre (g)	0.7
Minerals	
calcium (mg)	22
phosphorus (mg)	62
iron (mg)	1
sodium (mg)	2
potassium (mg)	278
magnesium (mg)	20
zinc (mg)	0.3
iodine (mg)	0.03
chlorine (mg)	510
sulphur (mg)	536
silicon (mg)	950
bromine (mg)	2.02
Vitamins	
A(IU)	900
B_1 (mg)	0.18
B_2 (mg)	0.2
B_3 (mg)	1.5
B_5 (mg)	0.13
B_6 (mg)	0.04
B_{12} (mcg)	0
folic acid (mcg)	30
biotin (mcg)	0.4
C (mg)	26
D (mg)	0
E (mg)	2.5
Organic acids	
citric (%)	0.11
malic (%)	0.1
oxalic (%)	0.0052
Water (%)	91.7
Digestion time (hrs)	2¼

Asparagus salad

Don't suffocate asparagus with elaborate sauces. It's an outstanding vegetable which shines in its own right and needs only a modicum of help.

1½lb (750 g) asparagus
1 cup Greek yoghurt
1 tablespoon grainy mustard
2 tablespoons finely chopped chives
1 tablespoon finely chopped fennel
½ tablespoon finely chopped tarragon
freshly ground black pepper

Cook and cool the asparagus, dipping the spears in cold water as soon as they are out of the saucepan. Combine the remaining ingredients. Place the asparagus in long ranks down a shallow dish and pour the dressing down the middle. Chill. Garnish with watercress and miniature pink radishes.

AUBERGINE

Family: *Solanaceae*
Genus: *Solanum*
Species: *Solanum melongena*

Although one generally tends to think of the aubergine as a Mediterranean plant, in fact it originated in northern India, then spread to China where it grew 12,000 years ago. Originally it was the size and shape of an egg (hence the name egg-plant). It spread to Europe and South America, but was not widely known until the seventeenth century and it did not become really popular until after World War II, when we suddenly became interested in Mediterranean cookery. Unhappily it is virtually impossible to grow in Britain as it demands so much sunshine, although it now grows extensively all round the shores of the Mediterranean, from Spain through southern France, Italy, Greece, Turkey and into the countries of the Middle East, as well as along the northern coast of Africa.

The egg-plant produces a firm, elongated fruit, purple in colour and varying in shape from round to oval and tear-shaped forms. There is also a white variety which looks like the egg of some gigantic bird, with a translucent glow, but this is more often used for decorative purposes than for cooking. The inner flesh of the aubergine is white, with tiny soft seeds, and it is this part which is eaten as a vegetable. There is a small hard calyx at the stalk end.

Aubergine does not have a pronounced flavour and requires lemon juice, herbs and seasoning in order to bring out its delicate taste. It marries particularly well with tomatoes, courgettes and sweet peppers.

As aubergines are generally imported they are almost always available. To prepare an aubergine, simply remove the stalk with a sharp knife, and wash the shiny skin or wipe it with a damp cloth. Depending on how it is to be cooked, it should then be cut in half or in quarters, or sliced or chopped, and usually the peel is left on. The inside of the vegetable is then sprinkled with salt and left to drain in a colander for about half an hour which gets rid of the slightly bitter

taste it sometimes has. If possible, choose fairly young aubergines before the seeds have had time to form. Before cooking, rinse off the salt thoroughly and pat dry in a soft cloth or with a paper kitchen towel.

Aubergines can be cooked whole, baked in the oven like potatoes, in which case they will take about 45 minutes in a moderate heat and can be tested with a skewer. This method is only usually used when the inner pulp is wanted for a purée, as with Middle Eastern hors d'oeuvres. They can be boiled, or cooked under the grill, but in most cases they are cut in slices unpeeled and fried in oil in a frying pan. Do this one layer at a time in batches as they consume huge quantities of oil. After cooking, drain them well on soft paper and keep in a warm place until needed.

Nutritional and medicinal properties

Aubergines are valuable for their vitamin B content, particularly B_1, B_2 and B_3, and for vitamin C, and they contain a little iron, calcium and carbohydrate. They are low in calories, but remember that they absorb enormous quantities of fat. They are helpful for constipation, colitis, stomach ulcers and nervous conditions.

Imam bayildi *(serves 6)*

This is a Turkish speciality and literally translated means 'the imam fainted'. Widely conflicting stories are told about the origins of its name. From one quarter we have

100 g AUBERGINE (raw)	
Calories	25
Protein (g)	1.2
Carbohydrate (g)	5.6
Cholesterol (g)	–
Fat (g)	0.2
Fibre (g)	0.9
Minerals	
calcium (mg)	12
phosphorus (mg)	26
iron (mg)	0.7
sodium (mg)	2
potassium (mg)	214
magnesium (mg)	16
zinc (mg)	–
iodine (mg)	0.017
chlorine (mg)	670
sulphur (mg)	445
silicon (mg)	–
bromine (mg)	–
Vitamins	
A(IU)	10
B_1 (mg)	0.05
B_2 (mg)	0.05
B_3 (mg)	0.6
B_5 (mg)	0.22
B_6 (mg)	0.08
B_{12} (mcg)	0
folic acid (mcg)	20
biotin (mcg)	–
C (mg)	5
D (mg)	–
E (mg)	–
Organic acids	
citric (%)	0
malic (%)	0.17
oxalic (%)	0.0069
Water (%)	92.4
Digestion time (hrs)	3½

greedy man fainted from over eating.

Whatever the truth it is a dish worth fainting for. My husband used to cook it expertly for me to welcome me home after a long day's work but sadly as he now works even harder than I do we seldom eat it these days.

3 large aubergines
a little salt
freshly ground black pepper
¾ pint (400 ml) olive oil
3 large onions
12 oz (325 g) tomatoes
2 cloves garlic
½ teaspoon ground cinnamon
½ teaspoon allspice
1 heaped tablespoon chopped
    parsley
1 heaped tablespoon finely
    chopped pine kernels

Cut the leaf bases from the aubergines, wipe them and put them in a large saucepan. Add enough boiling water to cover them, secure with a lid and boil for 10 minutes. Drain them and plunge them into warm water. Leave for 5 minutes. Then cut the aubergines in half lengthways and scoop out most of the flesh with a sharp-tipped spoon, leaving a ½ in (1 cm) shell. Set aside the scooped-out flesh. Arrange the shells in a buttered ovenproof dish and sprinkle with a little salt and freshly ground pepper. Pour 4 tablespoons olive oil into each shell and cook in the centre of a preheated oven at 350°F (180°C, gas mark 4) for 30 minutes.

While the shells cook, peel and finely chop the onions, skin and chop the tomatoes, peel and

the contention that the dish acquired its name when an imam (Muslim priest) fainted with pleasure on being served these aubergines by his wife; from another that the imam fainted when he heard how expensive the ingredients were (although the only really expensive ingredient is the olive oil); from yet another that the roughly chop the garlic. Heat 2 tablespoons oil in a pan and fry the onions and garlic slowly for 5 minutes. Then add the tomatoes, spices and parsley and black pepper to taste. Simmer this mélange gently until the liquid has been reduced by half – about 20 minutes. Chop the reserved aubergine flesh and add it to the frying pan with the pine kernels and cook for a further 10 minutes.

Remove the aubergine shells from the oven, fill them with the tomato mixture and serve hot or cold, garnishing with more chopped parsley. Sometimes I used to have a little grilled cheese on the top – an inexcusable offence in a purist's eye, but enjoyable.

AVOCADO

Family: *Lauraceae*
Genus: *Persea*
Species: *Persea americana*

Avocado is strictly the fruit of a tree belonging to the laurel family and not a vegetable. It is native to Central and South America and was originally cultivated by the ancient Aztecs and later by the Incas. Martin Fernandez de Encisco described it in 1519 after an expedition to Colombia, and it began to receive serious attention in 1900 when George Cellon and other Florida horticulturalists established orchards. From Florida it spread to California, South Africa, Australia and the Mediterranean, especially Israel; the latest recruit to the ranks of new

growers is Turkey where plantations should be on-stream in a few years time.

Several hundred varieties of avocado are now known although horticulturally they fall into three categories: Mexican, West Indian and Guatemalan. The appearance of the skin ranges from a thick glossy green to a very wrinkled black or purple. The flesh when ripe has a delicate nutty flavour and the texture of soft butter, and is a beautiful gentle green colour. To stop it discolouring remove the stone and rub the flesh with lemon juice.

Choose your avocado with care, holding the fruit gently and applying only the lightest pressure to determine the degree of ripeness. It should be slightly soft at the end and generally firm just bordering on soft, and should be without bruises or black marks. Avocados can be bought unripe and ripened on a sunny window-sill. The stone can be grown into a pretty plant: fill a bottle with water and place four toothpicks across its mouth so that they form a cradle for the stone, the base of which should be just in the water; once the stone has germinated and the root grown down some inches into the water, transfer to a pot.

Nutritional and medicinal properties

Avocados are always eaten raw and are best combined with a sharp taste as a good foil for their creamy blandness. The nutritional value varies according to their geographic origin but they are extremely rich in protein, vitamins A and B, potassium, and folic acid, and have some vitamin C. They contain a rare digestible oil which is not found in other fruits. The high fat and calorific content of avocado make it unsuitable for people trying to slim.

Avocados are, on the other hand, excellent for the malnourished, and I often recommend them to patients who have stomach ulcers or ulcerative colitis. Their richness make them good for male impotency, constipation, insomnia and nervousness.

100 g AVOCADO (Californian)

Calories	171
Protein (g)	2.2
Carbohydrate (g)	6
Cholesterol (g)	0
Fat (g)	17
Fibre (g)	1.5
Minerals	
calcium (mg)	10
phosphorus (mg)	42
iron (mg)	0.6
sodium (mg)	4
potassium (mg)	604
magnesium (mg)	45
zinc (mg)	–
iodine (mg)	–
chlorine (mg)	645
sulphur (mg)	505
silicon (mg)	22
bromine (mg)	–
Vitamins	
A(IU)	290
B_1 (mg)	0.11
B_2 (mg)	0.2
B_3 (mg)	1.6
B_5 (mg)	1.07
B_6 (mg)	0.42
B_{12} (mcg)	0
folic acid (mcg)	56.7
biotin (mcg)	3.2
C (mg)	14
D (mg)	0
E (mg)	1.2
Organic acids	
citric (%)	0
malic (%)	0
oxalic (%)	0
Water (%)	73.6
Digestion time (hrs)	1¾

Avocado delight
(serves 6)

Kelly Holden gave me this recipe when I was visiting her to give her a cold-sheet treatment. She didn't actually pass it on at the time because part of the treatment involves lying tightly wrapped up in a cotton sheet which has been dipped in ice-cubes. But before she bravely subjected herself to this she'd taken the trouble to prepare me an avocado lunch and the result was delicious – a lovely contrast of crunchy and smooth.

3 oz (75 g) cashew nuts, roasted and cooled
8 oz (225 g) curd cheese (or cottage cheese – but it's not so nice!)
1 large clove garlic, crushed
sea salt and freshly ground black pepper
2 ripe avocados
juice of ½ lemon
2 tablespoons chopped fresh chives
a few crisp lettuce leaves, shredded

dressing
½ teaspoon tomato purée
½ teaspoon brown sugar or honey (more if sweeter taste preferred)
¼ teaspoon paprika

2 tablespoons cider vinegar
6 tablespoons olive oil
sea salt and freshly ground black
*   pepper*

Grate the cashew nuts (preferably in the grinder attachment of a liquidizer or in a food processor), and add the curd cheese, garlic and a little salt and pepper. Mix well and form into about 24 small balls (the size of hazelnuts). Cool in the fridge to firm slightly. Make the dressing by mixing together the tomato purée, sugar, paprika and vinegar. Gradually add the oil, and season with salt and pepper. Just before serving, peel the avocados, remove their stones and cut the flesh into 1 in (2.5 cm) cubes. Put it in a bowl with the lemon juice, chives and lettuce. Add the curd cheese and cashew balls. Mix everything well. Pour the dressing over the mixture and serve plain, or with melba toast.

BANANA

Family: *Musaceae*
Genus: *Musa*
Species: *Musa sapientum*; *Musa paradisiaca* (plantain)

There are over 30 different species and 300 varieties of banana, differing greatly in size and colour. They enjoy hot, damp tropical climates. They originated from south-east Asia but soon spread to the western coast of Africa. They were brought to the Americas via the Canary Islands, and the United States developed a commercial market for them in the nineteenth century.

Today bananas are one of the world's most important fruits, valued for their flavour, excellent nutritional value and year-round availability. The chief sources of commercially produced bananas are still in Central America, but the finest flavoured ones come from south-east Asia.

The sages of ancient India used to sit in the shade of the banana tree, hence the botanical name *Musa sapientum* (*sapientia* is Latin for wisdom). Pliny, the Roman historian, records that the Greeks accompanying Alexander on an expedition to India enjoyed bananas. The banana was said to be the fruit the serpent used to tempt Eve in the Garden of Eden – not the mythical apple – hence the botanical name of the plantain, *Musa paradisiaca*. Hindu legend confirms this by calling it the forbidden fruit, and suggests that Adam and Eve covered themselves with the leaves of the tree after losing their innocence.

In the UK we are familiar with two types, the **Jamaican banana**, which is long and fairly large with a mild flavour, and the **Canary banana**, which is smaller with a more pronounced sweeter flavour. Other varieties of banana include the **Green dwarf banana** (*Musa cavendishii*) and the large **plantain banana**, eaten unripe but cooked in its own skin in the West Indies.

Bananas are imported while green and ripened in a special warehouse. They are still unripe if green at the tip and should be kept at room temperature until they turn yellow or yellow with brown spots. Keep them away from draughts and treat them with care as they bruise easily.

Nutritional and medicinal properties

Bananas are high in carbohydrate, potassium, folic acid and vitamin C. They contain a large amount of starch which changes to sugar as they ripen and unripe bananas are starchy and potato-like, and consequently indigestible. Contrary to popular myth, bananas are not particularly fattening. An average banana contains 85–90 calories, which makes it lower in calories than a good-sized serving of cottage cheese, besides which the banana is not only easily digestible but helps the body to store protein. A banana a day will give you one fifth of the recommended daily intake of vitamin C and the amount of B_6 in bananas is comparable to that in the equivalent weight of liver.

Bananas are used naturopathically as a dietary method of controlling allergic-type reactions. Their protein content is of such a benign nature that allergy sufferers adding a banana to their diet find it reduces the distressing symptoms of runny nose and puffy eyes. Calcium, phosphorus and iron are richly present in bananas. Indeed there is even more iron in them than there is in apple. Under the skin of unripe bananas, there is an antibiotic-type substance, hence the custom of cooking them in their skins in the West Indies and the Pacific islands. Like apples, bananas contain pectin, which helps to digest other foods, and they are very useful for normalizing bowel function in patients with either chronic constipation or chronic diarrhoea. Banana actually helps to increase the quantity of bacteria in the intestine, particularly if it is mixed with plain yoghurt.

Bananas are recommended for colitis, intestinal ulcers and coeliac disease. They are also excellent for oedema because kidneys that are under-functioning, sluggish or slow as a residual symptom of disease can be helped to function better as a result of the fruit's high potassium content. Bananas are extremely nutritious when mashed and given ripe to babies, and have the added

100 g BANANA

	Fresh	Dried
Calories	85	340
Protein (g)	1.1	4.4
Carbohydrate (g)	22.2	88.6
Cholesterol (g)	0	–
Fat (g)	0.2	0.8
Fibre (g)	0.5	2
Minerals		
calcium (mg)	8	32
phosphorus (mg)	26	104
iron (mg)	0.7	2.8
sodium (mg)	1	4
potassium (mg)	370	1477
magnesium (mg)	33	132
zinc (mg)	0.2	–
iodine (mg)	0.012	–
chlorine (mg)	270	–
sulphur (mg)	120	–
silicon (mg)	–	–
bromine (mg)	0.54	–
Vitamins		
A(IU)	190	760
B_1 (mg)	0.05	0.18
B_2 (mg)	0.06	0.24
B_3 (mg)	0.7	2.8
B_5 (mg)	0.26	–
B_6 (mg)	0.5	–
B_{12} (mcg)	0	–
folic acid (mcg)	10.9	–
biotin (mcg)	–	–
C (mg)	10	7
D (mg)	0	–
E (mg)	0.4	–
Organic acids		
citric (%)	0.23	–
malic (%)	0.37	–
oxalic (%)	0.0064	–
Water (%)	75.7	3
Digestion time (hrs)	3	–

advantage of coming in a nice germ-proof, dirt-proof skin. One pound of banana flour, made from the dried unripe fruit, is as nutritious as double the amount of wheat flour. Dried bananas have four times the nutritional value but less vitamin C than fresh bananas.

Banana breakfast whip
(serves 2)

This recipe is from the Gislingham Natural Therapeutic Centre in Suffolk where I teach student herbalists from time to time. Many of them arrive as ardent carnivores in great trepidation at the thought of a strict vegan weekend. This breakfast always dispels their fears.

12 almonds or hazelnuts
1 large ripe banana, sliced
1 teaspoon soy milk powder
1 teaspoon honey
1 tablespoon oats
orange juice
pinch of crushed cardamon seeds
*   or ground cloves*
pinch of freshly ground black
*   pepper*

Grind the nuts in the grinder attachment of a liquidizer. Add the rest of the ingredients, adjusting the orange juice to give a smooth creamy consistency. Serve alone or with muesli (see page 150).

BARLEY

Family: *Gramineae*
Genus: *Hordeum*
Species: *Hordeum vulgare*

Barley was widely used by the Greeks, Romans and Hebrews, and was used as currency as long ago as 4000 BC. Grains 5000 years old were found at Al Fayyum in Egypt. Its popularity in Europe as a vital bread cereal waned during the Middle Ages, when it was superseded by wheat and rye. Today a quarter of the total crop grown in Britain is used for brewing beer, whisky and vinegar. The grains are sprouted as part of the malting process, which increases the vitamin and enzyme content.

The plant looks like wheat and the single grains usually grow in three rows on each side of the spike of the top of the plant stem, making it so-called six-row barley. There is a rarer two-rowed barley, *Hordeum distichum*, much favoured in Britain, as well as an irregular form.

Wholegrain brown barley (or Scotch or pot barley), where only the outer husk is removed, makes a chewier grain which takes some time to cook (1 cup in 3 to 4 cups of water will usually take 1½ hours at a slow simmer). However, it is nutritionally superior, and is used in casseroles and soups like Scotch broth, as a stuffing for haggis and as an accompaniment for beans and nuts.

Pearl barley is steamed, rounded and highly polished so that the two outer layers are removed, often with the endosperm, making it nutritionally inferior and particularly low in B vitamins. By this stage it has lost 85 per cent of the fat, 97 per cent of the fibre and 88 per cent of the mineral constituents of the original barley. It is added to soup and stews.

Barley flakes are flattened barley grains used in porridge, gruel and vegetarian paté. They taste deliciously light and nutty and are easy to work with.

See also: Flour, Grains.

Nutritional and medicinal properties

Wholegrain barley is rich in protein and has substantial amounts of calcium, iron, potassium and phosphorus. The same amount of pearl barley contains only about two-thirds of the protein and mineral content and half the amount of B vitamins.

Barley is nutritious and easily digested and encourages healthy hair and nail growth. It will also soothe stomach ulcers.

Barley water

This is a wonderful tonic for convalescents, invalids and lactating mothers. It supports the kidneys and cleans out gravel, relieves diarrhoea, improves nail condition and is useful in fevers. It is believed to help asthma because of the hordenine it contains, which is an anti-spasmodic. When animals are sick, barley water can beneficially be substituted for their usual drinking water.

100 g BARLEY	Wholegrain (pot or Scotch) (raw)	Pearl (raw)
Calories	348	360
Protein (g)	9.6	7.9
Carbohydrate (g)	77.6	83.6
Cholesterol (g)	–	–
Fat (g)	1.1	1.7
Fibre (g)	0.9	6.5
Minerals		
calcium (mg)	34	10
phosphorus (mg)	296	210
iron (mg)	2.7	0.7
sodium (mg)	–	3
potassium (mg)	296	120
magnesium (mg)	37	20
zinc (mg)	–	2
iodine (mg)	–	–
chlorine (mg)	–	110
sulphur (mg)	240	110
silicon (mg)	–	–
bromine (mg)	–	–
Vitamins		
A(IU)	0	–
B_1 (mg)	0.21	0.12
B_2 (mg)	0.07	0.05
B_3 (mg)	3.7	–
B_5 (mg)	–	0.05
B_6 (mg)	0.44	0.22
B_{12} (mcg)	–	0
folic acid (mcg)	–	20
biotin (mcg)	–	–
C (mg)	–	–
D (mg)	–	–
E (mg)	–	0.2
Organic acids		
citric (%)	–	–
malic (%)	–	–
oxalic (%)	–	–
Water (%)	10.8	10.6
Digestion time (hrs)	3¾	–

Pour 1½ pints (900 ml) water over 1 oz (25 g) whole barley grains and boil until the quantity is reduced to half. Add the zest and rind of a lemon for flavour. Sweeten with honey if desired. To make a laxative, add 1 oz (25 g) diced figs while boiling. Strain and drink at room temperature.

BASIL

Family: *Labiatae*
Genus: *Ocimum*
Species: *Ocimum basilicum*

This is an annual herb, with shiny green leaves some 2 inches long and small white flowers. It grows wild in tropical and sub-tropical parts of the world. The plant grows 2 feet high in rich, moist soil and likes plenty of sun. It needs to be raised freshly from seed each year. If any attempt is made to grow it in adverse conditions, it will only become rank and tough. It withers quickly and is best used when young. There are over fifty different varieties of basil, varying in shape and colour of leaf, as well as size of plant. It was once native to India and Persia. In India, basil is considered to be sacred and *Ocimum sanctum* is the plant that Hindus will swear on (they call it tulsi).

Basil was introduced to Europe from the East in the sixteenth century and spread to America in the seventeenth century. In Tudor times, a pot of basil was given to departing visitors. In the West, basil is a symbol of fertility although in Crete it is considered a bad omen and an agent of the devil. For centuries there has been controversy over its powers.

Basil features in literature, notably in the *Decameron* of Boccaccio, in the story of Lisabetta, whose tears watered a pot of basil in which she had buried the head of her murdered lover.

The **common (or sweet) basil** with tooth-edged leaves is the type most used for cooking. The leaves have a sweet, strong aroma with a spicy clove-like taste when fresh. When dried, it is only a shadow of its former self, and the flavour diminishes to a rather stale curry taste. Dried basil simply cannot be compared to its fresh counterpart. Fresh basil will keep briefly in the refrigerator sealed in an air-tight container, but considering how short its season is, it is probably best to preserve it as the Italians do in oil and salt. Both items absorb the flavour readily, and pass it on to food to which they are added.

Basil goes beautifully with tomatoes and courgettes and excels itself in stuffings, herb butters and rice dishes. Perhaps one of the most delicious uses of basil is in *pesto genovese*. The basis is always basil with garlic salt, olive oil, parmesan or masado cheese, and pine nuts or skinned walnuts, all pounded together into a thick sauce.

Dwarf basil grows only 6 inches high and is mainly a decorative plant. The flavour is definitely inferior to that of true sweet basil. **Lemon basil, Italian basil** and **curly basil** are largely ornamental. So-called wild basil is not basil at all but a relative of calamint which itself is often confusedly called basil thyme. It is nothing like as sweet as basil in flavour.

Nutritional and medicinal properties

Basil contains an essential oil, comprising mainly estragol, which is also present in French and Russian tarragons. It sometimes (depending on the variety) contains thymol and it also contains basil camphor which gives it its specific fragrance and taste.

Basil is used as an anti-spasmodic, carminative and stomachic in treating gastrointestinal problems like stomach cramp, vomiting, constipation and enteritis. It is also used to treat whooping cough, head colds, headaches and warts. Its weak sedative action is sometimes used in the treatment of nervous headaches or anxiety.

Tomato and basil sorbet

Because tomatoes vary so much in sweetness and liquid, it is hard to suggest a quantity, but 2 lb (1 kg) will serve about four people. If the tomato is not sweet enough you may have to add a level tablespoon tomato purée.

Skin and seed about 2 lb (1 kg) ripe tomatoes. Liquidize the flesh. Add salt, and pepper, and (if necessary) enough purée to make it slightly sweet, then 4 fresh basil leaves. Liquidize again.

Whip up 3 egg whites until stiff, and fold them into the purée. Freeze the mixture for 4 hours in small moulds. Decant by quickly dipping each mould in hot water, and serve slightly thawed on beds of lettuce and fresh basil leaves.

BEETROOT

Family: *Chenopodiceae*
Genus: *Beta*
Species: *Beta vulgaris*, var. *esculenta*

Beetroot has been popular in Europe since Elizabethan times and featured widely in Renaissance cooking, prized for its colour. A native of the Mediterranean, it was introduced to northern Europe at the end of the sixteenth century, extolled as 'the Great and Beautiful Beete'. It is now particularly popular in Russia and Poland.

There are an amazing number of different varieties of beetroot, ranging from giant carrot-shaped objects to flat, squat turnip look-alikes, and varying in colour from purple through gold to white. The four main varieties are white beet, red beet, Swiss chard and mangel-wurzel. **White beet** accounts for a third of the world's sugar production. **Red beet** is the bulbous, dark-red beet with which we are familiar. Oddly it is hard to find raw beetroot in our shops; we tend to sell it already boiled. Red beet can be eaten raw: scrub and peel it (the skin is quite tough), then grate it and mix with an equal quantity of grated carrot and an equal quantity of grated apple – delicious with a spicy vinaigrette dressing. **Swiss chard** is a variety grown for its green leaves, which are even more nutritious than the root. **Mangel-wurzel** is grown for animal fodder.

Beetroot thrives in fairly cool

climates and needs cool weather to go deep red. It is available all year round but its season is from late summer to early spring. The round globe variety is available in summer and early autumn, the long-rooted type in late autumn and winter.

Choose young, tender, fresh roots, and if growing your own lift them out of the soil carefully as they bleed easily; brush off the earth and twist off the leaves (which, if still tender, can be cooked and served separately). Scrub the roots gently

100 g BEET

	Common red beetroot (raw)	Beet greens (raw)	Beetroot (boiled)
Calories	43	24	32
Protein (g)	1.6	2.2	1.1
Carbohydrate (g)	9.9	4.6	7.2
Cholesterol (g)	0	–	–
Fat (g)	0.1	3	0.1
Fibre (g)	0.8	1.3	0.8
Minerals			
calcium (mg)	16	119	14
phosphorus (mg)	33	40	23
iron (mg)	0.7	3.3	0.5
sodium (mg)	60	130	43
potassium (mg)	335	570	208
magnesium (mg)	25	106	25
zinc (mg)	0.4	–	0.4
iodine (mg)	0.009	–	–
chlorine (mg)	295	–	–
sulphur (mg)	50	–	–
silicon (mg)	200	–	–
bromine (mg)	0.34	–	–
Vitamins			
A(IU)	20	6100	20
B_1 (mg)	0.03	0.1	0.03
B_2 (mg)	0.05	0.22	0.04
B_3 (mg)	0.4	0.4	0.3
B_5 (mg)	0.12	–	–
B_6 (mg)	0.05	–	–
B_{12} (mcg)	0	–	–
folic acid (mcg)	90	–	50
biotin (mcg)	tr	–	tr
C (mg)	10	30	6
D (mg)	–	–	–
E (mg)	–	–	–
Organic acids			
citric (%)	0.11	–	–
malic (%)	–	–	–
oxalic (%)	0.138	0.916	–
Water (%)	87.3	90.9	–
Digestion time (hrs)	2¾	2	–

under running water, then boil until tender. To test pierce with a skewer. Allow up to 2 hours for small roots. Alternatively bake just as you would a potato and serve with fresh dill and Greek yoghurt.

Nutritional and medicinal properties

Beets are rich in fibre and potassium and the green leaves are high in vitamin A, iron and calcium as well as other trace minerals and vitamin C. Indeed they are higher in iron and other trace minerals than spinach. Beetroots make a wonderful liver cleanser and a good blood builder, and so will help with skin problems, constipation and other digestive disorders. They were once used to treat TB, obesity and gonorrhoea. Watch you don't overdo it as they are also high in oxalic acid, and remember that canned and pickled beetroot is very high in salt.

Bortsch

Even my husband, who can't abide beetroot, will eat this. It's the classic Russian soup, slightly piquant in taste and very nutritious.

beetroot	garlic to taste,
onions	crushed
carrots	tomatoes
celery	muscovado
parsnip	sugar
freshly ground	tomato purée
black pepper	fresh parsley,
vegetable stock	chopped
cabbage	arrowroot
(coarsely	pepper
shredded)	Greek yoghurt

The vegetables should be used in the following proportions: half the total quantity should be beetroot, and of the remaining half, one third should be onion, one third carrot, and the last third equally divided between celery and parsnip.

Cut the beetroot, onions, carrots and parsnips and celery into matchsticks and pack into a 5 in (12.5 cm) diameter pudding basin by way of measurement. Tip into a pot, cover with stock and simmer for half an hour. Meanwhile coarsely shred the cabbage and fill the bowl again, adding garlic to taste, and add to the rest of the vegetables. Simmer for a further 20 minutes.

Skin, de-seed and chop coarsely sufficient tomatoes to half-fill the bowl. Add to the mixture, then add sugar and tomato purée to taste, enough to sharpen the flavour. Simmer for 10 more minutes. Add a handful of chopped parsley. Thicken with a little arrowroot mixed into the yoghurt. Season with pepper. Serve hot with extra yoghurt offered in a separate bowl.

BLACK-EYED PEA

Family: *Leguminosae*
Genus: *Vigna*
Species: *Vigna unguiculata*

The black-eyed pea, so called because of the black spot or 'eye' on one side, has become popular all over the world. It is also known as the cowpea, kaffir bean or yard-long bean, because of a variety whose pods grow up to 3 feet long. In some countries, the young tender shoots are eaten as a vegetable and the dried seeds can be ground into a coffee substitute.

See also: Pulses, Sprouted seeds.

Nutritional and medicinal properties

Like the other members of the bean family, black-eyed peas are a valuable source of protein and contain a variety of vitamins and minerals.

Spinach and peas

This is a traditional Middle Eastern dish and chard is often used instead of spinach.

5 oz (150 g) black-eyed peas
salt and black pepper
1 lb (500 g) fresh spinach,
*   shredded, or 8 oz (225 g) frozen*
*   leaf spinach, unthawed*
1 onion, finely chopped
5 tablespoons olive oil

Cover the peas with water and bring them to the boil, then reduce the heat and simmer until tender (about 20 minutes). Check that you don't overcook and produce mushy peas. Add the seasoning just before the end of the cooking time.

Meanwhile, wash the fresh spinach, having already cut out any thick stems, and drain well. If you're using frozen spinach squeeze all the water out of it. (Hands are easiest for this operation.)

Fry the onion in the oil till soft. Add the spinach and fry until well cooked, stirring as you do so. Adjust the seasoning, then stir in the drained beans and warm them through. Serve hot or cold.

BRAN

It is astonishing to think that as recently as the 1960s a leading London specialist was treating his diverticular patients with bran in secret simply because he feared the ridicule of his colleagues. In 1974 Denis Burkitt addressed a conference of British doctors strongly advocating natural fibre as a remedy for diverticulitis and other 'diseases of civilization' and subsequently there was a rush on bran in all the shops. The most popular bran as we know it is the tough outer pericarp layer of wheat grain, which is removed together with the germ during milling to produce white flour, but there are also other forms of bran available, including rice bran, soya bran and oat bran. All bran, whatever its source, is a rich source of high-quality protein, B vitamins and phosphorus.

Wheat bran is the most common bran widely available and contains 16 per cent protein, 11 per cent natural fibre, and 50 per cent carbohydrate. **Oat bran** is much finer, with a smoother texture than wheat bran, and functionally the big difference is that the fibre of oat bran is water-soluble, whereas wheat bran fibre is insoluble.

Water-soluble oat-bran fibre has been found to reduce blood levels of LDL cholesterol, the type associated with fatty deposits. The active agent in the fibre is oat gum, which gives cooked rolled oats their characteristic stickiness. This cholesterol-reducing effect is entirely absent in wheat bran but wheat bran is the more effective of the two as a stimulant of the bowel. If you use oat bran as a substitute for wheat bran in recipes it will produce a denser, moister and silkier product. **Soya bran** is twice as powerful as wheat bran in its action and is extremely fine in texture so has the added advantage of not scraping the gut as it passes through. **Rice bran** sometimes called rice polishing, is a valuable source of vitamins B₁ and B₁₂.

Nutritional and medicinal properties

My only problems with bran as far as medical treatment is concerned are that it can cause a lot of flatulence and with very tender and inflamed colons can actually scour them and make the situation worse, besides which it is now recognized as inhibiting the absorption of iron in certain people. So I tend to prescribe psyllium seeds or flax seeds (marketed commercially as Linusit Gold). I also remind patients that cellulose fibre, although not a direct substitute for cereal fibre, is an excellent and positive addition to the diet and is contained in most fruits and vegetables. Bran itself can easily be added to soups, casseroles, bread and cakes. If eaten alone it should always be thoroughly moistened first.

If you are just starting on bran, introduce it into the diet very slowly beginning with just a couple of teaspoons and gradually increasing

100g BRAN WITH SUGAR AND MALT EXTRACT

Calories	240
Protein (g)	12.6
Carbohydrate (g)	74.3
Cholesterol (g)	0
Fat (g)	3
Fibre (g)	7.8
Minerals	
calcium (mg)	70
phosphorus (mg)	1176
iron (mg)	4–12
sodium (mg)	1060
potassium (mg)	1070
magnesium (mg)	–
zinc (mg)	16.2
iodine (mg)	–
chlorine (mg)	150
sulphur (mg)	65
silicon (mg)	–
bromine (mg)	–
Vitamins	
A(IU)	0
B₁ (mg)	0.1
B₂ (mg)	0.29
B₃ (mg)	17.8
B₅ (mg)	2.4
B₆ (mg)	0.82
B₁₂ (mcg)	0
folic acid (mcg)	100
biotin (mcg)	14
C (mg)	tr
D (mg)	–
E (mg)	–
Organic acids	
citric (%)	–
malic (%)	–
oxalic (%)	–
Water (%)	8.3
Digestion time (hrs)	–

to 3 level teaspoons a day. Unlike laxatives bran will not work suddenly – it may take a few weeks to help establish regularity, during which time it may also cause some quite violent intestinal gas. I don't much like elderly people or pregnant women to use bran if they have not tried it before and prefer to direct them to the aforementioned seeds.

In order to explain to a patient how to recognize if they are getting enough fibre in the diet, I always question them about the consistency of their stools – an approach which invariably causes either a great deal of embarrassment or hilarity. A large floating stool means that there is sufficient fibre in the diet and a small compact one which sinks means there is not enough.

Two excellent books I would recommend for further reading on the subject are *Taking the Rough with the Smooth* by Dr Andrew Stanway and *Don't Forget Fibre in Your Diet* by Dr Denis Burkitt.

Diabetics and those with a tendency towards poor blood sugar tolerance, like hypoglycemics, may also benefit from bran, particularly from oat bran, because these types of fibre slow down the emptying of the stomach during digestion, so reducing the rise of sugar as food is turned into available energy in the blood stream.

Bran from wheat is rich in protein, carbohydrate, fibre, phosphorus iron, sodium, potassium, vitamins B_2, B_3 and B_6 and folic acid.

Bran muffins *(makes 12)*

This is a very palatable way to add fibre to the diet and is popular with children.

6 fl. oz (175 ml) skimmed milk
2 tablespoons vegetable oil
½ tablespoon black strap molasses
1 tablespoon clear honey
2 oz (50 g) raisins
4 oz (100 g) wholemeal flour
1 teaspoon baking powder
1 teaspoon bicarbonate of soda
1 oz (25 g) oat bran
1 egg

Heat gently together the milk, oil, molasses, honey and raisins. Meanwhile, sieve the flour, baking powder and soda together and stir in the oat bran. Remove the liquid from the stove, whisk in the egg and pour the liquid into the flour mixture, blending quickly.

Pour the batter into 12 well-greased large bun tins or paper cases and bake for 15–20 minutes in an oven preheated to 400°F (200°C, gas mark 6). These muffins are best eaten while still warm.

BRAZIL NUT

Family: *Lecythidaceae*
Genus: *Bertholletia*
Species: *Bertholletia excelsa*

The Brazil nut is also known as the pará nut or cream nut. It has become one of the most popular nuts in the world, especially in the USA, although very few are eaten in Brazil.

The Brazil nut tree is an

enormously tall evergreen found in a forest near the Amazon and its tributaries in northern Brazil. The nuts are contained in a thick, spherical, hard, woody fruit which may be up to 6 in (15 cm) in diameter and weigh 3–4 lb (1.3–1.8 kg). This encapsulates anything between twelve and twenty-four nuts, set out rather like the segments of an orange. The nut kernels are rich in oil and the oil itself can be used for salads.

There are many types of Brazil nuts but the more delicate nuts are not transported since they do not survive shipping.

See also: Nuts.

Nutritional and medicinal properties

Brazil nuts are high in calories and fat and are a rich source of protein, containing many vitamins and minerals.

Brazil nut and spice fudge

This sweet will generally satisfy even the most hardened sugar addict and because it is so satisfyingly chewy a little goes a long way.

1 teaspoon black peppercorns
1 whole nutmeg, grated
1 teaspoon cummin seeds
4 sticks cinnamon
12 stoned dates
12 dried figs
12 almonds
18 brazil nuts
4 oz (100 g) unsalted butter
8 oz (225 g) thick honey

Pulverize the spices with a pestle and mortar. Chop the dried fruit and nuts finely. Mix the spices and fruit into the butter and add the honey. Roll into small balls.

BREAD

This section is inspired by Colin Tudge's book, *Future Cook* (Mitchell Beazley, 1980).

Early bread was unleavened and sometimes made of crushed acorns or beech-nuts. Potato breads, banana breads and cassava breads are local specialities dependent upon the varying availability of different ingredients, but most bread is based on fermented cereals. Plant seeds are excellent food for the omnivore, but because the seed is also hard and dry it is understandably difficult to digest, although nutritionally it is unimpeachable. Ancestors of ours who ate seeds have skulls which show teeth that are worn flat at the tender age of 20. The answer was to grind the grain into flour and then bind this together in some way.

Bread is a homogeneous lump of carbohydrate glued together by water acting on starch or mucilage. The earliest bread was a mixture of flour and water dried in the sun on flat stones. The Egyptians first invented ovens and discovered the secret of making leavened bread. Initially this may well have been an accident – the result of yeast spores from the air becoming trapped in bread dough. Yeasts create gases and alcohols that account for the way in which dough rises and for its fragrance. Fermentation helps to pre-digest bread, as does cooking, a factor that means some people prefer unyeasted or naturally risen bread, because the enzymes and bacteria present in them help fragile digestions.

For most of history bread was made from the whole grain and so included all the protein, fibre, minerals and vitamins that whole grain contains. True, it was sometimes of very dubious quality – made from mouldy or poor grains, badly milled or unevenly cooked – and it was often deliberately adulterated by millers and various middlemen, but when the bread was palatable people ate it in copious quantities, not just because they liked it, but because it was at least affordable, although it did not really become cheap until this century. People who had access to good bread did not starve but neither did they get fat. They escaped the whole range of deficiency diseases and did not suffer from that insidious list of the current 'diseases of civilization' including the number one killer, heart disease.

The move to crush grains with artefacts instead of long-suffering teeth was, technologically, one of the most significant that human beings have ever undertaken. The conversion of grain into meal and flour has, over the past 6000 years, been a pre-eminent technical preoccupation of civilized societies. Initially the mortar and pestle were used, but only one batch of grains could be worked on at a time and it was very slow work. The quern, through which the passage of grain flows continuously, was a great step forward. The first querns were saddle ones: the top stone was lifted and allowed to slide down the one underneath, shearing rather than simply crushing the grain in-between. Then came the rotary quern which was in general use in Britain by about 100 BC. Animal power was subsequently introduced so that bigger stones could be used.

Then came the introduction of water power and water-wheels, which turned vertically, altering the angle of rotation to 90 degrees, so that the great whirring cogs of wood and iron spun more efficiently. This was followed by the introduction of windmills, which were widespread in Britain by the fourteenth century.

In the nineteenth century came the technology which is still in use. Grain was channelled into the grinder on one side and then sheared by rollers with finely adjustable mechanical precision to produce a flour of any grade required at the switch of a handle – roller-milling had arrived.

Roller-milling has the advantage of being so versatile that it can produce almost any flour the miller chooses. Its disadvantage is that it removes the endosperm, producing an aesthetically pleasing white flour, but one which is nutritionally deficient. However, roller-milled flour gained in popularity because it could be stored for long periods of time without going rancid. Until the last two centuries only the rich indulged in white bread as we would recognize it. Until the seventeenth century the wheat went to make the bread of rich town-dwellers, while the peasants ate rye, barley and oatcakes.

Raised bread is preferred in Europe and the United States but unleavened bread is still popular in Asia and Africa. In the early days of bread-making spontaneous fermentation was used. However, advances were made when yeast was discovered to grow a fermented mash from beer-making. The first compressed yeast of this type was available in England in 1792. By 1800 it was being used all over England and northern Europe. Large-scale commercial production of bread became possible when Charles Fleischmann, an American, introduced in 1868 an improved type of distiller's compressed yeast in which the cells were separated from the liquid and compressed into cakes. This was followed by the isolation of single yeast cultures by 1883. Coupled with the development of new yeast strains and improved manufacturing conditions this led to the modern methods of commercial bread manufacture being well entrenched by 1915.

Yeast is a living material and therefore needs to be handled skilfully. This is why the technique of unleavened bread is so exacting. A century and a half ago, when cottage ovens were small and their fuelling expensive and uncertain, cooks wisely left bread-making to the baker. But now that bakers' bread is often so poor – much of it fit only for putty – and domestic ovens work so precisely it is perhaps a task that many competent cooks should take up again enthusiastically. Experienced bakers like to talk about the 'art' in making bread and about the mysteries of the process. Some have become so high-flown they have talked of a mystical element – the alchemy of baking. Certainly it can be artful and there are subtle aspects hidden from even the most skilled baker, but don't let the so-called art of baking intimidate you. If you can cook then you can certainly make a loaf of bread.

Scotland is famous for its **oatcakes** and **bannock**, made from oats and barley. Germany, the USSR and Scandinavia produce black **rye bread**, sometimes using barley and potato flour as well. India produces **millet cakes** and **chapatis** which are a simple unleavened form of bread used instead of cutlery, as a wrap to carry vegetables and curries, and as a mop to soak up juices. Mexico and Latin America concentrate on **tortillas**, unleavened bread made from corn. In Brazil **cassava bread**, made from cassava root, is made. In the Middle East **pitta**, a flat unleavened bread, is popular. It splits open in the middle to form a bag for beans, hummus, falafel, vegetables or olives.

See also: Flours, Grains.

Granary bread *(makes 3–4 large loaves)*

This was given to me by Jean Demaine who presented me with a loaf which tasted so good I had to have the recipe.

2 oz (50 g) fresh yeast
1½ pints (900 ml) (or perhaps a
   little more) tepid water
3 teaspoons salt
3 lb (1.5 kg) Granary flour
3 oz (90 g) unsalted butter

Dissolve the yeast in a little of the water. Mix the salt with the flour (keeping a little flour back for kneading and shaping), then rub the fat into the flour. Make a well in the flour and add the yeast and the rest of the water, then leave for 10 minutes for fermentation to begin. Bring the mixture together to form

100 g BREAD

	Rye	White*	Wholewheat
Calories	246	272.7	246
Protein (g)	9.2	8.1	10.6
Carbohydrate (g)	52.5	50.9	48.2
Cholesterol (g)	0	0	0
Fat (g)	1.1	3.2	3
Fibre (g)	0.4	0.2	1.5
Minerals			
calcium (mg)	75.8	84.8	100
phosphorus (mg)	148.5	97.9	230
iron (mg)	1.6	2.5	2.4
sodium (mg)	563	512	532.4
potassium (mg)	146.5	106	276
magnesium (mg)	116.2	22.2	–
zinc (mg)	–	–	–
iodine (mg)	–	–	–
chlorine (mg)	–	–	–
sulphur (mg)	–	–	–
silicon (mg)	–	–	–
bromine (mg)	–	–	–
Vitamins			
A(IU)	0	tr	tr
B$_1$ (mg)	0.18	0.2	0.27
B$_2$ (mg)	0.06	0.02	0.12
B$_3$ (mg)	1.5	2.4	2.8
B$_5$ (mg)	–	–	–
B$_6$ (mg)	0.09	–	–
B$_{12}$ (mcg)	0	–	0
folic acid (mcg)	15.8	–	–
biotin (mcg)	–	–	–
C (mg)	0	tr	tr
D (mg)	–	–	–
E (mg)	2.4–3.3	–	0.3
Organic acids			
citric (%)	–	–	–
malic (%)	–	–	–
oxalic (%)	–	–	–
Water (%)	35.5	35.6	36.4
Digestion time (hrs)	–	–	–

* Made with 3% non-fat dried milk and enriched flour.

a soft dough and knead until the surface of the dough is smooth. This will take about 10 minutes. Cover with a cloth and leave to rise until the dough has doubled its size (approximately 45–60 minutes). Re-knead the dough and divide it into three or four greased bread tins. Leave to rise again until the dough has doubled in size (approximately 20–30 minutes). Bake in a hot oven 400–450°F (200–230°C, gas mark 6–8) for 30–60 minutes depending on the size of each loaf.

BROAD BEAN

Family: *Leguminosae*
Genus: *Vicia*
Species: *Faba Vicia faba*

The ancient Egyptians believed that broad beans contained dead men's souls and were therefore unclean, so they were only eaten by peasants. In Greece and Rome beans were used for casting votes when electing magistrates and other public officers. The beans were thrown into a hat, the white ones for yes votes and the darker ones for no votes. So when Pythagoras said his followers should not eat beans he may well have meant that his disciples should resist the lure of political office.

The broad bean is the white, flat seed of the plant. In France the beans are cooked inside the young pods. In Brazil they are roasted and ground into flour.

See also: Pulses, Sprouted seeds.

Nutritional and medicinal properties

Broad beans are a good source of protein and contain calcium and iron together with some vitamins.

Broad beans with summer savory

The savory facilitates the digestion of the beans and the nutmeg and lovage add an interesting 'bite'!

1 onion, finely chopped
1 clove garlic, finely sliced
olive oil
2 lb (1 kg) shelled broad beans
1 tablespoon chopped fresh
   parsley
½ teaspoon chopped fresh lovage
1 heaped teaspoon chopped fresh
   summer savory
1 pint (600 ml) vegetable stock
Greek yoghurt
nutmeg, freshly grated

Sauté the onion and garlic in a little oil till soft. Add the beans, herbs and stock and simmer till the beans are cooked. Stir in enough yoghurt to thicken the stock and grate a little nutmeg over the top. Serve hot with brown rice or wedges of wholemeal bread.

BROCCOLI

Family: *Cruciferae*
Genus: *Brassica*
Species: *Brassica oleracea* var.
   italica

Broccoli is a form of cauliflower and both vegetables stem from wild cabbage, broccoli being the earlier of the two and originating in Italy where it is still very popular and much appreciated for its affinity with eggs and butter. It was brought to England in 1720 and taken to America in colonial times.

Of the two main types of broccoli, **calabrese** produces individual loose heads and has a fine, delicate aromatic flavour. **Asparagus broccoli** is the purple sprouting variety. Later developments produced a large-headed variety of asparagus broccoli, with a compact flower like a small cauliflower except that it is generally purple or green though occasionally one can find white varieties. This type is usually cooked standing up like asparagus.

Calabrese is in season during the summer while sprouting broccoli is in season from late winter to early May, but as the UK imports so much it can often be bought throughout the year. It is grown extensively in Italy, France and Spain as well as Britain.

Sprouting broccoli, because of its tough stalks, is best cooked in two stages, chopping up the stems first and laying them in a fairly broad pan and laying the flower heads over the top for the last 6 minutes. If the heads are still ready first, simply lift them out gently with tongs and keep them warm. Serve with unsalted butter and lots of black pepper.

Nutritional and medicinal properties

Cooked frozen broccoli is similar to fresh but has slightly less vitamin C (73 milligrams to 100 grams of the vegetable). It is a good source of fibre, potassium, vitamins A, B_2 and C, calcium, iron and potassium, and is low in calories unless of course you cheat and lavish it with sauces. Broccoli is good for constipation, toxaemia, neuritis, hypertension, and to brighten up a sluggish digestive

100 g BROCCOLI (raw)	
Calories	32
Protein (g)	3.6
Carbohydrate (g)	5.9
Cholesterol (g)	–
Fat (g)	0.3
Fibre (g)	1.5
Minerals	
calcium (mg)	103
phosphorus (mg)	78
iron (mg)	1.1
sodium (mg)	15
potassium (mg)	382
magnesium (mg)	24
zinc (mg)	0.6
iodine (mg)	0.003
chlorine (mg)	–
sulphur (mg)	–
silicon (mg)	–
bromine (mg)	–
Vitamins	
A(IU)	2500
B_1 (mg)	0.1
B_2 (mg)	0.23
B_3 (mg)	0.9
B_5 (mg)	1
B_6 (mg)	0.21
B_{12} (mcg)	0
folic acid (mcg)	130
biotin (mcg)	0.5
C (mg)	113
D (mg)	–
E (mg)	–
Organic acids	
citric (%)	0.21
malic (%)	0.12
oxalic (%)	0.0054
Water (%)	89.1
Digestion time (hrs)	3

system. People with underactive thyroids should avoid it, as it exacerbates the problem.

The enchanted broccoli forest

This is a wonderfully imaginative recipe from a cook-book (of the same name as the recipe written by Mollie Katzen (Ten Speed Press, 1982). My only variation is that, because foil is made of aluminium and therefore poisonous, I use a cut-up, spread-out roasting bag to cover the broccoli before covering it with foil so that the foil isn't actually in contact with the vegetables.

2 *cups brown rice*
3 *tablespoons butter*
1 *cup chopped onion*
1 *large clove garlic, crushed*
½ *teaspoon salt*
lots of freshly ground black
  pepper
cayenne pepper, to taste
¼ *teaspoon dried mint*
½ *teaspoon dill*
3 *large eggs*
½ *cup finely chopped parsley*
1½ *very full cups grated Cheddar*
1 *lb (450 g) fresh broccoli*
juice of 1 lemon

Cook the rice in 3 cups of water until just done (about 30 minutes). Meanwhile sauté together in 1 tablespoon of the butter, over a medium heat and stirring well, the onion, garlic, salt, spices and herbs (except the parsley) – until the onions are soft and translucent (about 8–10 minutes). Add this

mixture to the cooked rice, stirring well.

Beat together well the eggs, parsley and cheese, and stir into the drained rice. Spread this mixture evenly in a buttered 10×6 in (25×15 cm) baking dish.

Cut the broccoli into neat spears, shaving off any tough outer skin, and steam it until barely tender. Drain it and refresh it in water. Then arrange the broccoli spears upright on the bed of rice mixture, so that the flowering tips form the tree-tops and the stalks are firmly embedded in the rice. Melt the remaining 2 tablespoons butter and combine the melted butter with the lemon juice. Drizzle this mixture over the trees.

Cover firmly but very gently with greaseproof paper or a washing bag and then foil, and bake for 30 minutes in an oven preheated to 325°F (170°C, gas mark 3).

BRUSSELS SPROUT

Family: *Cruciferae*
Genus: *Brassica*
Species: *Brassica oleracea* var.
             gemmifera

At the seedling stage a Brussels sprout plant resembles a cabbage but it grows to 2 or 3 feet tall, sprouting miniature cabbages from a tall, woody stem. Dwarf varieties are now common. Unlike most other members of the same family it does not form a head, but only a loose rosette of leaves at the top of the stem, which must be left until all the sprouts (there are usually two pickings) have been harvested. Brussels sprouts should be picked and eaten while tight and very small.

The plant's European origins are obscure. It was recorded growing in Belgium as early as 1587 but it was almost certainly around for hundreds of years prior to this. It was introduced to England by the Flemish refugees fleeing from the Spanish Inquisition.

Brussels sprouts are in season from September to April and are grown extensively in Britain, Holland and Belgium. Tiny sprouts need little preparation beyond washing but the bigger ones need to have a few of the coarse outer leaves stripped away and the stem trimmed and cut with an X-shaped cross so that the stalk will cook more quickly. Cook briskly for 10 minutes in boiling water. Drain, return to the pot to dry out a little, and serve with unsalted butter and plenty of black pepper.

Nutritional and medicinal properties

There is so little difference between cooked fresh Brussels sprouts and frozen ones that they can be regarded as nutritionally identical. Rich in vitamins A, B and C, as well as calcium and potassium, and a good source of fibre, they have a fine nutty flavour.

Recommended for catarrh, obesity, constipation and pyorrhoea, Brussels sprouts are said to be a good general tonic.

100 g BRUSSELS SPROUTS		
	Raw	Boiled
Calories	45	36
Protein (g)	4.9	4.2
Carbohydrate (g)	8.3	6.4
Cholesterol (g)	–	0
Fat (g)	0.4	0.4
Fibre (g)	1.6	1.6
Minerals		
calcium (mg)	36	32
phosphorus (mg)	80	72
iron (mg)	1.5	1.1
sodium (mg)	14	10
potassium (mg)	390	273
magnesium (mg)	29	–
zinc (mg)	0.5	0.4
iodine (mg)	–	–
chlorine (mg)	275	–
sulphur (mg)	3530	–
silicon (mg)	–	–
bromine (mg)	–	–
Vitamins		
A(IU)	550	520
B_1 (mg)	0.1	0.08
B_2 (mg)	0.16	0.14
B_3 (mg)	0.9	0.8
B_5 (mg)	0.4	0.28
B_6 (mg)	0.28	0.17
B_{12} (mcg)	0	0
folic acid (mcg)	110	87
biotin (mcg)	0.4	0.3
C (mg)	102	87
D (mg)	–	–
E (mg)	–	0.4–0.9
Organic acids		
citric (%)	0.24	–
malic (%)	0.2	–
oxalic (%)	0.0059	–
Water (%)	85.2	–
Digestion time (hrs)	4	–

Brussels sprout sauce for pasta *(serves 3)*

It is hard to know what to do with sprouts apart from serving them plain. This is an interesting variation and goes well with wholemeal pasta or baked potatoes.

8 oz (225 g) tiny Brussels sprouts
1 oz (25 g) unsalted butter
¼ cup diced onion
½ lb (225 g) mushrooms, sliced
plenty of freshly ground black
    pepper
1 teaspoon dried tarragon
1 dessertspoon grainy mustard
1 tablespoon rice flour
1 cup hot milk
½ teaspoon grated horseradish
    root, bought prepared or
    freshly grated
a little Parmesan cheese

Steam the Brussels Sprouts till barely tender and set aside. Melt the butter and in it gently sauté the onions and mushrooms till soft, towards the end adding – and stirring in well – the pepper, tarragon and mustard. Stir in the rice flour, then gently drizzle in the hot milk, stirring well. Cover and cook over a very low heat for 5 minutes, stirring occasionally.

Stir in the horseradish and sprouts. Pour the Brussels sprout sauce over pasta. Offer the Parmesan.

BULGAR

Family: *Gramineae*
Genus: *Triticum*
Species: *Triticum vulgare*

Bulgar wheat is wheat which has been parboiled, dried and broken up, so it has lost a few of its nutrients along the way (1 ounce contains 2.5 grams of protein compared to wheat's 3.7 grams), but it has a wonderful nutty flavour

which I enjoy even more than rice, and there are obviously others who feel the same way as it is now becoming a popular staple in many parts of the world. Originally it was an ancient wheat that survived in Eastern Europe but it has since gained much popularity in the Balkans and in the Middle East and is readily available here. Genghis Khan was particularly fond of bulgar dishes and fermented bulgar alcohol, and in the Bible Ruth stood among the bulgar, called 'alien corn', when she left her homeland.

Nowadays most bulgar is made commercially by machines but in spite of modern steel-milling the seed is structured in such a way that the wheatgerm and bran are readily retained. **Parboiled (or parched) bulgar** is parboiled before pearling, and is marketed as 'precooked' or 'parched' on the label, indicating that the grains are quick-cooking. Bulgar is interchangeable with wheat and rice and works well in risottos, pilafs and paellas.

See also: Flour, Grains.

Nutritional and medicinal properties

Bulgar wheat retains much of the original nutritional content of the wholewheat grain. It is easy to digest and therefore invaluable for young children and invalids. It is a good source of iron and phosphorus and contains traces of the B vitamins.

Bulgar pitavi

This is an adaptation of a classic Turkish dish which makes an interesting alternative to rice or noodles. Even today bulgar is the staple food of Armenians, many Anatolians and Kurds.

2 large onions
4 tablespoons oil
14 oz (400 g) bulgar
1 pint (600 ml) stock made with a
  vegetable stock cube
sea salt
4 oz (100 g) pine nuts
2 heaped tablespoons sultanas

Brown the onion in the oil. Stir in the bulgar and fry for a few seconds which will emphasize the final nutty flavour of the dish. Add the stock and a little salt, cover and simmer gently for 20 minutes, checking from time to time to see if the stock needs replenishing. Check the seasoning and stir in the nuts and sultanas. Leave covered and undisturbed for 10 minutes until all the stock has been absorbed, then serve in heated bowls.

100 g BULGAR

	Made from hard winter wheat	Made from white wheat
Calories	354	357
Protein (g)	11.2	10.3
Carbohydrate (g)	75.7	78.1
Cholesterol (g)	–	–
Fat (g)	1.5	1.2
Fibre (g)	1.7	1.3
Minerals		
calcium (mg)	29	36
phosphorus (mg)	338	300
iron (mg)	3.7	4.7
sodium (mg)	–	–
potassium (mg)	229	310
magnesium (mg)	–	–
zinc (mg)	–	–
iodine (mg)	–	–
chlorine (mg)	–	–
sulphur (mg)	–	–
silicon (mg)	–	–
bromine (mg)	–	–
Vitamins		
A(IU)	0	0
B$_1$ (mg)	0.28	0.3
B$_2$ (mg)	0.14	0.1
B$_3$ (mg)	4.5	4.2
B$_5$ (mg)	–	–
B$_6$ (mg)	–	–
B$_{12}$ (mcg)	–	–
folic acid (mcg)	–	–
biotin (mcg)	–	–
C (mg)	0	0
D (mg)	–	–
E (mg)	–	–
Organic acids		
citric (%)	–	–
malic (%)	–	–
oxalic (%)	–	–
Water (%)	10	9
Digestion time (hrs)	3¾	–

BUTTER

This is an entirely natural food which at its purest, if it is free of preservatives, is made only with cream which is then solidified into milk fats. The average composition of butter is 81.5 per cent milk fat, 15.9 per cent water, up to 2.5 per cent salt, and up to 2 per cent milk protein and other residues. One pound of butter requires the cream of at least 18 pints of milk. One third of all the milk produced in the world is made into butter.

Butter is an ancient idea. There is some suggestion that wandering herdsmen carrying milk in goatskins found that the skins acted as churns and turned the milk into butter. Butter is mentioned in the Bible and was known to the ancient Greeks and Romans who used it medicinally to spread on burns. Women used it for hairdressing.

Butter can be made from any milk, including that of the goat, sheep and buffalo. Originally butter was made by the swinging-bag method and it was not until much later that it was churned in earthenware. Modern butter-making began with the development of a wooden 'dasher' – a stick with a round, blunt end – which was plunged up and down in a churn. In the nineteenth century the churn and dasher were a household necessity, until a method of centrifugal separation was developed around the middle of the century. All milk contains fat suspended in tiny globules in it. When the milk is stirred vigorously at an appropriate temperature the fat globules collect together as butter granules. The remaining liquid after the fat has been separated is called butter-milk (*see* Milk).

In commercial butter-making, cream is pasteurized by heat and then tempered at a cool temperature. This is churned as sweet cream or soured by the addition of lactic-acid bacteria in a process called ripening. The butter is separated from the butter-milk and washed in cold water, drained and salted and then churned again to mix the fat, moisture and salt. If worked too long the butter loses its grain, turning oily and greasy. Butter ranges in colour from deep gold to white depending on the type of milk used. Cows fed on rich pasture give a yellower milk than those fed on dry fodder. Often butter is dyed yellow to be more appealing. Freshly made butter is worked into prints or blocks.

There are two main types of butter – **sweet cream butter**, made from fresh cream, which has a mild delicate flavour and is used for pastry, biscuits and fine doughs and **lactic butters** were a special bacterial culture is added to enhance the flavour and develop a milk-acid flavour. This butter has a fine texture, creams easily and has a good rich flavour. It is excellent for cakes, especially spicy ones like ginger and Dundee cake, and makes good caramels, fudges and toffees. Both types of butter generally have salt added for flavour. Unsalted butters deteriorate more rapidly than salted butters.

See also: Margarine.

Nutritional and medicinal properties

Butter is a concentrated form of energy food and is extremely high in calories. It is also rich in vitamin A and contains calcium and vitamin D.

Clarified butter

Also known as butter or ghee, this is made from sweet butter, which has a very low melting point. It is produced at a low temperature and is extremely stable, at least as stable as sesame oil, and has 30 per cent polyunsaturated fats compared to sesame oil's 44 per cent. It has a nice way of enhancing food flavours as no vegetable oil can and Dr Roger Williams believes it has a mysterious ability to protect against atherosclerosis. It is easily made at home.

Bring a pound of sweet butter to the boil and then lower the heat to simmer. The white foam, which is a combination of water and milk solids, boils fat out of the butter and this needs to be

100 g FAT

	Salted butter	Unsalted butter	Margarine
Calories	715	715	720
Protein (g)	tr	tr	0.7
Carbohydrate (g)	tr	tr	0.7
Cholesterol (g)	217	217	0
Fat (g)	81	81	81
Fibre (g)	0	0	0
Minerals			
calcium (mg)	20.9	20.9	20.3
phosphorus (mg)	23.1	23.1	16.1
iron (mg)	0.14	0.14	0
sodium (mg)	818.2	9.7	986.7
potassium (mg)	25.2		23.1
magnesium (mg)	2.1	2.1	9.1
zinc (mg)	–	–	–
iodine (mg)	–	–	–
chlorine (mg)	–	–	–
sulphur (mg)	–	–	–
silicon (mg)	–	–	–
bromine (mg)	–	–	–
Vitamins			
A(IU)*	3035	2035	3295
B_1 (mg)	tr	tr	–
B_2 (mg)	0.03	0.03	tr
B_3 (mg)	0.04	0.04	tr
B_5 (mg)	tr	–	–
B_6 (mg)	tr	tr	tr
B_{12} (mcg)	tr	tr	–
folic acid (mcg)	2.1	2.1	–
biotin (mcg)	tr	–	–
C (mg)	0	0	–
D (mg)	41.9	41.9	306.3
E (mg)	2.1	2.1	–
Organic acids			
citric (%)	–	–	–
malic (%)	–	–	–
oxalic (%)	–	–	–
Water (%)	15.5	–	15.5
Digestion time (hrs)	–	–	–

* Value for vitamin A is the year-round average.

skimmed off. Some of the milk solids will also sink to the bottom as the water that holds them is driven off. The sinking milk solid should be allowed to accumulate undisturbed, turning a golden brown. If you use heat which is too high, these solids will scorch and so ruin the flavour of the clarified butter. The sound of boiling changes to the hissing sound of frying when all the water is evaporated and the bubbling has stopped, a process which takes about 20 minutes. Remove the clarified butter from the stove and then carefully pour it off, leaving the sediment behind. Store it in a covered container that keeps light out – it will not then go rancid or need to be refrigerated. A pound of butter makes 1¾ cups clarified butter. Clarified butter makes an excellent dressing for vegetables and can be used as a seal for vegetable patés and terrines.

Home-made butter

You can produce your own home-made butter, starting with chilled cream and shaking it in a glass jar for about 45 minutes. (A blender is not the answer here as it will spin too fast.) When churned or shaken the cream creates a large lump. Pour the contents of the jar through a strainer and press the remaining solid lump of butter into the desired shape with the flat edge of a knife. Refrigerate. Some food mixers have attachments which will make butter from fresh cream for you.

CABBAGE

Family: *Cruciferae*
Genus: *Brassica*
Species: *Brassica oleracea*

The word 'cabbage' covers an enormous range of plants that have been cultivated throughout Europe and western Asia for thousands of years and includes cauliflower, broccoli, kale, Brussels sprouts and kohlrabi, as well as the many different varieties of what we actually call cabbage, all developed for their root, leaves, flowers and even their stems. The cabbage we think of as cabbage is a cross between wild and sea cabbage, the ancestor of which was used in Neolithic times. The Romans brought the open-hearted cabbage to England and this has since remained the most popular variety.

In Britain Anglo-Saxons called cabbage cole-plants or worts and served it in pottage stewed with a marrow bone and flavoured with

saffron or cinnamon. The value of cooking cabbage very lightly to preserve its goodness was recognized even in medieval times when the shredded leaves were simply cooked in butter in a closed earthenware pot set in boiling water.

Cabbage is generally classed according to season and type. **Green cabbage** [*Brassica oleracea* var. *bullata*) is the best-known of the cabbages. It grows particularly well in England, and can be smooth- or curly-leaved (for example the Savoy cabbage, which has a delicate flavour and is in season from September to May). Try it simmered in milk, thickening the liquid – once the cabbage is cooked – with a beaten egg yolk, and seasoning well with freshly ground black pepper and a dash of grated nutmeg. Serve it with croutons of toast and savoury custard lavished all over it – a delicious light meal in itself.

Red cabbage (*Brassica oleracea* var. *capitata*) is the result of *Brassica* cross-breeding and its dark crimson leaves are particularly rich in vitamin C. It is available as an autum-to-winter vegetable, in season from September to May, and is particularly delicious eaten raw with apple slices, pineapple chunks and nuts. If you're boiling it add the juice of half a lemon, to stop the leaves being leached of colour and turning an ugly mauve, and cover it tightly as it has a rather unpleasant smell. It is better to braise it with butter and vegetable stock in the oven with juniper berries, garlic or caraway seeds, adding a little red wine vinegar and some honey at the end. Thicken the juices with yoghurt stabilized with a little arrowroot.

White cabbage makes the classic coleslaw and if eaten raw needs to be served with vegetables that are as hard and as crisp as the cabbage itself – celery, apple, horseradish, carrot. Chinese cabbage (*Brassica pekinensis*) looks like a cross between a cos lettuce and a cabbage and will happily substitute for either. The head stuffs well as it is strongly made and an ideal shape. The Chinese stir-fry the leaves. Add a tiny bit of raw sliced ginger to enhance the taste. It is lower in calories and has less vitamin C than its green cousin but has the same mineral content.

Nutritional and medicinal properties

Cabbage is a good source of vitamins A, C, B_1, B_2, B_3 and D. It is also high in iron, potassium and calcium. However much water it is cooked in, it loses the same amount of nutrients – a quarter of the original calories, half of the vitamins B and C, all of the vitamin B_6 and folic acid and one third of the sodium, potassium and phosphorus.

In the ancient world cabbage water, taken either internally or externally, was considered a panacea capable of alleviating everything from freckles to drunkenness, and some even went so far as to say the mere act of slicing it made one feel better. Nowadays we acknowledge its muscle-building and blood-purifying properties and fresh raw cabbage juice is an excellent treatment for gastric ulcers and anaemia. The chlorine and sulphur in it cleanse the internal mucosa and so it is also helpful for kidney and bladder problems, diabetes, skin problems and asthma. It is also very low in calories and so a good bulky filler for slimmers, though a dressing of any sort obviously increases the calories. Very excessive intakes of cabbage juice can cause goitre, so for gastric ulcers take only 450 ml spread throughout the day.

Sauerkraut

Zig Rudevics, married to a Polish woman, passed on his wife's family recipe to me and gave me the added tip of washing the sauerkraut well before serving so that the salt intake is radically reduced. Because sauerkraut is fermented it is very rich in benign bacteria which will help to repopulate and protect the colon.

Grate a whole white cabbage finely on a mandoline. Pack it in layers in a plastic bucket, generously sprinkling sea salt between the layers. Cram it all down as tight as you can and cover with a plate which completely encompasses the top, and weight it down with something heavy. Store in a cool place. After six weeks, tip off the juice and discard any cabbage that has rotted (it will do so from the top down). Transfer the sauerkraut into jars, with the juice, so that each jar is really tightly packed and full, and screw the lids on firmly.

Before serving, wash the sauerkraut thoroughly in a sieve under running water to get rid of most of the salt. It is nice served very simply with some added freshly grated carrot and apple, olive oil and black pepper.

100 g CABBAGE (raw)	Common	Chinese	Red	Savoy
Calories	24	14	31	24
Protein (g)	1.3	1.2	2.0	2.4
Carbohydrate (g)	5.4	3.0	6.9	4.6
Cholesterol (g)	0	–	–	–
Fat (g)	0.2	0.1	0.2	0.2
Fibre (g)	0.8	0.6	1.0	0.8
Minerals				
calcium (mg)	49	43	42	67
phosphorus (mg)	29	40	35	54
iron (mg)	0.4	0.6	0.8	0.9
sodium (mg)	20	23	26	22
potassium (mg)	233	253	268	269
magnesium (mg)	13	14	–	–
zinc (mg)	–	–	0.3	0.3
iodine (mg)	0.009	0.016	–	–
chlorine (mg)	1045	–	1051	1003
sulphur (mg)	1710	–	958	1041
silicon (mg)	110	–	38	607
bromine (mg)	1.05	–	–	–
Vitamins				
A(IU)	130	150	40	200
B_1 (mg)	0.05	0.05	0.09	0.05
B_2 (mg)	0.05	0.04	0.06	0.08
B_3 (mg)	0.3	0.6	0.4	0.3
B_5 (mg)	–	–	0.32	0.21
B_6 (mg)	0.16	–	0.21	0.16
B_{12} (mcg)	0	0	0	0
folic acid (mcg)	6–42	–	90	90
biotin (mcg)	–	–	0.1	0.1
C (mg)	47	25	61	55
D (mg)	0	–	–	–
E (mg)	0.1	–	–	–
Organic acids				
citric (%)	0.14	–	–	–
malic (%)	0.10	–	–	–
oxalic (%)	0.0077	0.0073	–	–
Water (%)	92.4	95.0	90.2	92
Digestion time (hrs)	3	–	3¾	–

CARAWAY

Family: *Umbelliferae*
Genus: *Carum*
Species: *Carum carvi*

This is a biennial which grows over 2 feet high, with creamy-white flowers and feathery leaves. It is a member of the carrot family. It grows wild in Europe and temperate parts of Asia (including Turkey, Iran, North Africa and India) but it is not native to Britain and has naturalized itself in America. It is grown commercially in Holland and occurs throughout most of Europe, particularly Russia and the Balkans, and North Africa. The seeds are flattened and oval in shape and provide an aromatic odour when bruised. They have a pleasantly spicy, rather strong taste. The flavour of the leaves is much milder, something between parsley and dill.

Caraway has been used since the time of the ancient Greeks who prescribed it for pale young girls to bring pinches of colour to their cheeks. The seeds were at one time much more important in English cooking than they are now and some adults may have traumatic childhood memories of the obligatory 'seed cake'. Personally I rather like it which is why I offer an old recipe for it here. It goes very nicely with a glass of madeira. In Elizabethan times, roast apples were always served with caraway and Falstaff was invited to 'a pippin and a dish of caraways' by Master Shallow (*Henry IV, Part II*).

In the Middle Ages, caraway leaves were used chopped into soups and salads and are still sometimes used like this in Norway. Caraway is extremely popular in Germany and Austria and these countries use it, it seems, in almost everything including cakes, bread, and cheese, cabbage and potato dishes, as well as in various meat dishes. It is also eaten in sugar as a digestive called 'sugar plums'. It is used with cummin – the two are often confused – as an ingredient of the liqueur kümmel, and of anisette and schnapps. The root of the caraway plant is also used as a vegetable in some parts of Europe, but these are spindly and somewhat awkward to harvest.

Nutritional and medicinal properties

Caraway yields a volatile oil, the chief constituent of which is carvone, which makes up over half of the total. Caraway grown in northern climates contains noticeably less oil than that grown further south. It also contains fibre, limonene, minerals, protein and wax. The volatile oils promote digestion and prevent flatulence.

For this reason, caraway is an excellent aid to digestion. It is taken for indigestion, gas, colic and nervous conditions. Simply infuse 1 oz (25 g) of the crushed seeds in a pint of freshly boiled water and steep for 20 minutes. Take the tea in frequent doses of 2 teaspoonfuls until relief is obtained. This is particularly useful to prevent griping in babies. Caraway is also useful for congestive bronchitis and colds in the chest. Chew 2 grams of the dried seeds, three times daily. It has in the past been used to promote the onset of menstruation, relieve uterine cramps and increase lactation.

Seed cake

I know caraway seed cake smacks of maiden aunts and sweet sherry but you'll be pleasantly surprised when you try it. It is less bland and predictable than Madeira cake and complements a cup of herbal tea spiked with lemon nicely.

6 oz (175 g) butter
6 oz (175 g) brown sugar
3 eggs, beaten
8 oz (225 g) wheatmeal flour, sifted
1 teaspoon baking powder
1 heaped teaspoon caraway seeds a little milk

Cream the butter and sugar together until light and creamy. Beat the eggs in gradually. Fold in the flour, baking powder and seeds, and add a little milk if necessary to get a good dropping consistency. Put it in a buttered and floured 7 in (18 cm) cake tin and cook in an oven preheated to 350°F (180°C, gas mark 4) for 1½ to 1¾ hours.

CAROB

Family: *Leguminosae*
Genus: *Ceratonia*
Species: *Ceratonia siliqua*

This is also known as the locust-bean, locust-seed or Saint John's bread. The fruit of a dark green evergreen tree which grows wild in the Mediterranean, carob is much used in the Middle East and in Chinese cooking. The tree looks rather like a small apple tree with red and yellow flowers and produces a brown leathery pod 4–10 inches long which is both edible and ornamental. I first encountered such a tree in Greece and enjoyed taking a pod or two on my way down to the beach as dessert for lunch.

I had always assumed that when John the Baptist lived in the wilderness on locust and wild honey he was actually eating the locust insect. This may have been part of my childhood upbringing because I distinctly remember in Dar-es-Salaam young boys bringing round tin cans of long-legged dragonflies which came out in their hundreds after the rain. I also remember getting soundly spanked when I bought a can and ate the contents. But they were offered for the purposes of eating! However, the locust John ate was the carob pod.

The whole pod has a sweet, rather natural flavour and can be used in cooking or made into syrup. A gum extracted from carob seed is used like gum tragacanth in industry. Bread made from carob flour is called locust bread.

Nutritional and medicinal properties

Carob is an excellent, well-balanced food rich in vitamin A and the B-complex vitamins and it contains valuable minerals, particularly calcium and phosphorus, as well as iron, copper and magnesium. The flower is recommended for non-specific diarrhoea and is good for weak babies who can't keep food down. It is a natural pectin and recent research has shown that this makes it useful for

100 g CAROB FLOUR	
Calories	180
Protein (g)	18
Carbohydrate (g)	80
Cholesterol (g)	–
Fat (g)	1.4
Fibre (g)	7.7
Minerals	
calcium (mg)	343
phosphorus (mg)	80
iron (mg)	0
sodium (mg)	–
potassium (mg)	–
magnesium (mg)	–
zinc (mg)	–
iodine (mg)	–
chlorine (mg)	–
sulphur (mg)	–
silicon (mg)	–
bromine (mg)	–
Vitamins	
A(IU)	–
B_1 (mg)	–
B_2 (mg)	–
B_3 (mg)	–
B_5 (mg)	–
B_6 (mg)	–
B_{12} (mcg)	0
folic acid (mcg)	–
biotin (mcg)	–
C (mg)	–
D (mg)	–
E (mg)	–
Organic acids	
citric (%)	–
malic (%)	–
oxalic (%)	–
Water (%)	11.2
Digestion time (hrs)	–

diarrhoea and stomach upsets. Use one tablespoon of powder to 8 fluid ounces of water.

Carob is interchangeable with chocolate though I cannot pretend it tastes exactly the same. It has a distinct advantage over chocolate in as much as all cocoa-bean products contain caffeine and need to be artificially sweetened with sugar which carob does not. Cocoa beans are also high in oxalic acid, which is known to have the ability to lock in calcium and make it unavailable to the body. Chocolate is generally processed with harsh alkalis and contains theobromine both of which are toxic to the liver. I think of carob with its 50 per cent natural sugars, not as second-best chocolate but as first-rate food.

Carob honey biscuits (*makes 16*)

Those who crave chocolate biscuits are assured that these make a very satisfying substitute.

4 oz (100 g) butter
⅔ cup honey
2 eggs
1 teaspoon vanilla essence
½ teaspoon salt
4 oz (100 g) carob powder
6 oz (175 g) wholewheat flour
1 teaspoon baking powder
1 cup chopped, toasted hazelnuts
3 tablespoons milk

Cream the butter and honey together and beat in the eggs, then beat in the essence and salt. Sift together the carob powder, flour and baking powder, and stir in the nuts and milk.

Turn the mixture into a 9 in (23 cm) square well-oiled baking tin, and bake for 30 minutes in an oven preheated to 350°F (180°C, gas mark 4). Cut into squares while still warm. When cool, store in an air-tight container.

CARROT

Family: *Umbelliferae*
Genus: *Daucus*
Species: *Daucus carota*

Native to Afghanistan, carrots were cultivated in the Mediterranean before the Christian era and were used by the Greeks and Romans as medicine. They spread north to Germany and France and by the thirteenth century had reached China. By the sixteenth century they were widely cultivated in Britain. In Tudor times sweet carrot pudding, impregnated with dried fruit and spices, was popular, as was a lighter version including eggs and cream. Sweet grated carrots added to the traditional Christmas pudding recipe will greatly reduce the need to add sugar. Indeed there was a time in Europe when carrots were used as a commercial source of sugar.

There are many different varieties of carrot, ranging from the white-rooted primitive plant of Asia to the small purple-rooted carrot of Egypt and the elegant long-rooted carrot of Japan, as well as the medium-length orange root so popular in Europe and the USA. The different shapes and colours tend to indicate different nuances of flavour. Carrots are grown extensively in Europe and are available all the year round. Britain adds to what it produces by importing supplies from Holland.

Nutritional and medicinal properties

New carrots, particularly the first thinnings, not only taste wonderful but are better for you than woody winter carrots. Carrots are immensely rich in carotene (provitamin A) and contain significant amounts of vitamins B_3, C and E, and sodium, calcium phosphorus, potassium, fibre and folic acid. They are very high in sugar (hence their sweet taste).

Carrots are best scrubbed not peeled as all these precious nutrients are stored close to the surface. The old adage that carrots make you see in the dark contains some truth because carotene is essential for the health of the eyes and carrot juice is excellent for preventing eye, throat, tonsil and sinus infections as well as for protecting the lungs, liver, kidneys, glands and genital organs – lack of vitamin A leaves the internal mucosa vulnerable to bacterial attack.

Cooked carrots obviously lose some of their nutrients including one third of their potassium. Ordinary canned carrots are far too high in salt, but diet canned carrots have less salt than fresh ones.

Creamed carrots *(serves 6)*

Pat Thursfield served this to me one Sunday lunch. It's unbelievably

100 g CARROTS (raw)	
Calories	42
Protein (g)	1.1
Carbohydrate (g)	9.7
Cholesterol (g)	0
Fat (g)	0.2
Fibre (g)	1
Minerals	
calcium (mg)	37
phosphorus (mg)	36
iron (mg)	0.7
sodium (mg)	47
potassium (mg)	341
magnesium (mg)	23
zinc (mg)	0.4
iodine (mg)	0.012
chlorine (mg)	318
sulphur (mg)	445
silicon (mg)	166
bromine (mg)	1.4
Vitamins	
A(IU)	11000
B$_1$ (mg)	0.06
B$_2$ (mg)	0.05
B$_3$ (mg)	0.6
B$_5$ (mg)	0:25
B$_6$ (mg)	0.15
B$_{12}$ (mcg)	0
folic acid (mcg)	7.6
biotin (mcg)	0.6
C (mg)	8
D (mg)	0
E (mg)	0.5
Organic acids	
citric (%)	0.09
malic (%)	0.24
oxalic (%)	0.0330
Water (%)	88.2
Digestion time (hrs)	2¼

simple and transforms the humble carrot from Morris Minor status to that of a purring Rolls-Royce.

Boil and drain 2 lb (900 g) carrots. Purée them, adding 2 or 3 large boiled potatoes. Add a little butter and plenty of black pepper. Serve very hot.

CASHEW-NUT

Family: *Anacardiaceae*
Genus: *Anacardium*
Species: *Anacardium occidentale*

It was the Portuguese who first took cashew-nuts from their native habitat in Brazil to East Africa and from there to Mozambique and India. India is now the largest exporter of cashews in the world.

The trees sometimes reach 40 feet in height, supporting large, leathery, green leaves, up to 6 inches long and 4 inches wide. Each fruit contains one nut. The cashew tree is related to poison ivy and the nut shell contains an irritating poison which can cause skin blisters on contact. For this reason the outer layer has to be removed by roasting or steaming to get rid of the acrid fluid before the nut is safe to eat. The cashew is attached to a pedicle called an 'apple' or 'cashew pear' and in its native Brazil is often simply detached from the nut itself so that only the 'apple' is consumed. The nut is white, sweet and kidney-shaped and extremely versatile as far as its culinary uses are concerned, capable of being salted, roasted, creamed, made into liquor (as it is in Goa in India) or used in sauces for its bland, sweet flavour.

See also: Nuts.

Nutritional and medicinal properties

Cashew-nuts are good body-builders and easily digested when

raw (having first been deprived of their acrid fluid) and so help in cases of emaciation and in building good teeth. Boiling them in oil or salting them makes them harder to digest, so they are best eaten in their natural state. They go best with acid fruit and non-starchy vegetables rather than sweet fruit and heavy starch. Like all nuts cashews contain a great deal of unsaturated fatty acid, mostly in the form of oleic acid.

Cashew cream

This is a cream substitute. It's expensive and no less calorific than cream, but it tastes good, goes with all sorts of fruit and is the ideal alternative for those whose sinues go on strike at the first sniff of real double cream.

4 oz (100 g) unsalted cashews
4 oz (100 g) cottage cheese
1 tablespoon honey
¼ pint (150 ml) water

Blend all the ingredients together in a liquidizer until smooth.

CAULIFLOWER

Family: *Cruciferae*
Genus: *Brassica*
Species: *Brassica oleracea* var.
              botrytis

Cauliflower was first cultivated in the Middle East and arrived in Europe in the thirteenth century. It came to England from Cyprus at the beginning of the seventeenth century. Originally the head was only the size of a tennis ball. Ironically modern freezing firms are experimenting with dwarf varieties to ease the headache of packing. One grower of a large cauliflower in England in the seventeenth century was so proud of his achievement he had one carved on his tombstone.

Mark Twain denigrated the cauliflower as 'nothing but cabbage with a college education', but its delicate flavour is well worth the careful handling it requires to emphasize it.

Cauliflowers need a uniform cold climate to grow well, and are obtainable all year round but are best in season during May and June. Fresh cauliflower is incomparably better in flavour than frozen florets and is best of all eaten raw, as it tastes delightfully nutty, rather like walnuts. If you are cooking a whole cauliflower, cut an X in its base to speed the cooking of the stalk.

Nutritional and medicinal properties

Cauliflower is not quite so rich in vitamins and minerals as some of its relatives but contains good amounts of phosphorus, sulphur, calcium and sodium and vitamins A and C. In fact an average helping of cauliflower supplies half the daily recommended vitamin C requirement (though the amount recommended is far too low in my opinion). The tender pale green leaves that encase the head are rich in minerals, so leave some of these on.

Cauliflower has a high sulphur content which may cause indigestion and poor food assimilation, so do not combine it with other sulphur-rich foods like onions.

Cooked frozen cauliflower retains two-thirds of its calories, half its protein, two-thirds of its carbohydrate and loses one third of its vitamins.

Cauliflower is a good blood purifier and helps asthma, kidney and bladder disorders, hypertension, gout, constipation and biliousness. Eaten raw it will strengthen bleeding gums.

Cauliflower salad

If you've never eaten cauliflower raw try this.

¾ cup olive oil
¼ cup red-wine vinegar
1 clove garlic, crushed in a little salt
freshly ground black pepper
1 medium cauliflower, cut into small florets
2 teaspoons finely shredded fresh marjoram
1 cup coarsely grated carrots
½ cup minced fresh parsley
¼ cup minced red onion
½ cup toasted slivered almonds

Combine all the ingredients except the parsley, onion and almonds in a deep bowl and chill for three hours. Just before serving mix in the rest. Serve with crusty hot herb bread or garlic bread for a light lunch.

100 g CAULIFLOWER	Raw	Boiled
Calories	27	22
Protein (g)	2.7	2.3
Carbohydrate (g)	5.2	4.1
Cholesterol (g)	0	0
Fat (g)	0.2	0.2
Fibre (g)	1	1
Minerals		
calcium (mg)	25	21
phosphorus (mg)	56	42
iron (mg)	1.1	0.7
sodium (mg)	13	9
potassium (mg)	295	206
magnesium (mg)	24	–
zinc (mg)	0.3	0.2
iodine (mg)	–	–
chlorine (mg)	310	–
sulphur (mg)	1186	–
silicon (mg)	337	–
bromine (mg)	0.7	–
Vitamins		
A(IU)	60	60
B_1 (mg)	0.11	0.09
B_2 (mg)	0.1	0.08
B_3 (mg)	0.7	0.6
B_5 (mg)	0.6	0.42
B_6 (mg)	–	–
B_{12} (mcg)	–	–
folic acid (mcg)	39	49
biotin (mcg)	1.5	1
C (mg)	78	55
D (mg)	–	–
E (mg)	–	–
Organic acids		
citric (%)	0.21	–
malic (%)	0.39	–
oxalic (%)	–	–
Water (%)	91	–
Digestion time (hrs)	2¼	–

CELERIAC

Family: *Umbelliferae*
Genus: *Apium*
Species: *Apium graveolens* var. *rapaceum*

Celeriac has only recently become popular in Britain. It originated in the Mediterranean and is available all year round, though it is at its best from November to February. The large swollen root, brown on the outside and white inside, can be eaten raw or cooked. Younger, paler roots have a delicately aromatic flavour reminiscent of celery without its stringy texture. Older darker ones taste decidedly more pungent.

Peeled celeriac can be cut in slices or chunks and boiled, drained and puréed with a little butter and seasoning. The taste is improved by the addition of an equal quantity of mashed potatoes. Slices can be parboiled, buttered and made into fritters. Or young celeriac can be peeled, grated and eaten raw with a dressing.

Nutritional and medicinal properties

As the celeriac root is the storehouse of energy for the long-stemmed plant it is high in calories and carbohydrates. It is also high in sodium and potassium, and is very rich in iron (0.6 mg), but it has almost no vitamin A.

Celeriac remoulade

This is a classic French hors d'œuvre. Instead of using sour cream I've substituted thick Greek yoghurt. It works just as well and is less calorific.

1 celeriac, pared and coarsely grated

sauce
the yolks of 2 hard-boiled eggs and 2 raw yolks
pinch finely ground black pepper
1 tablespoon Dijon mustard

100 g CELERIAC (raw)	
Calories	40
Protein (g)	1.8
Carbohydrate (g)	8.5
Cholesterol (g)	–
Fat (g)	0.3
Fibre (g)	1.3
Minerals	
calcium (mg)	43
phosphorus (mg)	115
iron (mg)	0.6
sodium (mg)	100
potassium (mg)	300
magnesium (mg)	–
zinc (mg)	–
iodine (mg)	–
chlorine (mg)	845
sulphur (mg)	295
silicon (mg)	210
bromine (mg)	0.42
Vitamins	
A(IU)	–
B_1 (mg)	0.05
B_2 (mg)	0.06
B_3 (mg)	0.7
B_5 (mg)	–
B_6 (mg)	–
B_{12} (mcg)	–
folic acid (mcg)	–
biotin (mcg)	–
C (mg)	8
D (mg)	–
E (mg)	–
Organic acids	
citric (%)	–
malic (%)	–
oxalic (%)	–
Water (%)	88.4
Digestion time (hrs)	3½

2 tablespoons white-wine vinegar
½ pint (300 ml) sunflower oil
¼ pint (150 ml) Greek yoghurt
fresh parsley, chopped, to decorate

Mash the boiled egg yolks to a paste in a mortar. Beat in the raw egg yolks to make a smooth paste, and continue to beat while adding the seasoning and mustard. Add the vinegar gradually (at this stage a liquidizer helps) and drop in the oil slowly. Stir in the yoghurt. Pour the sauce over the grated celeriac and mix. Decorate with the parsley.

CELERY

Family: *Umbilliferae*
Genus: *Apium*
Species: *Apium graveolens*

Celery is a popular vegetable related to parsley and parsnips. The plant grows 20–30 inches (50–75 centimetres) tall and bears curly yellow-green leaves at the top. The long, stiff, crisp-ribbed leaf stalks are the part of the plant eaten. Celery enjoys moist, fertile soil but grows slowly.

It was used originally in Egyptian rituals and was known to the Greeks and Romans. The wild celery of the European salt-marshes was very popular with the Romans. Garden celery was developed from this variety, mainly by the Italians, during the seventeenth century. Even when blanched, the original celery was exceedingly bitter and it was the breeding out of this bitterness which was the great contribution of the Italians. Before, celery was only used as a flavouring in pottage or for its medicinal qualities.

Celery came into widespread use in Britain and America only during the nineteenth century. Home-grown celery is now available in the UK from September to February and is best after the first frosts. It is imported all year round. It grows extensively in Belgium, Spain, Italy and Israel, as well as the coastal Mediterranean.

Today there are many horticultural varieties of celery, some of which are naturally white and called self-blanching, while others are green but without any bitterness. There are summer and winter varieties, as well as varieties grown for the root, like celeriac. Until recently, the most popular type of celery was banked up with earth to keep the stems white and this was traditionally available in autumn from Lincolnshire and the Fens. Self-blanching has put a stop to this by and large. **Pascal celery** is a heavy green-ribbed variety. **Golden celery** is blanched and white with yellow ribs, and for obvious reasons contains less chlorophyl.

As a flavouring, celery is particularly valuable in soups and stews. In northern countries the large salad types of celery are used but in the Mediterranean the smaller leafy green and bitter types of celery are more popular. Celery leaves may be dried and are a source of essential oil of celery. Celery seed is also used for flavouring but is rather bitter and needs to be used sparingly. Celery salt is salt flavoured with celery and is widely available.

Nutritional and medicinal properties

In summary, celery does not have much food value. On the other hand, boiling hardly affects the food value there is – though it does slightly reduce the number of calories. Freezing doesn't seem to make much difference either.

Celery was once widely recommended for the treatment of rheumatism and I have used it with a great deal of success on certain rheumatic patients. It is excellent for those trying to lose weight, though it is also good for stimulating the appetite. The fresh juice is a strong diuretic and is good for nephritis. Celery is also helpful for high blood pressure, catarrh, diarrhoea, diabetes and acidosis as it eats the acid in the body and raises the alkali levels, thereby clearing the complexion. It is one of the best sources of organic calcium and so is useful for strengthening the nervous system and helping insomniacs. A decoction made of the celery leaves was once used as a footbath to help chilblains, and in the past it has had a reputation as an aphrodisiac.

Celery with walnut dip

When you get tired of dipping celery into salt, braising it, or stuffing it with cream cheese try this. It makes a delicious change and a most unusual starter.

3 oz (75 g) skinned walnuts
3 cloves garlic
¼ pint (150 ml) olive oil
1 head celery

Pound the walnuts in a mortar with the garlic and gradually stir in the olive oil, drop by drop, stirring hard until the mixture becomes a thick sauce. (A liquidizer speeds up the process.) Serve as a dip for raw celery, offering bread rolls as well.

100 g CELERY (raw)	
Calories	17
Protein (g)	0.9
Carbohydrate (g)	3.9
Cholesterol (g)	0
Fat (g)	0.1
Fibre (g)	0.6
Minerals	
calcium (mg)	39
phosphorus (mg)	28
iron (mg)	0.3
sodium (mg)	126
potassium (mg)	341
magnesium (mg)	22
zinc (mg)	0.1
iodine (mg)	0.007
chlorine (mg)	1780
sulphur (mg)	650
silicon (mg)	430
bromine (mg)	17.60
Vitamins	
A(IU)	240
B_1 (mg)	0.03
B_2 (mg)	0.03
B_3 (mg)	0.3
B_5 (mg)	0.40
B_6 (mg)	0.06
B_{12} (mcg)	0
folic acid (mcg)	8.5
biotin (mcg)	0.1
C (mg)	9
D (mg)	0
E (mg)	0.5
Organic acids	
citric (%)	0.01
malic (%)	0.17
oxalic (%)	0.056
Water (%)	94.1
Digestion time (hrs)	3¼

CHEESE

Cheese is made by clotting milk by adding rennet from either animal or vegetable sources. The clots (curds) contain protein and fat and many of the other nutrients in milk such as calcium and vitamins. After a while they are gently cut and the liquid (whey) is drained off. The curds are then soldered and pressed into a firm cake and left to mature in a cool place.

Traditionally rennet is the enzyme employed to coagulate milk for cheese. The traditional form of rennet is derived from calves' stomachs. It is both expensive and objectionable to lacto-vegetarians. Hence rennet is being replaced by a vegetable-derived enzyme sometimes described by the misnomer 'vegetable rennet'. If it is rennet it does not come from a vegetable source. No matter — what is important is to know what is meant by the term. No-one knows how people first discovered the use of rennet, but nomads were often shepherds and were forever carrying things in pouches made of sheeps' stomachs and perhaps such transport solidified their lunch beautifully.

The casein – the principal protein in milk – once curdled forms a three-dimensional lattice-work which holds milk fats and the whole coagulum is called curd. If you squeeze out the surplus moisture from this curd, you have the beginnings of a primitive cheese. If you pickle the cheese in saline or with bacteria or fungus, you have true cheese. The liquid remaining after the curd is removed from the milk is the whey and contains very little fat, but it does contain the milk sugar (lactose) and some of the non-casein-soluble proteins. These can in turn be coagulated to form whey cheeses, of which perhaps the best known is the Norwegian Mysost.

There are countless different ways of producing curd and of extracting the whey afterwards – from cutting and straining, to hanging in wicker baskets or perforated jars – and there are many kinds of organisms, both bacteria and fungi, that will ferment the finished curd. These organisms operate either on the surface, as with Camembert, or sunk deep into the fabric of the cheese, as with blue-veined cheeses. There are many ways of modifying each kind of fermentation, through temperature, length of maturation and so on. Each modification effects the ultimate flavour of the finished cheese. It is not possible to make every kind of cheese from every kind of milk but each principal class of milk gives rise to its own very wide catalogue of cheeses.

One can, however, loosely classify cheeses into six main groups. The **soft cheeses**, either unripened or ripened, include low-fat varieties such as cottage cheese and high-fat varieties such as cream cheese. Ripened soft cheeses include Bel Paese, Brie, Camembert and Neufchâtel. Of the **semi-soft cheeses**, some – such as Munster – are ripened by bacteria. Others are ripened both by bacteria and by surface fungi – these include Port

Salut. Some are ripened mainly by penicillin moulds injected deep into the cheese – examples are Roquefort, Gorgonzola, Blue Stilton and Wensleydale. The **hard cheeses** are ripened by bacteria.

Some do not contain big trapped bubbles – for example Cheddar, Cheshire and Cacciocavallo. Those ripened by bacteria but spattered with cavities include Swiss Emmental and Gruyère. The **very**

100 g CHEESE

	Cheddar	Pasteurized processed	Blue Roquefort	Camembert
Calories	398	370	368	299
Protein (g)	25	23.2	21.5	17.5
Carbohydrate (g)	2.1	1.9	2	1.8
Cholesterol (g)	100	87	84	105
Fat (g)	32.2	30	31.5	26
Fibre (g)	0	0	0	0
Minerals				
calcium (mg)	750	697	315	105
phosphorus (mg)	478	771	339	184
iron (mg)	1	0.9	0.5	0.5
sodium (mg)	700	1136	–	–
potassium (mg)	82	80	–	111
magnesium (mg)	45	45	–	–
zinc (mg)	4.0	3.2	–	3
iodine (mg)	–	–	–	–
chlorine (mg)	–	–	–	–
sulphur (mg)	–	–	–	–
silicon (mg)	–	–	–	–
bromine (mg)	–	–	–	–
Vitamins				
A(IU)	1310	1220	1240	800
B_1 (mg)	0.03	0.02	0.03	0.04
B_2 (mg)	0.46	0.41	0.61	0.75
B_3 (mg)	0.1	tr	1.2	0.8
B_5 (mg)	0.3	5	2	1.4
B_6 (mg)	0.08	0.08	0.12	0.22
B_{12} (mcg)	1	0.8	0.62	1.3
folic acid (mcg)	12.4	11	–	60
biotin (mcg)	1.7	2	1.5	6
C (mg)	0	0	0	0
D (mcg)	0.26	0.2	0.2	–
E (mg)	1–1.6	1	0.7	–
Organic acids				
citric (%)	–	–	–	–
malic (%)	–	–	–	–
oxalic (%)	–	–	–	–
Water (%)	37	43.8	40	47.5
Digestion time (hrs)	–	–	–	–

hard cheeses, which need grating, include Parmesan and Spalen. The **processed cheeses**, which are made with dried skimmed milk powder and include citrates and phosphates as additives, are hard or semi-hard cheeses which are not to my mind particularly palatable. The **whey cheeses** include Primost and Mysost.

See also: Milk.

Edam type	Parmesan type	Stilton type	Cottage	Cream (full-fat soft)	Swiss	Swiss pasteurized processed
304	408	462	86	374	370	355
24.4	35.1	25.6	17	8	27.5	26.4
tr	tr	tr	2.7	2.1	1.7	1.6
–	29.7	–	5.6	1.2	98	85
22.9	29.7	40	0.3	37.7	28	26.9
–	–	–	0	0	0	–
740	1220	360	90	62	925	887
520	770	300	175	95	563	867
0.21	0.37	0.46	0.4	0.2	0.9	0.9
980	760	1150	290	250	710	1167
160	150	160	72	74	104	100
28	50	27	–	–	–	–
4	4	–	0.47	0.48	–	–
–	–	–	–	–	–	–
–	–	–	–	–	–	–
–	–	–	–	–	–	–
–	–	–	–	–	–	–
–	–	–	–	–	–	–
–	–	–	10	1540	1140	1100
0.04	0.02	0.07	0.03	0.02	0.01	0.01
0.4	0.5	0.3	0.28	0.24	0.4	0.4
–	–	–	0.1	0.1	0.1	0.1
0.3	0.3	–	–	–	–	–
0.08	0.1	–	–	0.005	0.075	0.043
1.4	1.5	–	–	0.2	1.8	1.2
20	20	–	–	–	–	11
1.5	1.7	–	–	–	–	–
0	0	0	0	0	0	0
0.179	0.274	0.312	–	–	–	–
0.8	0.9	1	–	–	0.4	–
–	–	–	–	–	–	–
–	–	–	–	–	–	–
–	–	–	–	–	–	–
43.7	28	28.2	–	–	–	–
–	–	–	–	–	–	–

Nutritional and medicinal properties

Most people think of cheese as natural because the process is strictly controlled by law. and no additives are allowed, but do bear in mind that dairy herds are given antibiotics and other medicines in substantial quantities. If you want to be sure of buying really organic cheese, look for the word 'organic' on the labelling. A true organic cheese should come from a cow which is not rattling with chemicals and emerge at about 101.5°F (38.6°C). It is then immediately chilled to 50°F (10°C) or less or held at that temperature to prevent the multiplication of bacteria until it is dumped into the cheese vat. Then it is heated to 88–90°F (31–32°C) to activate the starter and the temperature is increased to 99–103°F (37–39°C) to separate the whey from the curd and so produce the proper moisture levels. Since certain amino-acids are destroyed at 104°F (40°C), milk should not be heated to above 103.5°F (39.7°C).

Watch for preservatives like sorbic acid in Cheddar and Cheshire cheese. Edam may contain sodium nitrate or sodium nitrite while the rinds may contain colourings. Anatto is a vegetable dye used in Red Leicester and carotene is used in Double Gloucester and some hard goat's cheeses to give an orange marble effect. The processed cheese and cheese spreads or cheese-flavoured spreads are made by heating cheeses from various sources and blending them together to obtain a consistent result. Emulsifying agents, lactic and acetic acid, salt and flavourings are added. The cheese is then heat-fixed so that it cannot mature any further and the flavour will not change. Many hard cheeses are flavoured with added ingredients like garlic, onions and beer.

Cheeses vary enormously nutritionally, but as a group they can be considered a very potent food. Cheddar, the most common type of cheese in the West, on the whole appears nutritionally in the middle of the range of cheeses. Cheddar, with 398 calories per 100 g, is horrendously calorific but the drier Parmesan (408) and Stilton 462) outstrip it. Cheddar is 25 per cent protein and only Parmesan with its 35 per cent is richer, while the watery cottage cheese is 17 per cent protein, and cream cheese with 8 per cent protein contains much less. Cheddar is very fatty – 32 per cent, which is slightly more than most of the other hard cheeses. Edam contains less than 25 per cent fat. Cream cheese is nearly 38 per cent fat while cottage cheese contains only 0.3 per cent. Cottage cheese emerges with the most favourable ratio of protein to fat but it really does need to be tarted up to taste anything like palatable.

Protein and calcium are the chief nutritional features of cheese, and many cheeses contain significant amounts of vitamins A, B_2 and D.

Milk is the most common of all food allergies and cheese, if anything, cause more allergies even than milk. It should not be assumed that either milk or cheese is necessary, even for children. Symptoms of cheese and milk intolerance are excess of mucus, susceptibility to colds and sinus problems, and indigestion accompanied by flatulence. Solutions to the problem include boiled milk, yoghurt or butter-milk, or better still no milk at all. Milk and cheese are undeniably rich nutritional sources, but the many alternatives to both should be considered by people who experience allergies to them. Above all bear in mind there is no such thing as a sacred food, not even milk.

Greek salad *(serves 6)*

The only cheese I can ever eat with impunity is feta cheese – everything else causes me chronic mucus problems. It is made with ewe's milk and since half the world now seems to emigrate to Greece for their holidays is becoming readily available by popular demand here.

8 oz (225 g) feta cheese
1 cucumber
1½ lb (750 g) tomatoes
a few black olives
shredded lettuce or *cabbage*
* (optional)*

dressing
1 tablespoon wine vinegar
4 tablespoons olive oil
1 teaspoon oregano or *marjoram*
* or mint*
freshly ground black pepper

Dice the cheese and cucumber. Peel the tomatoes and chop them roughly. Stone the olives and put them in a bowl with the cheese, cucumber and tomatoes. Make the dressing by mixing the dressing ingredients together and pour it over the salad. Toss well and serve with hot pitta bread. If using lettuce or cabbage, line the bowl with it and then put the rest on top.

CHERVIL

Family: *Umbilliferae*
Genus: *Anthriscus*
Species: *Anthriscus cerefolium*

There are several other plants also sometimes called chervil, but garden chervil is the close relative of the common cow parsley, and its natural habitat is southern Russia, the Caucasus and the Middle East. It is a delicate plant, much less robust than parsley, which it slightly resembles, and it has a distinctive aroma of its own, somewhat reminiscent of liquorice or anise.

It has small fragrant leaves and grows to about 3 feet high. It is one of the best herbs for growing in window-boxes; if you sow regularly in warm conditions indoors you will have a supply of fresh leaves throughout the winter. The leaves are fern-like, lacy and a downy grey colour. The plant has small white flowers on top of hollow stems. It can be grown from seed or by root division and is fairly adaptable. It will tolerate both damp and shade.

In the old days, the large dark-brown seeds were blended into a wax for floor polish to perfume wooden floors. The roots were valued for their aromatic and stimulant properties and were used as a pot-herb. At a pinch, sweet cicely can be used in its place, because it has almost the same anise flavour. It is a herb which has to be used fresh, either chopped or in tiny sprigs. Add it right at the end of cooking any dish so that its delicate flavour is preserved. It goes particularly well with egg and cheese dishes and in soups and salads, and, because it's so pretty, it makes a nice garnish. It can be used in place of sugar to sweeten tart fruit like gooseberries, plums and rhubarb, though to be effective it does have to be used in large quantities. The delicate anise flavour goes well with cabbage and parsnip.

The green seeds, which come at the beginning of the summer, can be used as an interesting flavouring for salads, and later in the year the ripe seeds can be stored for winter use in vegetable stews and soups. In Germany the ripe seeds are ground up like pepper and used as a condiment and they are also popular in Middle European cooking.

Nutritional and medicinal properties

Chervil contains a volatile oil which stimulates the metabolism. The fresh roots are antiseptic and used to be prescribed by herbalists for girls during puberty. However, there is some division on this because some herbalists now feel that the root itself is poisonous.

The distilled water of chervil is a diuretic and acts on the kidneys. A warm poultice applied locally will ease painful joints. It was popular for soothing gout at one time.

Bonne femme soup

A sturdy, unpretentious soup, best served with wholemeal croutons.

3 leeks, chopped (use as much of the green spear as possible)
4 carrots, diced
1½ oz (40 g) butter
1 lb (450 g) potatoes, diced
2½ pints (1.5 litres) vegetable stock
seasoning
cream
chopped chervil

Cook the leeks and carrots in the butter gently for about 10 minutes, then add the potatoes, stock, a pinch of salt and a few twists of black pepper. Cook slowly for half an hour.

Liquidize, then taste the soup and adjust the seasoning. Add the cream to taste. Serve with croutons and a good sprinkling of chopped chervil.

CHESTNUT

Family: *Fagacea*
Genus: *Castanea*
Species: *Castanea dentata* (American); *Castanea sativa* (European)

The common European or Spanish chestnut is *Castanea sativa*, but many other species are widely cultivated, from North America to China and Japan.

The shiny, brown, sweet chestnut

is encased in a prickly, green outer husk. Chestnuts are sweet and floury when cooked and in many regions of southern Europe are eaten every day as part of their diet. The Italians grind them into flour for bread making.

Marron chestnuts, from France are superior to other varieties. Chestnuts vary in flavour, sweetness and their ability to keep, but they can most easily be judged by whether the brown inner covering will peel off easily. The trick is to split the casing and roast the nuts in the oven. You should be able to split the casing and break it away easily, but a brown, bitter, astringent skin may still adhere to the nut. Sometimes this will come away if the nut is fried in a little hot oil but no amount of treatment will strip the skin cleanly from a poor variety.

The European sweet chestnut should not be confused with the horse chestnut tree, *Aesculus hippocastanum*, whose fruit is not suitable for human consumption.

See also: Nuts.

Nutritional and medicinal properties

Chestnuts which are raw should be approached with caution because of their high tannic-acid content. They make good body-building material and are helpful for strengthening gums.

Chestnut pudding
(*serves 6*)

This is a good dessert to serve in winter – rich, but not overwhelming.

4 oz (100 g) dark carob chocolate, grated
4 oz (100 g) butter
3 tablespoons rum
12 oz (325 g) tinned unsweetened chestnut purée
4 oz (100 g) brown sugar
¼ pint (150 ml) double cream
vanilla essence
2 egg whites
2 teaspoons icing sugar
grated carob bar for sprinkling

Melt the chocolate in a double boiler (or in a bowl over a pan of hot water), add the butter, stirring it in as it melts, and then the rum and the purée.

Dissolve the brown sugar in a little water and boil it briskly until it caramelizes. Whisk it into the chestnut mixture.

Oil a shallow 8 in (20 cm) round dish and spoon the mixture in, smoothing the top. Leave it in a cool place to solidify.

Whip the cream with just a touch of vanilla essence. Beat the egg whites until stiff and lightly fold them into the cream. Stir in the icing sugar. Pile the cream mixture on top of the chocolate mixture and scatter grated carob over.

CHICK-PEA

Family: *Leguminosae*
Genus: *Cicer*
Species: *Cicer arietinum*

The chick-pea is native to western Asia. It spread to the Middle East and India and is now grown in most of the warmer climates of the world.

In the Middle East chick-peas are often sold dry and roasted as nuts, and they can be ground and used as a substitute for coffee. There are two varieties, one beige or golden and the other dark brown. Chick-peas have a deliciously nutty flavour and an invitingly crunchy texture.

See also: Pulses, Sprouted seeds.

Nutritional and medicinal properties

Chick-peas are rich in iron, calcium and vitamins, especially vitamin C, and have been used to treat deficiency diseases in children.

Chick-peas with yoghurt

This is eaten for breakfast in the Middle East and is very sustaining – an exotic version in terms of protein of our baked beans on toast.

4 oz (100 g) chick-peas
salt and white pepper
3 cloves garlic, crushed
1 pint (600 ml) thick yoghurt
2 pieces wholemeal pitta bread
3 tablespoons pine nuts
1 tablespoon butter
2–4 tablespoons chopped fresh
  mint

Soak the chick-peas overnight. Next day, drain them and boil them in fresh water until tender (about 1¼ hours). Add the seasoning just before the end of the cooking time. Beat the garlic into the yoghurt. Toast the pitta bread and cut it open lengthways. Fry the pine nuts till golden brown in the butter. Tear up the pitta into small pieces and put them into the bottom of a deep serving dish. Pour the chick-peas (keeping back a few) over the bread, together with enough of the water in which the chick-peas have cooked to soak the bread thoroughly.

Pour the yoghurt over the chick-pea and scatter the mint on top. Sprinkle on the nuts and reserved chick-peas. Serve immediately with dishes of spring onions and fresh peppers cut into strips.

CHICORY

Family: *Compositae*
Genus: *Cichorium*
Species: *Cichorium intybus*

There is confusion between chicory and endive. In France chicory is called endive or Belgian endive and the French call our 'endive' chicory. Chicory (which is also known as succory or wild sùckery) is a native to Europe and west Asia where its use can be traced back to the Egyptians who, like the Arabians, used the blanched leaves as a salad. Cultivated chicory was first raised by the Belgian Brézier in the nineteenth century. He discovered that chicory root stored in the dark put out green shoots which eventually form crisp heads of white, faintly bitter leaves some 8 inches long, which give a nice touch of sharpness to salads.

The large taproot of some

varieties is grown to flavour coffee. The origin of the use of chicory in coffee is given as Sicily in 1769 or Holland around 1800. Apparently it was first used as an adulterant. By 1832, it was forbidden by law in England, but because the flavour was so popular it was reinstated in 1840 with the proviso that it be properly labelled. The best chicory coffee is not very bitter, and tastes rather like caramel because of the high sugar content of the root.

Nutritional and medicinal properties

Chicory is rich in inulin, like dandelion root, and contains mineral salts and vitamins B, C, K and P. It is a weak tonic, a diuretic and a laxative and was once used to help jaundice. It was also believed to protect the liver from the effects of too much coffee drinking, and certainly it makes a much more effective enema than coffee, opening up the haemorrhoidal portal vein so that waste products can be dumped from the liver. It increases glandular secretion slightly. Before the discovery of antibiotics it was used to treat TB.

Please note really excessive and continued use of chicory coffee may impair the function of the retina.

100 g CHICORY	Chicory	Chicory greens
Calories	15	20
Protein (g)	1	1.8
Carbohydrate (g)	3.2	3.8
Cholesterol (g)	–	–
Fat (g)	0.1	0.3
Fibre (g)	–	0.8
Minerals		
calcium (mg)	18	86
phosphorus (mg)	21	40
iron (mg)	0.5	0.9
sodium (mg)	7	–
potassium (mg)	182	420
magnesium (mg)	13	–
zinc (mg)	0.2	–
iodine (mg)	–	–
chlorine (mg)	275	–
sulphur (mg)	270	–
silicon (mg)	–	–
bromine (mg)	–	–
Vitamins		
A(IU)	tr	4000
B_1 (mg)	–	0.06
B_2 (mg)	–	0.1
B_3 (mg)	–	0.5
B_5 (mg)	–	–
B_6 (mg)	0.05	–
B_{12} (mcg)	0	0
folic acid (mcg)	52	–
biotin (mcg)	–	–
C (mg)	4	22
D (mg)	–	–
E (mg)	–	–
Organic acids		
citric (%)	–	–
malic (%)	–	–
oxalic (%)	–	–
Water (%)	95.1	92.8
Digestion time (hrs)	–	–

Gratin of chicory

I first had this as a starter at 'Marielle's' in Market Drayton, Shropshire. It won my heart because it arrived so hot I could warm my hands over it, unlike so much of the tepid food encountered in restaurants.

1½ lb (750 g) chicory
1 oz (25 g) butter
1 teaspoon lemon juice
2 eggs
¼ pint (150 ml) single cream
freshly ground black pepper
freshly grated nutmeg
2 oz (50 g) Gruyère cheese, grated

Tear the chicory into 1 inch (2.5 cm) slices. Cutting accentuates the bitterness. Sauté gently in the butter and lemon juice for 10 minutes, giving the pan an occasional shake. Drain. Beat the eggs, cream and seasoning together, and stir in cheese. Mix the chicory with this mixture and pour into a buttered dish. Cook for 15 minutes at 400°F (200°C, gas mark 6). Serve very hot.

CHIVES

Family: *Amaryllidaceae*
Genus: *Allium*
Species: *Allium schoenoprasum*

This is the only member of the onion family found wild both in Europe and North America, and although it was used for centuries it was not actively cultivated until the Middle Ages. It has thin, grass-like, hollow leaves and hardly any bulb. The plant is a perennial with purple flowers. Chives are easy to cultivate and enjoy almost any sort of soil. They can be grown from seed, or by separating the root. There is a large-leaf form known as the giant chive.

Chives are native to the cooler parts of Europe, including Britain, and they grow wild in Canada and parts of Asia.

Chives have a delicate onion flavour and make a nice garnish for soups, salads, omelettes and cheese dishes, as well as adding a subtle flavour. Their high volatile-oil content means that they do not dry well, but they can be successfully quick-frozen, or chopped and frozen in ice cubes.

Snip off the flowers before they develop because if you don't do so the leaves tend to deteriorate. You will find you can harvest the leaves as often as you like and they will still grow back vigorously.

There is a large and more strongly flavoured crunchy variety of chive, called Chinese chives (*Allium tuberosum*)

Nutritional and medicinal properties

Chives contain very similar health-giving properties to garlic but they are altogether milder. They are rich in vitamin C and sulphur. They are a digestive and have antiseptic properties.

Potato chive salad

This is simple but streets ahead of the usual gluey potato and mayonnaise slop one normally encounters.

1 lb (450 g) new potatoes
1 onion, skinned only
1 bay leaf
3 tablespoons French dressing
lots of chopped fresh chives

Wash the potatoes and rub away a little of the skin with the fingers, so that the flavour of the onion and herbs can penetrate. Boil them with the onion and bay leaf until tender but still waxy. Drain, and allow them to cool only enough to enable you to handle them. Cut into slices.

Chop up half the boiled onion and mix this in. Discard the other half and the bay leaf. Dress the salad while it is still warm and add lots of chives (which are most easily snipped with scissors – a knife tends to tear and bruise them). Serve cold.

COCONUT

Family: *Palmaceae*
Genus: *Cocos*
Species: *Cocos nucifera*

The coconut palm is a native of Malaysia, although it now grows on tropical coasts all over the world. It is a tall and graceful tree growing 40–100 feet high and has large feather-like leaves spreading from the top of its branchless trunk. Clusters of large round coconuts grow among the leaves of the trees. Each coconut has a light, smooth rind. Under the rind is 1–2 inches of a husk made of tough, reddish-brown fibre. The husk and rind surround a woody shell which has three soft spots or eyes at the end. The rind and husk are usually cut away before the nuts are sent to market.

The most important product of the coconut is copra, which is the dried, extracted kernel, or solid dried meat from which coconut oil is made. Copra is also used as a livestock feed, fertilizer and for desiccated coconut. Coconut oil is one of the most highly saturated vegetable oils and has a thick texture like margarine. It is not recommended since it contains 75 per cent saturated fatty acids and little linoleic acid. It also tends to be rather indigestible.

Coir is made from the husk and used for ropes, baskets, brushes, mats and crude roofs. The flowering stalks of the palm are tapped, yielding a sweet liquid which makes the drink toddy, a fermented distilled alcohol. Sugar and vinegar can also be made from this. The young buds are eaten as vegetables. The trunk is used in carpentry. When harvested the outer husk of the nut is green, the flesh soft and the water sweet and plentiful. As it dries the shell darkens, the flesh thickens and the water is reduced. So when buying, always choose a heavy coconut and shake it to see whether you can hear the movement of plenty of liquid inside. The less liquid the less fresh it is.

To crack a coconut, first pierce the eyes of the coconut and pour off the liquid. Heat in a hot oven at 400°F (200°C, gas mark 6) for 15 minutes, then remove and crack sharply with a hammer. The shell will break easily and fall away from the flesh. The flesh can then be grated or used as desired.

See also: Nuts.

Nutritional and medicinal properties

Coconut has less protein than other nuts and is unique in having a very high saturated fatty acid content – ounce for ounce even more than milk. The saturated fatty acid in coconut meat contains a high proportion of lauric acid, which is liquid at room temperature. Because of this property it is used to make artificial milk and modified cow's milk products and this is another good reason for being a hawk-eyed label reader if you are on a diet low in saturated fats.

Coconut is said to destroy tapeworms acquired through infected meat. It contains organic iodine and can prevent thyroid problems. It is also used to help with constipation, flatulence, dysentery and intestinal inflammation, as well as for body-building. In the tropics the milk is used to soothe sore throats and stomach ulcers. Coconut oil is widely used as a skin lubricant and is commonly used in Ghana on newborn babies

100 g COCONUT

	Cream	Meat	Dried	Milk	Water
Calories	334	346	662	252	22
Protein (g)	4.4	3.5	7.2	3.2	0.3
Carbohydrate (g)	8.3	9.4	23	5.2	4.7
Cholesterol (g)	–	–	–	–	–
Fat (g)	32.2	35.3	64.9	24.9	0.2
Fibre (g)	–	4	3.9	–	tr
Minerals					
calcium (mg)	15	13	26	16	20
phosphorus (mg)	126	95	187	100	13
iron (mg)	1.8	1.7	3.3	1.6	0.3
sodium (mg)	4	23	–	–	25
potassium (mg)	324	256	588	–	147
magnesium (mg)	–	46	90	–	28
zinc (mg)	–	0.5	–	–	–
iodine (mg)	0.009	–	–	–	–
chlorine (mg)	–	320	–	–	–
sulphur (mg)	–	85	–	–	–
silicon (mg)	–	–	–	–	–
bromine (mg)	–	–	–	–	–
Vitamins					
A(IU)	0	0	0	0	0
B_1 (mg)	0.02	0.05	0.06	0.03	tr
B_2 (mg)	0.01	0.02	0.04	tr	tr
B_3 (mg)	0.5	0.5	0.6	0.8	0.1
B_5 (mg)	–	0.2	–	–	–
B_6 (mg)	–	0.04	–	0.03	–
B_{12} (mcg)	–	0	–	0	0
folic acid (mcg)	–	28	–	–	–
biotin (mcg)	–	–	–	–	–
C (mg)	1	3	0	2	2
D (mg)	–	0	–	–	–
E (mg)	–	–	–	–	–
Organic acids					
citric (%)	–	–	–	–	–
malic (%)	–	–	–	–	–
oxalic (%)	–	–	–	–	–
Water (%)	54.1	50.9	3.5	65.7	94.2
Digestion time (hrs)	–	$2\frac{3}{4}$	$3\frac{1}{4}$	–	–

who are massaged daily with it for the first month or two of life. It is good for sunburn and for treating dry scalps as well as conditioning hair.

Coconut milk

Coconut milk is very popular in Eastern cookery and by this I do not mean the sweetish liquid in the middle of the coconut but milk or cream made by finely shredding the flesh, macerating it for a short time in hot water, and then squeezing out the cream.

To make your own coconut milk, grate the flesh of half a coconut into a mixing bowl, add ½ pint (600 millilitres) boiling water and leave it to stand for an hour; then strain it through cheesecloth, squeezing out the richly flavoured milk. Coconut cream substituted for cream in making a custard gives a delicious result. Coconut cream can also be bought ready-made in blocks from some delicatessens and Indian grocery stores.

COFFEE

Family: *Rubiaceae*
Genus: *Coffea*
Species: *coffea arabica*, *coffea robista* and others

Coffee is drunk by one third of the world's population and is thought to be the most popular single beverage on earth. It is uncertain whether it originally came from Ethiopia or the Yemen but legend has it that Ethiopian goatherds noticed that their animals stayed awake after eating the coffee plant and the usual story is that the plant was brought out of Ethiopia – to the Yemen initially – between the years 575 and 850, which would mean that it was not known in ancient Egypt, Greece or Rome. It is certain that by 1200 coffee had reached Arabia where it was called *kahwah*, originally a poetic name for wine in old Arabic.

In 1600 Francis Bacon knew of coffee as something used in Turkey, and in time coffee was introduced to Europe and the first coffee houses sprang up in London in 1652. The Arab expression 'Let's have a cup of coffee and talk politics' proved international as coffee houses were centres of serious discussion and the seedbed of many businesses. Lloyd's insurance brokers started at the coffee shop in Lombard Street in 1688. By the end of the century plantations had been started in Sri Lanka and the French took coffee to the West Indies, from where it reached Brazil in 1727. Brazil now produces half of the world's coffee, but it is grown in almost every country with a suitable climate.

There are twenty-five species of coffee and *arabica* is the original and still the most important. Others may have better disease resistance or heavier yields but their flavour is inferior. Coffee is a small laurel-like tree with white flowers which look like gardenias and smell like jasmine. The berries resemble bright red cherries when ripe, each generally containing two 'beans', growing flat-sides-together snugly enclosed in a parchment envelope. The pulp of the fruit surrounding this is sweet and much prized by monkeys who have been known to denude plantations.

Coffee is usually produced by allowing the berries to ferment slightly so that the flesh becomes squashy and is easily washed off. The beans are then dried, separated, cleaned and graded according to size. At this stage they are greenish or yellowish and have no coffee flavour. There are an enormous number of different types which, after washing, develop varying degrees of aroma, acidity and colour.

I often think it's a pity that coffee does not taste as superb as it smells when it is being roasted – unhappily its initial fragrance is due to the rapid loss of the most volatile of its essential oils. If coffee is under-roasted it fails to develop its true flavour, and if over-roasted it tastes distinctly bitter and smells flat. The best coffee is made from beans which are quickly and evenly roasted for 8–12 minutes at 390°F (200°C). In this process the caffeine is split from the tannin – and the sugar is caramelized. While the beans remain hot the flavour continues to deteriorate, so it is essential to cool them rapidly and once cooled to use them quickly, because even in this state the essential oils continue to evaporate insidiously. On grinding the essential oils disappear even more quickly, and the oxygen in the air also begins to destroy the flavour, so for those who appreciate the best coffee a small electric grinder is a must.

Ideally coffee should be made with water kept just below the boil to conserve the aroma of the beans. Countries such as France and Italy which go in for elaborate percolators and espresso machines buy in the worst coffee, while the best goes to America, Sweden and Germany. Fine grinding allows the flavour to emerge more easily and is more economical, but it makes the coffee difficult to clear. The best coffee is made in earthenware pots by filtration.

Nutritional and medicinal properties

Most people are now aware that caffeine is bad for you. A breakfast-sized cup of fresh coffee contains 100 mg of caffeine, and the same amount of instant 80 mg. Caffeine stimulates the central nervous system and brain. It panics the adrenal glands into releasing stored sugar into the bloodstream, but when the anticipated emergency doesn't materialize, there is no burst of physical action to use up the sugar-energy, the pancreas produces insulin to balance the sugar levels. When this routine is repeated five or six times a day it can result in an insulin overreaction which pushes blood-sugar levels down too far and results in irritability, fatigue, and even chest pains that mimic a heart attack. Another cup of coffee may temporarily relieve such symptoms, and so the addiction cycle begins.

The continual strain on the adrenals and the pancreas may lead to nervous problems, an inability to cope with stress and to hypoglycemia – a permanent state of low blood sugar. It has been suggested that coffee is a risk factor in heart disease and may be one of the causes of high blood pressure. Drinking coffee does release fats into the bloodstream, which is why many marathon runners drink

100 ml COFFEE

	Percolated (made with 60 g ground coffee)	Instant (made with 1 teaspoon coffee powder/ granules)
Calories	2	1
Protein (g)	0.2	tr
Carbohydrate (g)	0.3	tr
Cholesterol (g)	–	0
Fat (g)	tr	tr
Fibre (g)	–	tr
Minerals		
calcium (mg)	2	2
phosphorus (mg)	2	4
iron (mg)	tr	0.1
sodium (mg)	tr	1
potassium (mg)	66	36
magnesium (mg)	6	–
zinc (mg)	–	–
iodine (mg)	–	–
chlorine (mg)	tr	–
sulphur (mg)	–	–
silicon (mg)	–	–
bromine (mg)	–	–
Vitamins		
A(IU)	–	–
B_1 (mg)	–	–
B_2 (mg)	0.01	tr
B_3 (mg)	10	0.3
B_5 (mg)	–	–
B_6 (mg)	–	tr
B_{12} (mcg)	–	–
folic acid (mcg)	–	–
biotin (mcg)	–	–
C (mg)	–	–
D (mg)	–	–
E (mg)	–	–
Organic acids		
citric (%)	–	–
malic (%)	–	–
oxalic (%)	–	–
Water (%)	–	–
Digestion time (hrs)	–	–

black coffee before and even during a race. It raises the pulse rate and may in certain sensitive people cause irregular heart rhythm or palpitations. Its tannic-acid content can inhibit the proper digestion of protein and the absorption of iron.

However, **decaffeinated coffee** is not necessarily the answer to a coffee addict's prayers, unless it is carefully chosen. As early as 1900 a German, Ludwig Roselin, devised a technique that removed the caffeine from coffee but questions soon arose about the damage caused by chemical solvents used to do this. Happily none of the decaffeinated coffee sold in this country now uses trichlorethylene, which was banned by the American Food and Drug Administration because it was a suspected carcinogen. But other chemical solvents are used and some claim that the acids left behind may be just as dangerous as the original caffeine.

G. R. Lane's decaffeinated coffee is produced using a chemical solvent but they claim that 'the small amount which is present in the green coffee evaporates, leaving no trace in decaffeinated instant coffee'.

Café Hag, the brand leader in decaffeinated coffee in Britain, use the carbon dioxide process of decaffeinating their beans. They insist on keeping the exact method a secret, so whether any chemical solvents are used and any residues are left remains open to question.

Nestlé also import decaffeinated beans but these are not processed by chemicals. They are flushed several times with hot water under pressure and the water dissolves the caffeine and is washed away in the liquid. The green beans are then washed and marketed as freeze-dried instant coffee called Descaf, the decaffeinated equivalent of Nescafé. Decaffeinated coffee may still affect the digestive process because of the amount of tannic acid present.

Alternative **coffee substitutes** include roasted dandelion and chicory roots (either separately or mixed) which are actively beneficial and various grain coffees made from roasted rye, oats, millet, barley, wheat, figs and molasses.

The longer a bean is roasted the more niacin (vitamin B_3) it contains. A dark-roasted bean will contain three or four times the amount found in a 'regular' roasted one. The longer a coffee is brewed the stronger the brew. If brewed for 10 minutes, it will gain 2 more calories per cup. Instant black coffee contains very few nutrients.

Black coffee may be invaluable in certain cases of narcotic poisoning and in acute cases it can be introduced into the body by means of an enema. Max Gerson the famous therapist who had so much success treating cancer used this as part of his therapy. It is useful in cases of snakebite to ensure the victim does not become comatose.

See also: Chicory, Dandelion.

Turkish coffee

The only coffee I ever indulge in is Turkish, and I salve my conscience by reassuring myself that it is prepared in such a tiny cup that the dose of caffeine I'm imbibing is minimal and so can't be hurting me!

This type of coffee is traditionally prepared in a *jaswah* (Arabic) or *cezve* (Turkish), a fairly small long-handled metal-lined pot made of copper or brass, but it is possible to make it in a miniature pot on the stove. The amount of sugar depends on personal taste but the usual measure (called *orto* in Turkish, *magburt* in Arabic and *metrios* in Greek) is 1 teaspoon per person. Ask for 'Turkish' coffee beans and make sure they are very finely ground and absolutely fresh. The recipe below is for one person only, so for more people increase the proportions accordingly.

1 level teaspoon brown sugar
1 coffee-cup water
1 rounded teaspoon coffee

Correctly served Turkish coffee should be as frothy as possible and in order to achieve this it is never begun with anything other than cold water and it is never stirred after heating the water. So this is the correct way to make Turkish coffee according to Metin Peköz – and he should know, he's an excellent cook!

1. Put the coffee in the *cezve*.
2. Add the sugar and cold water.
3. Stir well until the sugar dissolves.
4. Put the *cezve* on slow fire over a low heat. If you heat it too quickly it will discourage the froth.
5. As the coffee froths up remove it from the heat and allow the froth to subside.
6. Return it to the heat until the froth reaches the brim. Remove again.
7. Repeat this process two more times.

Do not add more sugar and do not stir or you'll disturb the sediment at the bottom of the cup.

Variations include the addition of 1 crushed cardamon seed and 2 drops of orange-blossom water; or 2 drops of rose water; or ½ teaspoon powdered saffron and ½ a crushed cardamon seed but leaving out the sugar. The latter mixture is Bedouin and needs to be simmered very slowly for 20 minutes, without the usual removals from the heat, so that it becomes very thick. Normally no sugar is added to this version. Turkish coffee is always drunk in tiny sips and served very hot.

CORIANDER

Family: *Umbelliferae*
Genus: *Coriandrum*
Species: *Coriandrum sativum*

Coriander is a hardy annual growing 2 feet high with white, pink or pale mauve flowers. If the leaves are to be harvested, it is sown in the spring, in which case it ripens in August and September. For leaf purposes, it is sown in the summer. It is remarkably unfussy about soil and will grow easily in a window-box.

Coriander is native to southern

Europe and Asia Minor and is cultivated in the rest of Europe, growing extensively along the Mediterranean shores. It also grows in the United States, Central America and India. It is one of the most ancient herbs and is mentioned in the Book of Exodus: 'And the house of Israel called the name thereof manna, and it was like coriander seed, white; and the taste of it was like wafers made with honey.'

Coriander has been cultivated for well over 3000 years and is mentioned in the Egyptian Ebers Papyrus. The name is derived from *koris*, which is the Greek for bedbug, because the plant smells strongly of the insects – not very pleasant! Green coriander was first introduced into Britain by the Romans, and was used up until Elizabethan times, when it gradually fell out of favour. Happily, it is now being reintroduced by Pakistani and West Indian immigrants. Elsewhere, it was probably the most commonly used herb flavouring in the world, from Beirut to China, in southern Asia, in the Americas and in Mexico. In India, a common delicacy, green coriander chutney, is made using coconut, green chilli, salt and lemon as a basis.

The leaves are fan-like and feathery and make a pretty garnish. The seed itself is spherical and may be split into two. It varies when ripe from pale green to cream or brown. It tastes sweet and aromatic with a slight hint of orange peel. In India, the seeds are roasted before grinding which gives them a curry-like flavour. They are used, whole or ground, in curries, chillis, chutneys, desserts and cakes. The seeds are extensively grown in Russia, Hungary, North Africa, India and South America. They are also valued for their oil, which is extracted by steam distillation. This oil is used in bakery, liqueurs, confectionery and medicine. In Britain and North America, coriander seed is used as a pickling spice. In the Balkans, it is used for bread and it is also eaten as 'sugar plums'.

Coriander is vitally important in the cookery influenced by the Arabs, including the cuisines of the Middle East, North Africa, the Balkans, Spain and Portugal, and spread from the latter two countries into Mexico and South America.

Nutritional and medicinal properties

Coriander contains volatile oil (about 1 per cent) as well as fats, starch, sugar, protein, tannin, flavonoids, glycosides, vitamins, including niacin, riboflavin and thiamin, and minerals, particularly potassium and calcium. The leaves are higher in protein than the seeds but contain less oil.

Coriander is usually used to stop griping caused by senna or rhubarb, which will mask the unpleasant taste of other medicines. Chewing the seeds stimulates the secretion of gastric juices. The bruised seed can be applied externally as a poultice between pieces of gauze to relieve painful joints in rheumatism.

In China, ripe coriander seeds are sun-dried and then used to stop bleeding, to break up phlegm and to eliminate odours. There is a Cantonese folk remedy for treating bad breath, foul urine and female genital odour which requires fresh coriander herb to be used in soup. Its main use is for the treatment of haemorrhoids, dysentery, measles, indigestion, constipation and anal prolapse. A decoction is sometimes used as a mouthwash to relieve toothache and also for gargling.

Coriander mushrooms
(serves 3)

6 oz (175 g) firm button
mushrooms
lemon juice
3 tablespoons olive oil
1 heaped teaspoon coriander
seeds, crushed to a paste
2 bay leaves
salt
freshly ground black pepper

Rinse the mushrooms, wipe them dry and neaten the stalks by trimming. Slice them into quarters and squeeze a little lemon juice over them.

In a heavy-bottomed saucepan, warm 2 tablespoons oil and add the coriander. Heat for a few seconds, but keep the heat low. Add the mushrooms, bay leaves and seasoning. Let the mushrooms cook gently for a few minutes, then cover the pan and leave them, still on a very low heat, for a further 5 minutes. Uncover the pan. Decant everything into a serving dish. Drizzle more olive oil and lemon juice over the top. Serve warm or cold as a starter, with crusty bread to mop up the juices.

COURGETTE

Family: *Cucurbitaceae*
Genus: *Cucurbita*
Species: *Cucurbita pepo*

Courgettes, called zucchini in the United States and Italy, are baby marrows with edible green skins. They are best when picked very young, no longer than one's middle finger, and should be cooked whole in this state. Larger ones are still perfectly edible but need to be sliced crosswise when cooked. They originated in the warmer zones of America, especially in South America, and in Africa, and they were brought 400 years ago to Europe, where they were first grown in Italy.

Courgettes are dark to light green in colour, with a light speckle on the skin, and look a little like cucumbers. The flavour is extremely delicate, almost elusive, and becomes stronger when cooked with other flavours. They can be cooked in a variety of different ways – fried whole or in slices in butter or oil, poached or stewed in their own juice, or baked in the oven. They marry well with tomatoes and herbs such as basil, dill and chervil. They also go well with other Mediterranean vegetables like aubergines, sweet peppers, onions and garlic, as in the classic ratatouille. They taste excellent flavoured with cheese, which should be subtle and delicate like Parmesan or Gruyère – avoid strong English Cheddar at all costs. They can be peeled, or left unpeeled, and can be eaten whole or cut into slices. It is not necessary to slice, sprinkle with salt and drain young courgettes but this does enhance the flavour when they are older. The flower can be cooked and make a very pretty dish. They can be either dipped in butter and deep-fried, or stuffed with a light stuffing and fried or baked in the oven.

Courgettes are available all the year round. Those in the shops are home-grown in summer and autumn and imported from Italy during the rest of the year. They are widely grown in North Africa and the East and flourish well in all sunny countries.

Nutritional and medicinal properties

Courgettes are high in vitamin C and contain a great deal of water, so are very low in calories unless boosted by oil or butter.

Courgette soup *(serves 6)*

This is a very substantial soup – a meal in itself with a crusty piece of brown bread and particularly appropriate on one of those damp early summer nights.

3 tablespoons olive oil
2 onions, sliced
8 oz (225 g) courgettes, sliced
1 lb (450 g) tomatoes
2 small potatoes, peeled and diced
about 2 pints (1.25 litres) hot water
½ cup shelled and peeled broad beans

100 g COURGETTES (raw)	
Calories	17
Protein (g)	1.2
Carbohydrate (g)	3.9
Cholesterol (g)	0
Fat (g)	0.08
Fibre (g)	0.6
Minerals	
calcium (mg)	27.7
phosphorus (mg)	29.2
iron (mg)	0.39
sodium (mg)	0.8
potassium (mg)	200
magnesium (mg)	–
zinc (mg)	–
iodine (mg)	–
chlorine (mg)	–
sulphur (mg)	–
silicon (mg)	–
bromine (mg)	–
Vitamins	
A(IU)	323
B_1 (mg)	0.05
B_2 (mg)	0.09
B_3 (mg)	1
B_5 (mg)	–
B_6 (mg)	0.09
B_{12} (mcg)	0
folic acid (mcg)	–
biotin (mcg)	–
C (mg)	19.2
D (mg)	–
E (mg)	–
Organic acids	
citric (%)	–
malic (%)	–
oxalic (%)	–
Water (%)	–
Digestion time (hrs)	–

1½ oz (40 g) small, wriggly pasta bits
salt (if desired)
freshly milled black pepper
3 cloves garlic
3–4 leaves fresh basil
2 egg yolks
2 tablespoons Parmesan, preferably freshly grated

In a large deep saucepan warm the olive oil and sauté the onions till soft and transparent. Add the sliced courgettes, then 10 minutes later add all but two of the tomatoes. When they are softened put in the potatoes and pour the water over all. Simmer until the potatoes are nearly cooked. Add the broad beans, pasta and seasoning and continue simmering to cook the pasta.

Meanwhile grill the last two tomatoes and remove their blackened skins. In a mortar pound the garlic to a creamy paste, add the tomatoes and a small bunch of basil and continue to pound well. Add the yolks and beat hard so you have a thin mayonnaise. (A liquidizer will do all this efficiently except for the garlic and basil which need to be crushed with a pestle and mortar first).

Once the pasta in the soup is cooked stir the soup into the sauce ladleful by ladleful. Return the whole mixture to a saucepan and heat it very gently, stirring well all the time to ensure that the egg yolk doesn't curdle. Just before serving stir in the Parmesan.

CUCUMBER

Family: *Cucurbitaceae*
Genus: *Cucumis*
Species: *Cucumis sativus*; gherkins – *Cucumis auguria*

Cucumbers are usually long and thin with bright green skin encasing slightly sweet watery flesh with a seeded core which can be eaten unless the vegetable is old. (In which case scoop out the seeds, stew the cucumber in vegetable stock till soft, and fill with hot peas, asparagus tips or indeed any delicate vegetable filling.)

Cucumbers grew in Asia 4000 years ago and the ancient Egyptians, Greeks and Romans used them as food and medicine. The Chinese enjoyed them. The Israelites grieved over the lack of them in the desert. Charlemagne cultivated them in his herb garden. Columbus found them in Haiti and they were later discovered in Montreal and Florida. The Romans brought them to Britain but they sank into obscurity until the sixteenth century, when they began to be served pickled or cooked. They were never used raw except as decoration, the raw flesh being considered only fit 'as meate for mules and asses'. Gerard recommended cooked cucumbers for 'all manner of phlegm and copper faces, red and shining fiery noses of every sort of pimple and pumple'. And this still applies today. Cucumber makes a wonderfully soothing skin pack, used raw, for sunburn and problem complexions.

It was really only during the twentieth century that the cucumber became popular raw. Even then it was thinly sliced and soaked in salt, which naturally made it indigestible as the pieces were often swallowed whole. It is much better to eat raw cucumber shorn of its skin (which is often too tough to be appreciated and soaked in the residue of chemical sprays), unsalted and cut into thick slices. That way you can revel in its ice-cool crunchiness.

Fresh cucumbers are readily available all year round, the main harvest running from August to September. Cucumber bought outside this time are usually grown under glass. Smaller pickling cucumbers with their pale warty skins are available twice a year in spring and autumn. Reject tired-looking cucumbers – they should be firm all over (check the ends especially). Cucumbers grow all over the world but Hungary is especially well known for them.

Nutritional and medicinal properties

Cucumber has few nutrients; and no fat content or carbohydrates, which makes it ideal for slimmers. They are 95 per cent water and once peeled lose all their vitamin A and the few trace minerals they have, but hang on to their vitamin C, folic acid and fibre.

Cucumbers are an excellent diuretic and are high in potassium so do not strain the kidneys. Among the enzymes they contain is erepsin, an enzyme which helps digestion problems and which in Japanese medicine is used for the treatment of troubled intestines. Their high silicon and sulphur content helps hair to grow, especially when they are juiced and mixed with carrot or spinach juice, and helps mend splitting nails. Combined with carrot juice, cucumber juice is good for the type of rheumatism brought on by too much uric acid.

Cold cucumber soup

I've eaten cold cucumber soups which looked nice and tasted of dishwater. This one is foolproof. It's a lovely pale green and tastes delicious, but do remember to serve

100 g CUCUMBER (with skin)	
Calories	15
Protein (g)	0.9
Carbohydrate (g)	3.4
Cholesterol (g)	0
Fat (g)	0.1
Fibre (g)	0.6
Minerals	
calcium (mg)	25
phosphorus (mg)	27
iron (mg)	1.1
sodium (mg)	6.0
potassium (mg)	160
magnesium (mg)	11
zinc (mg)	0.1
iodine (mg)	0.037
chlorine (mg)	660
sulphur (mg)	690
silicon (mg)	800
bromine (mg)	4
Vitamins	
A(IU)	250
B_1 (mg)	0.03
B_2 (mg)	0.04
B_3 (mg)	0.2
B_5 (mg)	0.3
B_6 (mg)	0.042
B_{12} (mcg)	0
folic acid (mcg)	6.7
biotin (mcg)	0.4
C (mg)	11
D (mg)	–
E (mg)	0.1
Organic acids	
citric (%)	0.01
malic (%)	0.24
oxalic (%)	0
Water (%)	95.1
Digestion time (hrs)	3¼

it really chilled and garnish it imaginatively.

2 oz (50 g) butter
1 onion, peeled and chopped
2 potatoes, peeled and diced
3 pints (1.75 litres) vegetable stock
1 large cucumber
freshly ground black pepper
bunch of watercress
¼ pint (150 ml) plain yoghurt

Soften the onion in the butter, but don't brown it. Add the potatoes and the stock and simmer for 10 minutes. Wash the cucumber really well. Don't peel it as it is the peel that lends the soup its delicate green colour. Set aside a quarter of the cucumber for the garnish, and dice the rest and put it into the soup. Add the pepper and cook for a further 10 minutes till the cucumber is tender, then purée the soup. Adjust the seasoning. I hardly ever cook with salt, but you may like to add a little. Chill. Before serving garnish with finely chopped watercress and cucumber and a swirl of yoghurt. Serve with hot herb brown bread.

DANDELION

Family: *Compositae*
Genus: *Taraxacum*
Species: *Taraxacum officinale*

This is a common weed, which gardeners often regard as a pest, found in temperate climates throughout Europe and Asia and it was taken by colonists to America. Its name is a corruption of the French *dent de lion* because of the tooth-edged leaves. It has yellow flowers and a thick, dark root.

Dandelions as a salad plant are particularly useful in winter and may be cooked like spinach, preferably mixed with sorrel. They have a strong diuretic action — hence the popular name in France *pissenlit*. It is best to cultivate them because the wild dandelion tends to be tough and have rather a bitter taste. The leaves should be blanched. The flowers are used to make wine. Dandelion leaves are sometimes used as a food for silkworms, if no mulberry leaves are available. The root makes a valuable coffee, which contains no caffeine and acts as a superb gentle tonic for the liver.

Nutritional and medicinal properties

The leaves are particularly high in vitamins A and C and contain more iron than spinach, as well as potassium, potash and glutin. The raw leaves contain 14,000 IU vitamin A to every 100 g. There are also traces of vitamins B and D. The root contains triterpenes, sterols, choline and 25 per cent inulin as well as sugars, pectin, phenolic acids, gums, resins and vitamins.

Dandelion has a notable ability to clear obstructions and stimulate the liver to detoxify poisons. So dandelion acts as an excellent blood purifier and much of its beneficial action on the liver and the blood is as a result of its high content of easily assimilable minerals, especially in the root. Dandelion root will also clear obstructions of the spleen, pancreas, gall-bladder, bladder and kidneys and is of tremendous benefit to the stomach and intestines. The root is a specific for hypoglycemia (the result of the high inulin content). For this, drink a cup of dandelion coffee, made from the fresh roots, two or three times a day and follow a diet consisting of wholefoods, remembering to eat a small amount of protein (sunflower seeds are ideal) every 2½ to 3 hours. Dandelion-root tea is used to treat diabetes that has been acquired later in life. It is of benefit in helping to lower blood pressure. It's also useful for anaemia, and is a great nutritive for the nerves and the blood. The raw roots made into a decoction are more effective medicinally than the roasted roots but a small amount of roasted roots, or some chicory (which has similar properties), can be added for flavour.

In China, the powdered herb or fresh juice has been found to be most effective in treating upper respiratory tract infections, acute and chronic bronchitis, pneumonia, infectious hepatitis (serious cases can be cleared up within a week or two, when a diet is properly controlled), urinary tract infections, acute mastitis, acute pancreatitis, appendicitis and dermatitis, and for preventing post-operative infections. It has the advantage over modern antibiotics in such applications in that it causes fewer side-effects. Any side-effects there are, such as stomach upset and dizziness, disappear completely when the dandelion treatment is stopped.

In China, nasty sores which will not heal and snake or insect bites are treated by making a poultice of the fresh dandelion root and applying the mash directly to the affected areas. In Europe, a white sap is applied directly to warts as a long-term reduction treatment.

Dandelion root coffee

The instructions for harvesting the root are very specific because the precious insulin content of the root reaches its peak in November.

8 oz (225 g) dried dandelion roots
a few cardamon seeds (optional)

On one of those fine bright November days go out and dig up enough dandelion roots to make up 8 oz (225 g) once dried, which depends on how much water they contain and how much earth comes in clinging to their roots. Hold the roots under running water and scrub off any soil with a vegetable scrubbing brush. Cut off any tiny rootlets with a knife and slice any particularly thick roots to $\frac{1}{4}$ in (6 mm) thickness. Now spread them out to dry on a baking sheet in the oven in a very low oven – 225°F (110°C, gas mark $\frac{1}{4}$) or less. This will take about 20 minutes, depending on the original water content of the roots.

Test to see if completely dried by cracking a cooled root between the fingers. If it merely bends it needs more time.

Store in an airtight jar. Before use roast the stored root on a baking sheet for a few minutes in an oven heated to 400°F (200°C, gas mark 6), stirring with a wooden spoon from time to time to ensure the roots become evenly brown. Grind to medium fineness in a coffee grinder. Boil up one level teaspoon dandelion root to $\frac{1}{2}$ pint (300 ml) of water for 10 minutes and add a cracked cardamon seed at the end for extra flavour. Serve black with honey if desired. Dandelion root coffee, if properly made, is quite bitter; so even if you don't sweeten your drinks normally you may unbend in this instance, but honey soothes and heals the liver, as does dandelion, so a combination of the two is a real treat for this organ.

DILL

Family: *Umbelliferae*
Genus: *Anethum*
Species: *Anethum graveolens*

The common name, dill, is derived from the old Indo-European word meaning 'to blossom'. Dill is a native of southern Europe and western Asia. It is mentioned in the Bible and has been in use as a medicinal herb since the earliest times. Its use by the ancient Greeks and Romans spread to central Europe, in medieval times, and it was then taken to America by the colonists.

Dill is a member of the parsley family and has small yellow flowers with feathery leaves. The plant grows about 2–3 feet high, prefers a warm position, and needs good drainage as well as wind shelter. It is biennial.

It was the Anglo-Saxons who first discovered how useful dill weed could be for flatulence. During the Middle Ages, dill was thought to enhance passion but on the other hand it was popularly called 'meeting-house seed' and was eaten by hungry church-goers during long, boring sermons (presumably to keep passion under control!)

Dill is now grown all over the world and is particularly common as a weed, in the grain fields of Spain, Portugal and Italy. It grows in India, Europe and North America. The leaves taste a little like parsley but the seeds taste much more like bitter caraway. They are ⅛ inch long, brown, with yellow ridges and flattened edges with a slight wing to them. In fact the taste is so similar to caraway that the latter can be used in place of dill. It is extremely popular in Scandinavia – indeed the use of it is often overdone – and is also used in Russia, the Balkans, Rumania, Germany, Eastern Europe, Iraq and Turkey, but seldom in the UK.

Perhaps the best use of dill is in pickled cucumbers. The seeds also go well with cauliflower, cabbage (particularly sauerkraut) and as part of the stuffing for vine leaves. Try half a teaspoon of dill seed in a large apple pie.

Nutritional and medicinal properties

Dill seed contains 2.5–4 per cent volatile oil, composed mainly of carvone with lesser amounts of numerous other aromatic chemicals. It also contains coumarin, steroids, flavonoids, glucosides, phenolic acid, protein, fat, carbohydrates and minerals, particularly calcium and potassium, and vitamins, especially A and C.

In the West, dill seed is used as an anti-spasmodic, sedative, carminative, diuretic and stomachic. It stimulates poor appetite, soothes upset stomachs and helps with insomnia and flatulence. It is also used to promote lactation in nursing mothers. Oil from dill seed has been found, in animal experiments, to lower blood pressure, inhibit the growth of bacteria and relax spasms of the intestinal and uterine muscles.

In China, dill seed is believed to

benefit the spleen, kidney and stomach and is used mainly for treating gastrointestinal problems, including abdominal distension, colic, vomiting, lack of appetite and stomach-ache. Chew 4 g of the dried seed three times a day. It is a useful addition to prevent the griping caused by other medicines such as senna.

Dill cabbage
(serves 6)

This is a satisfying meal served piping hot with baked potatoes and some grated cheese.

1 white cabbage, finely shredded
2 eggs
2 tablespoons water
2 tablespoons fresh lemon juice
1 tablespoon honey
1 tablespoon dill seed or chopped dill leaves
salt
freshly ground black pepper
1 tablespoon butter

Boil the cabbage briskly until it is barely cooked, and drain really thoroughly. Whisk the eggs and add the water, lemon juice, honey and dill. Season and whisk again. Put a large saucepan on to a low heat and melt the butter in it. Pour the egg mixture into the saucepan and stir with a wooden spoon until it thickens. Stir the cooked cabbage into this dressing, mixing well.

DRIED FRUITS

When restored to juicy plumpness dried fruits come up sweet and full of flavour and so are particularly useful during the winter months when many fresh fruits are not so readily available. Fruits have been dried since ancient Egyptian times. The ancient method of sun-drying is still used today for most of the vine fruits, but many larger tree fruits are dried by artificial heat.

Some dried fruits, such as apples, apricots and peaches, are treated with sulphur dioxide or other chemicals before drying to preserve their colour and to improve their keeping qualities. Most commercially dried fruit is sprayed with mineral oil to improve its appearance, although this retards vitamin absorption by the body. The only way to prevent this is by washing the fruit in hot water. Levels of chemical residues and mineral oils are strictly controlled but I would advise that only fruit that can be guaranteed to be untampered with and dried simply by wind and air should be eaten. This is more likely to be the case if the fruit comes from Australia or California. Fruit labelled 'unsulphured' has *not* been treated with sulphur dioxide.

Tenderized (moisturized) dried fruit is made by blanching or soaking whole dried fruit and packing it at high temperatures into airtight bags. The fruit produced in this way is plump and ready to be used without soaking. **Dehydrated fruit** has a much lower moisture content than ordinary dried fruit and comes in very hard little chips or cubes. It needs to be reconstituted in hot water before use.

Unlike fresh fruit, dried doesn't have to be labelled with grade or class. So look for large even-sized fruits and (except for currants) the general rule is the bigger the better. Avoid any that is dirty or badly blemished but don't worry if it comes stuck together in a solid mass – it simply means it has not been sprayed with mineral oil. Dried fruit will keep for up to a year stored in a cool, dry atmosphere away from strong-smelling foods. Decant dried fruit into dark containers as sunlight tends to make the colours fade. Loose fruit and fruit from an open pack need to be transferred to airtight containers and remember not to mix fresh supplies with old ones. You'll find that some fruits develop a white bloom due to natural sugar crystallizing on the surface but it doesn't affect the flavour and will disappear when the fruit is soaked or cooked.

Unopened packs of tenderized fruit keep for up to a year, but when they are opened the fruit should be refrigerated and used within three months. Soaked or cooked dried fruits will keep for up to about four days in the fridge or up to six months frozen in rigid containers. In fact all dried fruit freezes extremely well.

Rinse unwashed fruit in cold water, drain and pat dry with absorbent paper. This is particularly important if the fruit is to be used in baking, because unless it is really dry it will sink. To reconstitute dried fruit cover with cold water – or you can use cider, wine, fruit juice or cold tea for a more interesting flavour – and leave over night. If you are in a hurry, simply bring the fruit to the boil in water and simmer for 10 minutes. Remove from the heat and soak for another hour. Eight ounces (250 grams) of dried fruit give between four and six good servings.

Apples are usually sold in rings or slices. They retain their vitamin C content when dried. **Apricots**, whole or halved, vary in quality and size. Look for large fleshy fruits. Brown spots on the skin are due to rain damage and are harmless. Apricot pieces and slab apricot – i.e. whole fruit or pieces pressed into a block – have a sharper flavour, are cheaper and are ideal for cooking and jam-making. Small wild apricots or hunzas are pale brown and dried complete with the stone. Mild and delicate in flavour, they are best soaked and cooked. **Bananas** are usually sun-dried in slices or halves and are deliciously sticky and chewy to eat. They may be eaten raw or used for puddings and baking. Do not confuse them with dried banana chips which are sweet and dehydrated or deep-fried slices of banana.

Dates of the best quality are large and plump with glossy, golden-brown skins. They are ideal as an ingredient of stuffing, but do check that all stones are removed first. 'Red dates', also known as jujubes, are not dates at all but fruits which are dried or candied and used in

Oriental and Indian cookery. The date has the highest natural sugar content of all dried fruits. **Figs** vary in size and colour. Look for large, pale or honey-coloured fruits. The natural sugar tends to crystallize on the surface soon after drying so figs may be coated with glucose to prevent this, in which case they will look very white. I would advise that all glucose-covered dried fruit be avoided as far as possible. **Pears** are usually sold in halves and quarters.

Peaches and **nectarines** are stoned and halved or cut into slices. They vary in colour from yellow to deep golden orange and are not as readily available as the other dried fruits. **Prunes** come from a special variety of plum and are well known for their laxative effect. Whole dried prunes are graded according to the number per kilogram (around 38 for jumbo or giant prunes to over 200 for breakfast prunes). The best quality come from South America and California. The prunes with stones keep their shape best during cooking but pitted prunes are quicker to soak. Prunes are also available chopped or minced and are ideal for puréeing and cooking.

All the vine fruits are simply dried grapes. **Currants** are made from small black seedless grapes. Large ones sometimes contain tiny pips. Seedless **raisins** are made from seedless white or red grapes. Stone raisins come from larger grapes and are flat and sticky. Dessert raisins are the most expensive of all and are eaten as they are. Muscatel raisins are usually sold dried in bunches.

You need to squeeze out the pips by gently rubbing them through the fingertips. To my mind they are the most delicious dried fruit of all. Baking raisins are seedless and coated in vegetable oil which is supposed to prevent scorching in caramelization during cooking. Personally I can't detect a significant difference and I certainly don't think they are worth the higher price. **Sultanas** are made from seedless white grapes and are usually dipped in alkaline solution to speed drying time. They are sweeter than currants and raisins. Mixed dried fruit, sometimes cake fruit, is a mixture of vine fruits.

Glacé and crystallized fruit should never be confused with dried fruit. They are made by soaking fruit in a sugar solution which gradually replaces the moisture in the fruit.

Drying fruit at home

Most instructions for drying fruit at home tend to include the old-fashioned suggestions for sulphuring and blanching. Sulphuring is done by leaving the food for hours in a box with burning sulphur. The primary reason for doing it is cosmetic because sulphured fruit doesn't darken much while drying. The sulphur also imparts a sour taste, and prevents the loss of some of the vitamin A and C while destroying the B vitamins – in all a negative net advantage. Blanched dried fruit is moister than unblanched, but blanching means that you dry a cooked fruit instead of a raw one, so unblanched dried fruit is superior in both flavour and nutrition.

To dry **apples**, first core the fruit and cut it into rings or halves and then into slices. Do not peel. Leave it out for 3–4 days in the sun, or 2–4 hours in a low oven.

Halve and pip **apricots** and leave them for 2–3 days in the sun, or 8–12 hours in a low oven. Dry **figs** whole. In coastal areas pick them when ripe, but if picking them inland leave them on the tree until they are two-thirds dried, then

100 g DRIED FRUIT

	Figs	Banana	Currants
Calories	274	340	243
Protein (g)	4.3	4.4	1.7
Carbohydrate (g)	69.1	86.6	63.1
Cholesterol (g)	–	–	–
Fat (g)	1.3	–	tr
Fibre (g)	5.6	2	6.5
Minerals			
calcium (mg)	126	32	95
phosphorus (mg)	77	104	40
iron (mg)	3	2.8	1.8
sodium (mg)	34	4	20
potassium (mg)	640	1477	710
magnesium (mg)	71	132	36
zinc (mg)	–	–	0.1
iodine (mg)	–	–	–
chlorine (mg)	100	–	16
sulphur (mg)	270	–	31
silicon (mg)	240	–	–
bromine (mg)	–	–	–
Vitamins			
A(IU)	80	760	–
B_1 (mg)	0.10	0.18	0.03
B_2 (mg)	0.1	0.24	0.08
B_3 (mg)	0.7	2.8	0.5
B_5 (mg)	–	–	–
B_6 (mg)	–	–	0.3
B_{12} (mcg)	–	–	0
folic acid (mcg)	–	–	11
biotin (mcg)	–	–	–
C (mg)	–	–	–
D (mg)	–	–	–
E (mg)	–	–	–
Organic acids			
citric (%)	–	–	–
malic (%)	–	–	–
oxalic (%)	–	–	–
Water (%)	23	3	22
Digestion time (hrs)	2½	–	–

leave them for 2–5 days in the sun, or 2–7 in a low oven. **Grapes** need 2–5 days in the sun, or 4–7 hours in a low oven.

Halve and pit **nectarines** and **peaches** and leave for 3–5 days in the sun, or 12–16 hours in a low oven. Rinse **plums** in hot tap-water to remove any spores, which can cause mould, and dry them whole. They need 4–5 days in the sun, or 12–16 hours in a low oven.

In all cases cool before testing for proper dryness. Dried fruit is ready

Sultanas	Apricot	Raisins	Prune	Californian date (natural dry)
250	260	289	255	274
1.8	5	2.5	2.1	2.2
64.7	66.5	77.4	67.4	72.9
–	–	0	–	–
tr	0.5	0.2	0.6	0.5
7	3	0.9	1.6	2.3
52	67	62	51	59
95	108	101	79	63
1.8	5.5	3.5	3.9	3
53	26	27	8	1
860	979	763	694	648
35	62	35	40	58
0.1	–	–	–	–
–	–	0.003	0.003	0.001
16	–	210	10	390
44	164	255	80	120
–	–	–	90	–
–	–	–	–	–
5	10900	20	1600	50
0.1	0.01	0.11	0.09	0.09
0.08	0.16	0.08	0.17	0.10
0.5	3.3	0.5	1.6	2.2
–	–	–	–	–
0.3	0.07	0.194	0.24	0.153
0	0	0	0	0
4	14	10.6	4.8	24.9
–	–	–	–	–
–	12	1	3	0
–	0	0	0	0
–	0.5	–	–	–
–	0.35	–	0	–
–	0.81	–	1.44	–
–	–	–	0.0058	–
18.3	25	18	28	22.5
–	–	2	3	2½

when the moisture is no longer evident but there is still pliability, before brittleness sets in. After allowing the fruit to cool, cut across to expose a cross-section. When you do so no moisture should appear, but the texture should still be leathery.

Christmas pudding
(serves 6–8)

This recipe is so sensational that my patients insist I pin it up on the noticeboard yearly, so that they can make it. It is very light, and no trouble at all to make, yet tastes appropriately rich and fruity – undoubtedly the best Christmas pudding I've ever eaten. Lexia raisins are juicier and plumper than the average raisin.

2 whole pieces candied peel
3 oz (75 g) wheatmeal
    breadcrumbs
4 oz (100 g) Muscovado sugar
3 oz (75 g) unsalted butter
rind and juice of 1 lemon
1 tablespoon skimmed milk
3 tablespoons brandy
¼ teaspoon freshly grated nutmeg
1½ teaspoons cinnamon
4 oz (100 g) ground almonds
8 oz (225 g) Lexia raisins
8 oz (225 g) sultanas
2 eggs, beaten

Pour boiling water over the peel and leave it to soften for 3–4 minutes. Drain, slice, then dice it very finely. Mix the breadcrumbs and sugar, then add the butter, lemon rind and juice, milk and brandy, and beat well. Add the spices, almonds, dried fruit and eggs and mix well again. Decant into a 1¾ pint (1 litre) basin. Cover with a disc of greaseproof paper and secure a roasting bag over the top, tied on with string. Steam for 4 hours and then for a further hour on the day.

None of this nonsense about making it months in advance and leaving it to mature – I put it together on Christmas Eve, and it still tastes as if it has an impeccable pedigree!

EGG

The amino-acid pattern of eggs is so well proportioned that they can be used as a reference point for judging the quality of protein in all other foods. They are particularly high in methionine, an amino-acid of which grains provide an inadequate intake. It is the cholesterol content of eggs that has made them controversial. Some researchers say that eating eggs does *not* raise blood cholesterol levels, while others say quite the opposite. Personally I think it is illogical to believe that any food that has played such an important part in human nutrition for centuries has suddenly this century begun to cause people to have heart attacks – unless the prevalence of heart disease bears some relationship to the drastic change in the *quality* of eggs. It has now been pointed out that even on a cholesterol-reducing diet, many doctors recommend an egg a day, and the idea that heart disease can be controlled by not eating foods such as eggs is

oversimplified and dangerous. Any food can become a liability if consumed excessively. It is increasingly being acknowledged that cholesterol consumption may have nothing at all to do with heart and circulatory problems. The cholesterol content of an egg ranges up to 200 mg while the lecithin content is 1700 mg. This is a ratio of nearly 1:9. The lecithin breaks up the fat into globules so that the body can neutralize the cholesterol normally. So I believe that the natural lecithin in the egg protects against the cholesterol build-up.

Of course the method of preparation of the egg can change all this. Egg fried in animal fat or margarine is more likely to raise the blood cholesterol level than egg boiled, poached, or fried in appropriate vegetable oils.

Free-range eggs are becoming increasingly popular. Research by the Ministry of Agriculture shows that battery eggs are 50 per cent lower in folic acid than free-range ones. However, factory-farmed eggs have more calcium and iron, depending on the feed used. Norwegian research shows that battery-hen eggs may have more antibiotics and residues of hormone injections and other drugs. The Farm and Food Society of Britain insist that the mental health of the animal laying the eggs is important in the final product quality. Free-range eggs may be fertile and the embryo chick forms a small red-brown clot in the yolk. A fertilized egg may contain many natural hormones. Good free-range eggs will have dark-yellow yolks, almost orange, but the deep colour in this instance will not be achieved by putting dye in the chicken feed, which is a common commercial practice. The shell of a good free-range egg will be thick and strong and a little bit hard to crack.

The white will be thick, not runny. And the yolk will stand up in a high mound without flattening out.

Stale eggs don't give such good results when cooked. The white becomes thin and watery and the yolk flabby which makes them

100 g EGGS	Raw whole	Raw white	Raw yolk
Calories	147	36	339
Protein (g)	12.3	9	16.1
Carbohydrate (g)	tr	tr	tr
Cholesterol (g)	–	–	–
Fat (g)	10.9	tr	30.5
Fibre (g)	–	–	–
Minerals			
calcium (mg)	52	5	130
phosphorus (mg)	220	33	500
iron (mg)	2	0.1	6.1
sodium (mg)	140	190	50
potassium (mg)	140	150	120
magnesium (mg)	12	11	15
zinc (mg)	1.5	0.03	3.6
iodine (mg)	–	–	–
chlorine (mg)	–	–	–
sulphur (mg)	180	180	170
silicon (mg)	–	–	–
bromine (mg)	–	–	–
Vitamins			
A(mcg) retinol	1140	–	400
B_1 (mg)	0.09	0	0
B_2 (mg)	0.47	0.43	0.43
B_3 (mg)	0.07	–	–
B_5 (mg)	1.8	0.3	4.6
B_6 (mg)	0.11	tr	0.3
B_{12} (mcg)	1.7	0.1	4.9
folic acid (mcg)	25	1	52
biotin (mcg)	25	tr	60
C (mg)	0	0	0
D (mg)	1.75	0	5.0
E (mg)	1.6	0	4.6
Organic acids			
citric (%)	–	–	–
malic (%)	–	–	–
oxalic (%)	–	–	–
Water (%)	74.8	88.3	51.0
Digestion time (hrs)	–	–	–

difficult to fry or poach without running or breaking. The white of older eggs also give less volume when whisked. Fresh eggs take longer to boil. To tell whether an egg is fresh for certain, put it in a bowl of cold water. If it was laid recently, it will have only a small air space and will remain at the bottom of the bowl. An old egg will start to tilt and rise to the top. Throw away any eggs which actually float, because they are bad. Warmth makes eggs go stale more quickly so

Dried	Fried	Poached	Omelette	Scrambled
564	232	155	190	246
43.6	14.1	12.4	10.6	10.5
tr	tr	tr	tr	tr
–	–	–	–	–
43.3	19.5	11.7	16.4	22.7
–	–	–	–	–
190	64	52	47	60
800	260	240	190	190
7.9	2.5	2.3	1.7	1.7
520	220	110	1030	1050
480	180	120	120	130
41	14	11	18	17
5	1.8	1.5	1.3	1.3
–	–	–	–	–
590	200	160	1540	1580
630	210	180	160	150
–	–	–	–	–
–	–	–	–	–
490	140	140	190	130
0.35	0.07	0.07	0.07	0.07
1.2	0.42	0.38	0.32	0.33
–	–	–	–	–
6.2	1.4	1.4	1.3	1.3
0.4	0.09	0.09	0.08	0.09
7	1.7	1.7	1.5	1.4
–	17	16	15	15
–	25	25	22	20
0	0	0	0	0
6	1.75	1.75	1.57	1.54
5.6	1.6	1.6	1.5	1.6
–	–	–	–	–
–	–	–	–	–
–	–	–	–	–
7	63.3	74.7	68.8	62.2
–	–	–	–	–

it is best to store them in a cool place or a refrigerator.

Other bird eggs account for a very small proportion of those eaten and are less widely available. Unlike for hens' eggs, there are no regulations covering their grading or labelling. Commercially produced duck eggs are sold in some supermarkets but quail, turkey, goose, gull, partridge and pheasant are more difficult to find.

Nutritional and medicinal properties

As well as the amino-acid content mentioned above, eggs are a good source of vitamin A and one of the few food sources of vitamin D. They are also a rich source of the B vitamins and of highly assimilable minerals. Of particular interest in eggs are the strong presence of inositol, choline and lecithin, all involved in cholesterol metabolism.

The membrane mixed with the shell of the egg contains avidin, an enzyme which interferes with the biotin in the egg, which is essential for proper cholesterol metabolism. Avidin can be neutralized simply by cooking the egg in hot water (160°F, 71°C) for five minutes, after which it is possible to eat it raw. All the usual methods of cooking also neutralize avidin but the less the egg is cooked the more valuable it is nutritionally. Rubbery, extremely hard-boiled eggs not only make the protein difficult to assimilate but also destroy amino-acids.

All hens' eggs of the same size and age have the same food value, whether they are white or brown, and whether they have light or dark yolks. Stale eggs have the same nutritional value as fresh, except that the older the egg is the less vitamin B_{12} it contains. Half the folic acid is lost in cooking.

How to make an omelette (*serves 2*)

I'm indebted to Colin Tudge for this health-giving suggestion about omelette making, which dispenses with the fat. It is offered in his excellent book *Future Cook* (Mitchell Beazley, 1980).

3 eggs
1 tablespoon milk
freshly ground black pepper
a pinch of salt

Break the eggs into a bowl, add the milk and seasoning and whisk until frothy.

Heat a large iron or non-stick pan (preferably one that has been well used), and when it is decidedly hot, pour in the beaten eggs. Stir lightly so the liquid on the top can run through to make contact with the hot metal underneath. Stop stirring when the surface is still moist, and there is little spare liquid, or you will not finish up with a properly integrated omelette. Serve flat or flip the omelette over on itself.

ELDERBERRY AND ELDERFLOWER

Family: *Caprifoliaceae*
Genus: *Sambucus*
Species: *Sambucus canadensis* or *Sambucus nigra*

Elders are part of the honeysuckle family. The common elders of North America and Europe are similar. They have clusters of white flowers which appear in June or July and develop into green berries, later turning red-brown and then shiny black. Elders grow prolifically in Europe, North Africa, western Asia, the Caucasus and southern Siberia. Note that several other trees which are called elder are not in fact members of the same family – for example, poison elder (a sumac) and box elder (a maple).

The leaves and berries give off a sickly-sweet odour which repels insects. Elderflowers have a flavour reminiscent of muscatel grapes and were once used to flavour inferior Moselle wines. Their inimitable flavour is so pronounced that merely dragging the flowers through jellies, jams or stewed fruit will ensure it is left behind. The leaves were once used to give a green colour to fats and oils. The berries are still used in wine-making, or as a fruit soup served with cooked apple and dumplings or fried bread. They taste quite strong, pleasant and rather bitter.

Nutritional and medicinal properties

Elderberries are a good source of vitamins A and C, and rich in phosphorus. The fresh flower-heads make a sweet, rather pleasant honey-flavoured tea which is often combined with peppermint and

100 g ELDERBERRIES	
Calories	72
Protein (g)	2.6
Carbohydrate (g)	16.4
Cholesterol (g)	–
Fat (g)	0.5
Fibre (g)	7
Minerals	
calcium (mg)	38
phosphorus (mg)	28
iron (mg)	1.6
sodium (mg)	–
potassium (mg)	300
magnesium (mg)	–
zinc (mg)	–
iodine (mg)	–
chlorine (mg)	–
sulphur (mg)	–
silicon (mg)	–
bromine (mg)	–
Vitamins	
A(IU)	600
B_1 (mg)	0.07
B_2 (mg)	0.06
B_3 (mg)	0.5
B_5 (mg)	–
B_6 (mg)	–
B_{12} (mcg)	–
folic acid (mcg)	–
biotin (mcg)	–
C (mg)	36
D (mg)	–
E (mg)	–
Organic acids	
citric (%)	–
malic (%)	–
oxalic (%)	–
Water (%)	79.8
Digestion time (hrs)	–

yarrow as a cold cure. They act as a gentle circulatory stimulant with a strong diaphoretic effect and so are very helpful in fever, as an expectorant, and as a mouthwash and gargle for mouth and throat inflammation. Served cold, they make an excellent diuretic. Fresh and frozen flowers are far more effective than dried ones. The berries are useful for constipation and to dispel flatulence.

Elderberry rob

This is a comforting hot drink to take in the winter if you feel you're going down with a cold.

Pick lots of elderberries – you'll know when they're ripe because the fruit turns and hangs downwards in tassels. Wash them and pack a casserole dish with them. Put the casserole into a hot oven till the juice runs. Strain off the juice and to every pint (600 ml) of it add 8 tablespoons honey and 1 large cinnamon stick. Cover and boil slowly till thick. Cool, fish out the cinnamon, and store tightly capped.

ENDIVE

Family: *Compositae*
Genus: *Cichorium*
Species: *Cichorium endivia*

The endive (or curly endive) is curly leaved, rather like a round lettuce in shape, pale yellow in the centre and darker green around the edges. The darker the leaves, the more bitter the taste. In the United States it is called chicory and in France *chicorée frisée*. There is another kind of endive called Batavian endive or escarole. This is paler in colour, has less curly leaves and is not quite so bitter. Endive is reputed to have been introduced to Europe from the East Indies although there is another suggestion that it may be indigenous to Egypt, and some place it as a plant that originated in southern Europe or in the Far East. Certainly the ancient Egyptians and Greeks knew it and the Romans introduced it to Britain. However, it was only cultivated seriously in northern Europe after the sixteenth century.

Endive is grown exactly like lettuce and does not like hot weather. Both curly and Batavian endives are sometimes tied together while growing in order to blanch the inner leaves, which are deliciously crisp. Curly endive is available in September and November while Batavian endive is available in the winter. Most of it is home-grown though the UK boosts its supplies occasionally by importing from Europe. Endives are excellent in salad and work just as well cooked.

Nutritional and medicinal properties

Endive is a good source of vitamins A and C and contains iron, calcium, sodium and phosphorus. The best news of all is that it is low in calories. Endives have been used to help asthma, tuberculosis, gout, diabetes, hypertension, catarrh, liver ailments, neuritis, acidosis, stomach gas and biliousness. A tea

100 g ENDIVE (raw)	
Calories	20
Protein (g)	1.7
Carbohydrate (g)	4.1
Cholesterol (g)	0
Fat (g)	0.1
Fibre (g)	0.9
Minerals	
calcium (mg)	81
phosphorus (mg)	54
iron (mg)	1.7
sodium (mg)	14
potassium (mg)	294
magnesium (mg)	10
zinc (mg)	–
iodine (mg)	–
chlorine (mg)	–
sulphur (mg)	–
silicon (mg)	–
bromine (mg)	–
Vitamins	
A(IU)	3300
B_1 (mg)	0.07
B_2 (mg)	0.14
B_3 (mg)	0.5
B_5 (mg)	–
B_6 (mg)	0.02
B_{12} (mcg)	0
folic acid (mcg)	63.7
biotin (mcg)	–
C (mg)	10
D (mg)	0
E (mg)	2
Organic acids	
citric (%)	–
malic (%)	–
oxalic (%)	0.0273
Water (%)	93.1
Digestion time (hrs)	3

made from the leaves was once drunk as a preventative measure against gall-stones.

Orange, endive and lamb's lettuce salad

This is a lovely winter salad and goes well with stuffed baked potatoes.

Cut a head of endive into 1 in (2.5 cm) lengths. Separate the lamb's lettuce leaves and divide the orange segments, collecting all the juice in a bowl as you do so. (The best way to prepare an orange in this way is to peel off the skin and pith together, and then run a sharp pointed knife down the side of each segment, leaving the fine membrane that covers them attached to the central core).

Make a salad dressing with the juice, 2 tablespoons grapeseed oil, freshly ground black pepper and a tablespoon thin yoghurt. Pour the dressing over the salad and serve immediately.

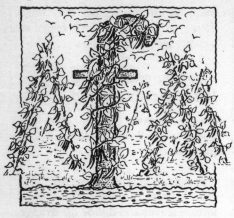

FENNEL

Family: *Umbelliferae*
Genus: *Foeniculum*
Species: *Foeniculum vulgare*

Fennel is a large plant which rockets up to 6 feet in height in a very short time, producing yellow flower-heads and bright green, feathery leaves. It is native to southern Europe and was much used by the Romans, who naturally brought it to Britain where it became well established before the Norman Conquest. It was widely used in cookery and medicine and for witchcraft. It was later taken to America and now grows there as a naturalized weed. Commercially fennel is grown for seeds in many countries, including France, Germany, Italy, India, Japan and America.

There are two main types of fennel, the first being **wild fennel** and the second **sweet fennel** (also known as florence). Fennel has a swollen bulb from which thick white stalks and green leaves grow. It tastes like anise and resembles celery in appearance. Wild fennel is grown for its stalks and its leaves. The flavour of fennel varies greatly according to the type. Wild fennel is slightly bitter and has no anise flavour. Sweet fennel lacks the bitter principle and tastes very strongly of anise. This is due to the large quantity of anethol, which makes up 90 per cent of the essential oil in anise itself. Sweet fennel is the type usually grown in Italy, France and Greece while bitter fennel is cultivated in central Europe and Russia.

Nutritional and medicinal properties

Fennel seed contains 2–6 per cent volatile oil, 17–20 per cent fat, and 16–20 per cent protein, and is relatively high in vitamin E, with traces of other vitamins and generous traces of calcium and potassium. It is an anti-spasmodic, calminative, diuretic, expectorant and stimulant. It has also been shown to have anti-bacterial and insecticidal properties.

One of the more interesting uses of fennel seed is the treatment of hernia of the small intestine. For this purpose a tea using 15 grams fennel seed is drunk while very hot. The patient then lies on his or her back with the legs together and knees half bent. If it is not possible to detect a response within half an hour the same dose can be repeated but generally the pain disappears about 30 minutes after treatment. Patients who do not respond 1 hour after this treatment often have to undergo surgery. Hernias successfully treated in this way are generally those formed no more than three days before – hernias of longer duration do not respond so readily. Fennel and ginger make an excellent digestive tea and will help with griping colic and flatulence. Fennel oil inhaled in a steam bath can vaporize mucus, loosening it and causing it to degenerate so that the eliminatory process can remove it through the bloodstream far more easily than can be done by coughing, sneezing or blowing the nose. This process is aided by fennel's high mineral content.

Stuffed fennel

This is Susan Campbell's excellent suggestion for a vegetarian supper in her *English Cookery New and Old* (Consumers' Association and Hodder & Stoughton, 1981).

2 lb (1 kg) fennel bulbs
4 oz (100 g) spinach, stemmed
  and blanched
2 shallots, finely chopped
olive oil
12 oz (325 g) cottage cheese,
  sieved
2 cloves garlic, crushed in a little
  salt
2 oz (50 g) dried wholemeal
  breadcrumbs
2 eggs
thyme, nutmeg, cayenne and
  parsley
1 pint (600 ml) homemade tomato
  sauce
grated Cheddar cheese

Divest the fennel bulbs of their hairy green stems and leaves with a sharp knife. Slice off the bottom of

100 g FENNEL	
Calories	28
Protein (g)	2.8
Carbohydrate (g)	5.1
Cholesterol (g)	0
Fat (g)	0.4
Fibre (g)	0.5
Minerals	
calcium (mg)	100
phosphorus (mg)	51
iron (mg)	2.7
sodium (mg)	0
potassium (mg)	397
magnesium (mg)	–
zinc (mg)	–
iodine (mg)	–
chlorine (mg)	–
sulphur (mg)	–
silicon (mg)	–
bromine (mg)	–
Vitamins	
A(IU)	3500
B_1 (mg)	–
B_2 (mg)	–
B_3 (mg)	–
B_5 (mg)	–
B_6 (mg)	–
B_{12} (mcg)	–
folic acid (mcg)	–
biotin (mcg)	–
C (mg)	31
D (mg)	–
E (mg)	–
Organic acids	
citric (%)	–
malic (%)	–
oxalic (%)	–
Water (%)	90
Digestion time (hrs)	–

each root and pull away the curved stalks. Reserve the innermost heart of the bulb for the stuffing. Soften the stalks by boiling in lots of water for about 10 minutes, and drain them well.

Finely chop the blanched spinach. Sauté the shallots in a little of the oil until soft and stir in the spinach. Leave to cool.

Mix the cottage cheese, garlic, breadcrumbs, eggs, finely chopped fennel hearts, spinach and remaining seasoning, and taste just to check. Put a spoonful of filling into each fennel stalk, and press the edges together to firmly capture the filling. Arrange seam-side-down in a buttered gratin dish.

Coat with tomato sauce and cover with grated cheese. Bake for 45 minutes to 1 hour in an oven preheated to 350°F (180°C, gas mark 4) until the sauce is reduced and the fennel heated through.

FLOURS

Most flours milled and consumed in this country come from wheat, some home-grown and some imported. The harder types which thrive in North America are generally preferred for bread, while the softer types typical of Britain are commonly used for animal feed and pastry. The crucial difference lies in the amount of gluten, of which there is an abundance in hard wheat, making it a 'strong' flour which produced taut, elastic dough that will encapsulate gas bubbles like a sponge and so rises easily. Soft wheat flours contain less gluten, so the dough will not puff up so spectacularly. The British baking industry has developed a technique for producing puffed-up loaves from soft wheat which are heavier but I think tastier. Besides which hard-wheat loaves soak up butter and other spreads like a sponge, making them nutritionally disadvantageous.

There are about 100 flour mills in Britain but the three giants – RHM, ABF and Spillers – produce 75 per cent of all wheat flour. White flour is flour from which the bran and germ have been removed. Brown or wheatmeal flour has the wheatgerm and some of the bran crushed and recombined with the white flour. Wholemeal flour has the whole grain. Rice, oats, millet, barley and buckwheat require a preliminary treatment to remove the husk, which is inedible, but wheat, rye and maize do not. Then the grains are scrubbed and – preferably – slowly stoneground. If the grains are ground with steel or roller plates the heat generated causes the wheatgerm oil to go rancid more easily and affects the flow of the flour.

Because **white flour** (72–74 per cent extraction) has most of the vitamins and minerals removed during the milling process, legislation passed in World War II compelled millers to add back certain nutrients like thiamin, nicotinic acid and calcium (in the form of chalk). Later, following a government report (COMA 1981) which considered that the original reason for adding nutrients to flour was no longer valid, the legislation was repealed, leaving manufacturers to add nutrients voluntarily instead of compulsorily. White flour which has not been chemically bleached with chlorine dioxide (the same bleach used to clean drains) has the word 'unbleached' on the packet. In the past white flour was often bleached with alum, arsenic or even ground-up bones from the graveyard!

The brownness of **brown (or wheatmeal) flour** (85–90 per cent extraction) depends on the amount of bran present – the more the darker. There is so much confusion in the public's mind about the terms 'wheatmeal' and 'wholemeal' that the Government has proposed that the term 'wheatmeal' should eventually be phased out, to be replaced simply by 'brown'. However, some brown bread is simply made from white flour coloured with caramel. If in doubt look for the words '100% wholemeal', then you will know that you are getting the bran.

Wholemeal flour (100 per cent extraction) contains all the grain and thus all the dietary fibre of the wheat. The only additive permitted is caramel.

Granary flour is the proprietary brand-name of a brown flour which has added malted wheat grain, giving it a characteristic nutty flavour.

Patent barley is pearl barley ground into fine flour and used for bread-making, generally half and half with wholemeal flour. **Barley flour** is made from the dehusked grain and **Barley meal** from the whole grain. Neither contains gluten and they are traditionally used in unleavened baking, making a heavier but more nutritious loaf than patent barley. Adding one part barley flour or meal to five parts wheat flour will give the latter a sweeter taste.

Buckwheat flour is coarse, quite heavy, speckled and gives a nutty flavour to breads. It makes the deliciously dark wafer-thin buckwheat crêpes characteristic of Brittany, and can also be used for muffin, pancake, biscuit and bread recipes, mixed with wheat or rice flour to lighten it.

Oat flour, which is fine oatmeal, is used for oatcakes, porridge and pastry, and one part oat flour added to three parts wheat flour gives crunchier scones and biscuits.

Rye flour, ranging in colour from dark to light brown, contains only a small amount of gluten. **Fine rye flour** is low in calories and used to make crispbread. **Wholemeal rye flour** is used to make dark, heavy, flat loaves and pumpernickel (a bread), both of which store extremely well and are much in favour in Scandinavia and northern Europe. For a lighter texture mix with strong wheat flour. It is also possible to obtain **'light' rye flour** which is sifted and consequently contains less bran.

Rice flour is one of the side products of the milling process and makes an excellent thickener. It produces delicate milk puddings. Combined with ordinary flour, it gives a crisp, dry texture to cakes and biscuits. **Ground rice** makes lovely instant puddings easily digested by babies.

Sorghum flour makes a simple unleavened bread, but the flour needs to be freshly ground or the oil in it quickly goes rancid. **Soya (or soy) flour** is made from specially prepared soya beans and is widely used in manufactured baked goods. It is also used to thicken soups and custards and gives a lovely creamy texture. For pastry, cakes and biscuits try using one part soya flour to five parts ordinary flour.

Sago flour is greyish and bland. It is used in bread and will bind slightly. **Yellow splitpea flour** is bright yellow and tastes strongly of peas, so needs to be used sparingly. It is an excellent thickener but remember it will add its yellow colouring to baking.

Potato flour (or farina) is very fine and white and tastes slightly of

100 g FLOUR

	100% wholemeal	85% brown	Breadmaking	72% white Household plain	Self-raising
Calories	318	327	337	350	339
Protein (g)	13.2	12.8	11.3	9.8	9.3
Carbohydrate (g)	65.8	68.8	74.8	80.1	77.5
Cholesterol (g)	–	–	–	–	–
Fat (g)	2	2	1.2	1.2	1.2
Fibre (g)	9.6	7.5	3	3.4	3.7
Minerals					
calcium (mg)	35	150	140	150	350
phosphorus (mg)	340	270	130	110	510
iron (mg)	4	3.6	2.2	2.4	2.6
sodium (mg)	3	4	3	2	350
potassium (mg)	360	280	130	140	170
magnesium (mg)	140	110	36	20	42
zinc (mg)	3	2.4	0.9	0.7	0.6
iodine (mg)	–	–	–	–	–
chlorine (mg)	38	45	62	45	45
sulphur (mg)	–	–	110	–	–
silicon (mg)	–	–	–	–	–
bromine (mg)	–	–	–	–	–
Vitamins					
A(IU)	–	–	–	–	–
B$_1$ (mg)	0.46	0.42	0.31	0.33	0.28
B$_2$ (mg)	0.08	0.06	2.03	0.02	0.02
B$_3$ (mg)	–	–	–	–	–
B$_5$ (mg)	0.8	0.4	0.3	0.3	0.3
B$_6$ (mg)	0.5	0.3	0.15	0.15	0.15
B$_{12}$ (mcg)	0	0	0	0	0
folic acid (mcg)	57	51	31	22	19
biotin (mcg)	7	3	1	1	1
C (mg)	0	0	0	0	0
D (mg)	0	0	–	–	–
E (mg)	1	tr	tr	tr	tr
Organic acids					
citric (%)	–	–	–	–	–
malic (%)	–	–	–	–	–
oxalic (%)	–	–	–	–	–
Water (%)	14	14	14.5	13	13
Digestion time (hrs)	–	–	–	–	–

potato. It does not bind well but works well with gluten-free flours. **Bulgar flour** is finely ground but heavy and needs to be refrigerated as its high oil content makes it easily go rancid. Dough made with bulgar flour has to be kneaded thoroughly because pre-cooking affects its gluten content.

Cornflour comes from maize. It is made from the hard and soft layers under the hard outer casing of the corn kernel, but without the nutrition germ. It makes a good smooth thickener, but has little nutritional value. Added to soft wheat flour it makes higher sponge cakes. Maize is also made into **maize flour (or cornmeal)**, which is yellow, may be milled coarsely or finely, and is used mainly for thickening soups and making porridge. It needs to be stoneground to ensure the best nutritive value. Some varieties have the germ taken out, so check before you buy. **Sifted (or bolted) cornmeal** is corn that has been hulled, ground and sieved, to give it a very fine texture.

Millet flour is low in gluten and is used to make the local bread of Ethiopia, *Injera*. It is a good thickener.

Gluten-free flours are maize, potato, sorghum, soya, rice and buckwheat, but it is also possible to buy specially modified wheat flours from which most of the gluten has been removed. Trufree flours have *all* the gluten removed, contain binders and bake just like ordinary flour. Some people are allergic to gluten and others (coeliacs, for example) simply cannot digest it. The Cantassium Company (225 Putney Road, London SW15 2P7) has a mail-order service for gluten-free ingredients and foods.

Self-raising flour contains a chemical raising agent distributed evenly throughout which releases carbon dioxide bubbles that expand during cooking and raise the mixture. There is generally 5 mg baking powder in every 100 g flour.

See also: Barley, Bulgar, Grains, Maize, Millet, Rice, Rye and Wheat.

GARLIC

Family: *Liliaceae*
Genus: *Allium*
Species: *Allium sativum*

Named from the Anglo-Saxon *gar*, meaning a lance, and *leac*, meaning a pot-herb, garlic probably originated in Asia but has been cultivated around the Mediterranean since the days of the ancient Egyptians. It is a relative of the onion and chive and is a member of the lily family. It is a perennial or biennial with sub-globular bulbs consisting of 10–20 cloves surrounded by silky, pink-white skin. The plant itself has long flat leaves and a bunch of snow-white flowers at the top, which grow from the bulb. The size of the bulbs varies, as do the size and number of cloves contained. Some are very small but there are giant forms. The flavour varies with both variety and climate, being sometimes mild, sweet and almost nutty and sometimes strong. Garlic grown in cold, damp climates tends to be rank and ill-flavoured.

Garlic prefers fairly rich, light, well-drained soil and plenty of sun. The bulbs can be broken up into individual cloves and planted about 2 inches deep and 6 inches apart in a row. In warm climates planting is done in the autumn but further north this must be delayed until the early spring. Once the tops have turned colour, the plants can be pulled and dried off for storage.

Garlic has been used for more than 5000 years. It was fed by Egyptians to their slaves to keep them strong and well and may have been the cause of the first strike when slaves refused to work one day because they were not given garlic. Garlic was supposed to be integral to the diet of athletes in ancient Greece and they were reputed to drink the juice in preparation for the Olympic games. Roman army doctors prescribed it to soldiers for intestinal and chest complaints and rubbed it directly on to wounds as an antiseptic. In World War I, when soldiers in the trenches were deprived of more conventional medicines, wounds were dressed with garlic and sphagnum moss.

Theophrastus of Eresus notes how ancient Greeks placed garlic at the crossroads as an offering to Hecate, the goddess of witchcraft and sorcery. Homer recounts how Ulysses escaped from the enchantress Circe by using garlic.

You will have noticed that in films garlic is portrayed as repelling vampires. This tradition could have sprung from the fact that the bite of mosquitoes often brought pain and death and garlic is known to have antiseptic and mosquito-repellant qualities. 'Vinegar of the four thieves', invented in Marseilles in 1772 as a remedy against the plague, contained a plentiful supply of garlic, together with other antiseptic herbs. The herbalist Culpepper recommended garlic for its anti-bacterial properties, and the Victorians lauded garlic as the 'Prince of Herbs'.

Good garlic should be hard, the cloves not shrunk away from the paper-like sheath, and there should be no discoloured spots. If you are forced to use faded cloves, all discoloured spots should be carefully cut out first because they give a bad taste to any dish. It is tempting to buy those wholesome-looking bunches of garlic strung together, but unless you are going to use a great deal in a short time it is far better to buy in small quantities, as garlic starts to lose its flavour and pungency very quickly. Store garlic in a cool, dry, dark and airy place away from other foods. Some kitchen shops and department stores sell earthenware garlic cellars with a lid and a hole in the sides, which keep the bulb well ventilated and preserve its freshness. Freezing is not recommended, except as an ingredient in a made-up dish, and even then it tends to intensify the flavour so only use half the normal quantity. Prolonged freezing will also make the dish slightly musty or bitter, so for best results eat it within a couple of months. Remember, even when frozen the taste and smell of garlic can be transferred to other foods, so seal carefully in airtight containers or double-wrap in freezer bags or freezer film.

A quick Spanish way of getting the garlic out of its skin is to put the cloves under a kitchen knife and squash them with a sharp blow before chopping. Alternatively, hold the point of the clove concave downwards against a plate and gently squash down with the thumb so that the flesh snaps loose from the paper-like casing. Then put the whole crushed clove, skin and all, into the dish and it can be fished out intact at the end before serving. If only a little flavour of garlic is required, simply rub the dish or bowl in which you are cooking with a clove or rub the clove over the food to be cooked.

Garlic's pungent flavour cannot, whatever you may have heard, be masked, whether it be by chewing parsley, eating coffee beans or drinking red wine. However, all of these, and especially cooking, will go some way towards subduing its pronounced flavour.

If using the **dried garlic**, which smells less pungent, use $\frac{1}{4}$–$\frac{1}{2}$ level teaspoon in place of 1 fresh clove. Chopped or minced dried garlic is then used in the same way as fresh, but must be soaked in a little water and drained before use. Dried products give an acceptable flavour but can sometimes taste rather musty.

Garlic salt is one of the most popular and least strong garlic products but some, like Sainsbury's and Lawry's, contain sugar, monosodium glutamate and parsley flakes and I would not recommend them. **Garlic pastes and purées** can be quite useful. Some, like Food Finders Garlic Purée, contain only fresh crushed garlic with a preservative. However, some people find the flavour of garlic presented in this way rather stale and once the container is opened, the smell of garlic tends to escape, even after the lid or cap has been firmly replaced.

Nutritional and medicinal properties

Fresh garlic contains about 0.2 per cent volatile oil, allin, alliinase (an enzyme that breaks down allanin), calcium, phosphorus, iron and potassium, thiamin, riboflavin, niacin and vitamin C. Garlic contains 70 per cent water, 23 per cent carbohydrate, 4.4 per cent protein, 0.7 per cent fibre and 0.2 per cent fat. Under normal conditions, alliinase and allin are separated from each other inside the garlic bulb. When the bulb is cut or crushed the two are brought together and alliinase turns allanin (a non-volatile, odourless sulphur amino-acid) into allicin, which is a pungent, volatile sulphur compound. It is also a powerful bactericide.

Garlic has a wide variety of biological effects, although not all active chemical constituents of garlic are known. It seems that the volatile sulphur-containing compounds are considered to be responsible for most of garlic's beneficial effects. Allicin, at a concentration of only 1 in 100,000 inhibits the growth of various bacteria, fungi and disease-causing amoebas. Garlic oil, juice or extract has anti-fungal and anti-bacterial qualities which inhibit some microbes and are deadly to others. Garlic kills amoebas that cause amoebic dysentery, and trichomonades that cause trichomoniasis, a vaginal parasitic infection. It inhibits the growth, or prevents the formation, of experimentally induced tumours in mice and rats. It lowers the blood sugar level in rabbits and the blood cholesterol in rabbits and humans. It reduces the blood pressure and prevents the formation of arteriosclerosis. Doctors Bordia and Bansal tested garlic on ten healthy patients in order to establish their blood cholesterol level. Initially the patients' blood cholersterol level averaged 221 mg per 100 ml, a level already higher than under the 200 mg per 100 ml considered safe as an indicator of heart-disease risk. The ten patients then ate a fatty meal, with plenty of animal fats, high in cholesterol. After three hours their average cholesterol level was 237 mg per 100 ml, which only dropped to the usual 221 mg very slowly. When they ate the same meal with garlic or garlic oil, their cholesterol levels did not rise at all. Indeed, they dropped by an average 16 mg. A Dr Piotrowski, at the University of Geneva, gave garlic to a hundred people with high blood pressure and it took only a week for 40 of the patients to show a significant drop in pressure.

The Japanese scientist Fujiwara has shown how garlic can increase the assimilation of B vitamins. The

Russian scientist Yanovich reported that he stopped the movement of bacteria in four minutes, by the introduction of garlic oil and the Russians use garlic vapour in most of their hospitals.

The Victorian Doctor Bowles prescribed a garlic poultice to be applied to the feet to kill stomach upsets. This may sound odd but the garlic permeates into the bloodstream. You can experiment by rubbing cloves of garlic into your feet – within a few minutes, on breathing out, you will smell strongly of garlic.

In China, garlic is also used to treat whooping cough, pulmonary TB, nose-bleeds, and snake and insect bites. The way it is used to stop nose-bleeds is rather interesting. First remove the skin from a clove, mash the garlic to a paste and form it into a small, round patty. Place this on the middle of the right sole, if the bleeding is from the right nostril, or on the middle of the left sole, if it is for the left nostril. If bleeding is from both nostrils, then two garlic patties can be applied, one on each sole. It is said to produce fast relief.

Deodorized garlic pearls are available, but they are not nearly so effective as the fresh cloves, or freshly made garlic oil. Some Chinese households prepare a garlic wine and have it handy for the cold season. The wine is prepared by soaking three peeled garic bulbs weighing about 1 oz each, in 6 fl oz (170 ml) rice wine, for at least a month. If you feel a cold coming on, you take 3 teaspoons of this wine before going to bed. To minimize the undesirable flavour, sugar is dissolved in boiling water before the garlic wine is added. It is said to be a most effective remedy.

To treat snake and insect bites, simply rub a crushed clove of garlic gently over the bitten area.

Garlic is useful in an oil for earaches and congested-middle-ear problems. It also acts as a digestive aid.

If treating serious infections chew at least 4–6 cloves daily until such time as the infection is under control. I hardly need add that you have to be aware that this is very anti-social, and I remember my hairdresser complaining bitterly when I was treating a sinus infection by eating at least twice this amount. The interesting thing was that I had stopped eating it at least four or five days previously and was unaware that my skin was still almost bleeding the garlic smell, it was so strong. For long-term treatment take 6 oil-of-garlic capsules daily. These are best taken with food so that the potent smell is not regurgitated. You can make your own oil of garlic by pressing 8 oz (225 g) peeled, minced garlic into a wide-mouthed jar with enough olive oil to cover. Close tightly and shake it a few times every day, allowing it to stand in a warm place for three days. Then press and strain it through a piece of muslin or fine cotton and store in a cool place in well-stoppered bottles.

Syrup of garlic may be prepared by placing 1 lb (450 g) peeled, minced garlic in a wide-mouthed

4 pint (2.25 litres) jar and almost fill the jar with equal quantities of apple cider vinegar and distilled water. Cover and let it stand in a warm place for four days, shaking a few times a day. Add 1 cup of glycerine and let it stand another day. Strain and, squeezing hard, filter the mixture through a muslin cloth. Add a cup of honey and stir until thoroughly mixed. Store in a cool place. This is excellent for coughs, colds, sore throats, bronchial congestion, heart weakness and nervous disorders. Take 1 tablespoon three times a day, before meals.

Warning Despite its many beneficial qualities, garlic may induce blisters, irritation and dermatitis, especially eczema in some individuals, so keep this in mind when handling or using garlic.

Pasta with garlic and fresh herbs

Fresh herbs are essential for this dish. Choose soft ones like basil, coriander, fennel and parsley. Of course the garlic lingers, so eat it with friends.

*1 lb (450 g) wholewheat pasta
  (any shape)*
3 tablespoons olive oil
6 cloves garlic, finely sliced
2 walnut-sized pieces butter
*6 oz (175 g) mixed fresh herbs,
  finely chopped*
1 teaspoon salt
lots of freshly ground black pepper
½ pint (300 ml) milk

Cook the pasta until *al dente*. Drain it well and return it to a clean saucepan. Heat the oil, fry the garlic until brown and tip it into the pasta. Toss the pasta using two forks. Add the butter and toss again. Add the herbs and seasoning and toss for a third time.

Now trickle in the milk slowly, continuing to toss. Once it forms a little sauce round the pasta you've added enough. Serve with a green salad.

100 g GARLIC	
Calories	137
Protein (g)	6.2
Carbohydrate (g)	30.8
Cholesterol (g)	–
Fat (g)	0.2
Fibre (g)	1.5
Minerals	
calcium (mg)	29
phosphorus (mg)	202
iron (mg)	1.5
sodium (mg)	19
potassium (mg)	529
magnesium (mg)	36
zinc (mg)	–
iodine (mg)	–
chlorine (mg)	–
sulphur (mg)	–
silicon (mg)	–
bromine (mg)	0.44
Vitamins	
A(IU)	tr
B_1 (mg)	0.25
B_2 (mg)	0.08
B_3 (mg)	0.5
B_5 (mg)	–
B_6 (mg)	–
B_{12} (mcg)	–
folic acid (mcg)	–
biotin (mcg)	–
C (mg)	15
D (mg)	–
E (mg)	–
Organic acids	
citric (%)	–
malic (%)	–
oxalic (%)	–
Water (%)	61.3
Digestion time (hrs)	2

GINSENG

Family: *Araliaceae*
Genus: *Panax*
Species: *Panax ginseng* (Oriental ginseng); *Panax quinque folius* (American ginseng)

Ginseng has a long fleshy root which is used medicinally. It is a low plant with tree leaves at the top, each leaf having five leaflets, and produces green-yellow flowers and scarlet berries. The root is obtainable in the West in straw-yellow pieces although the result of a special curing process produces a red form of root. It is fleshy but firm and wrinkled longitudinally. A good-quality root should taste clean, slightly sweet at first, then a little bitter. ·Inferior examples abound, so be cautious.

The plant grows in deep sandy soil away from stagnant water and it takes at least five years for the root to develop or seven years preferable. One crop depletes the goodness of the soil for ten years so naturally real ginseng is expensive.

Types of ginseng include **Chinese or Korean ginseng**, which is the true *Panax ginseng* and is now cultivated in Japan; **wild Chinese ginseng**, called Manchurian ginseng; and **cultivated ginseng** from China and Korea; **Siberian ginseng** (*Eleutherococeus senticosus*), which is sometimes sold as Asiatic ginseng and may be red or straw-yellow depending on the curing.

The two major ginsengs, American and Oriental, are quite different. American ginseng is regarded by the Chinese as having cooling properties as opposed to the warming, invigorating properties of Oriental ginseng. Both roots are harvested in the early autumn when the plant is at least six years old. They are carefully washed to avoid damaging them and dried in partial sunlight or in low artificial heat (the latter is generally the case with American ginseng). Oriental ginseng may be subjected to further curing including washing, steaming or soaking in water before drying. There are many types and grades of oriental ginseng and much depends on the source and age of the root and on the part of it which is used. It is the wild, old, well-formed, undamaged roots which are the most valued.

Nutritional and medicinal properties

The Japanese and Russians have done most of the research on the chemical composition of Oriental ginseng and have found that it contains numerous saponins, which are thought to be its active constituents. Oriental ginseng also contains – among other constituents – variable amounts of starch; steroids; pectin; sugars; vitamins, including B_1 to B_{12}, nicotinic acid, pantothenic acid and biotin; minerals, including zinc, manganese, calcium, iron and copper; choline, fats; and trace amounts of volatile oil. American ginseng differs from Oriental ginseng chemically because it contains ginsenosides not panaxoside.

Ginseng has been defined as an adaptogen, that is a substance that increases the body's resistance to outside stresses of various kinds without causing it to deviate from its normal functions. It achieves this balancing effect by normalizing the physiological functions of the individual as a whole and not by acting on one specific part or function of the body. The Chinese consider ginseng the king of all tonics and use it to stimulate the entire body energy to overcome stress and fatigue and to recover from weakness and deficiency. It has a very beneficial effect on the heart and circulation and is used to normalize blood pressure, reduce blood cholesterol and prevent atherosclerosis. It nourishes the blood and so is used to treat anaemia. It reduces blood sugar levels and thus is useful in managing diabetes and controlling hypoglycemia. Never use ginseng with any disease where there is inflammation, burning or high fever and it should especially never be taken by women with excessive menstrual flow.

American ginseng, which was introduced in China during the eighteenth century, acts as a fever breaker and is considered to benefit the lungs, dissipate heat, quench thirst and promote body secretions. It too is a tonic but it is used for different conditions, including coughs resulting from lung deficiencies which are marked by short difficult breathing and a dry throat, loss of blood, thirst, fever, irritability, tiredness, toothache and hangover. A tea made from the root is used to stop thirst and assist in cases of sunstroke. Put a teaspoon of ginseng powder in a cup of boiling water, leave for 5 to 10 minutes, and then drink the tea and eat the sludge.

Both ginsengs are available in tablet or in extract or powder form but it is safer to buy the root if you can get it from a Chinese herbalist.

For long-term use, decoct (*see* Herb teas) 400–800 mg of the dried root daily. Up to 2000 mg of the root may be taken daily for three weeks in any month for short-term use. Ginseng should never be mixed with caffeine.

GLOBE ARTICHOKE

Family: *Compositae*
Genus: *Cynara*
Species: *Cynara scolymus*

The Jerusalem and globe artichokes are two entirely different plants belonging to the same family. The globe, common, green, French or Paris artichoke is known as the true artichoke. It is a member of the thistle family.

Native to the western Mediterranean, it was taken to the eastern Mediterranean 2500 years ago where the young blanched flower-heads were greatly relished. The modern edible form with which we are familiar was first recorded in Italy in 1400. In Henry VII's time artichokes were served with boiled sparrows as a delicacy. Catherine de Medici served them at her wedding feast but they were presented in a rather more civilized way – wrapped in napkins.

The artichoke has a rosette of large, divided, toothed leaves in the centre of which grows a thick stem up to 5 feet in height which supports the famous globes. These look like large flower-buds in the shape of fat pine-cones with overlapping green leaves. If left unpicked they blossom into large violet flower-heads.

There are numerous different varieties, some – such as the **Brittany artichoke** – producing flat, round heads with smooth-sided leaves, while others have pointed heads and spikily sharp leaves like the **Paris artichoke**. The tender little flower-heads of the **Florence artichoke** can be boiled and eaten whole.

Buy globe artichoke when the buds are closed, and the leaves fleshy and close together. Don't be seduced by size – biggest isn't necessarily best. Old artichokes ferment and are indigestible, producing lots of gas.

Artichokes are in season from June to October and are grown extensively in France, Italy, Israel, Morocco, Egypt, Algeria and Spain.

To prepare an artichoke trim the stalks right down to the base, removing any discoloured leaves. Wash well under running water and leave to soak for a while in deep cold water. Drain upside down well before cooking. In a very large saucepan bring plenty of lightly salted water, with a little lemon juice added, to the boil and cook the artichokes briskly for 40–50 minutes. You can test whether they're done by pulling away one of the outer leaves. If it comes away easily the artichoke is ready. Lift them out with a large slatted spoon. Drain upside down. Serve hot with melted butter or hollandaise sauce, or cold with olive oil and lemon juice. They are at their best cool, about an hour after cooking.

Nutritional and medicinal properties

A large proportion of the carbohydrate in artichoke is insulin which is converted to sugars during storage, so the calorie content ranges from 10 to 53 for 100 grams after storage.

Artichokes are an excellent cholagogue, stimulating liver-cell regeneration, and are diuretic, so they are used for gall-bladder and biliary disease, and for any chronic liver condition (particularly albuminuria) and have long been used for diabetes mellitus and atherosclerosis. Because they have cholesterol-reducing properties they are also useful for high blood pressure and some types of heart complaint. A decoction made of the leaves is used medicinally.

Stuffed artichokes

These make a spectacularly impressive starter.

4 globe artichokes

stuffing
1 oz (25 g) butter
1½ cups finely minced hazelnuts
1 clove garlic, crushed

½ cup wholemeal breadcrumbs
freshly ground black pepper
½ cup dry white wine
2 tablespoons finely chopped
   fresh parsley
1 tablespoon chopped chives
¼ teaspoon thyme
½ teaspoon grainy mustard

4 oz (100 g) Cheddar cheese,
   grated
juice of 1 lemon

Cook the artichokes and cool. Pull out the central leaf cluster by grasping the tips, and scrape out the choke with a teaspoon. To make the stuffing, melt the butter and gently cook the nuts, garlic, breadcrumbs and seasoning for 8 minutes. Then add the wine, herbs and mustard and continue cooking for another 12 minutes. Stir in the cheese and lemon juice and mix to a paste. Stuff each artichoke firmly and generously. Bake in a covered casserole dish in a preheated oven at 325°F (170°C, gas mark 3) for 30 minutes.

GRAINS

Note   For details on the individual grains, *see* the following separate entries: Barley, Bulgar, Maize, Millet, Oats, Rice, Rye, Sorghum, Triticale and Wheat. *See also:* Flours.

Like eggs with their shell, white and yolk, cereals are made up of three parts:

The **protective husk** on the outside, made of fused layers of fruit and seed coat, consists of a tough cellulose skin and, like an egg-shell, strictly speaking has no food value as once eaten it can't be utilized and is eliminated in bowel movements. But it is a vital part of the grain because sticking to its inner surface are substances which contain vitamins, minerals, en-

100 g GLOBE ARTICHOKES	
Calories	9–47
Protein (g)	2.9
Carbohydrate (g)	10.6
Cholesterol (g)	–
Fat (g)	0.2
Fibre (g)	2.4
Minerals	
calcium (mg)	51
phosphorus (mg)	88
iron (mg)	1.3
sodium (mg)	43
potassium (mg)	430
magnesium (mg)	–
zinc (mg)	–
iodine (mg)	0.018
chlorine (mg)	206
sulphur (mg)	260
silicon (mg)	530
bromine (mg)	0.98
Vitamins	
A(IU)	160
B_1 (mg)	0.08
B_2 (mg)	0.05
B_3 (mg)	1.0
B_5 (mg)	0.21
B_6 (mg)	0.07
B_{12} (mcg)	0
folic acid (mcg)	30
biotin (mcg)	4.1
C (mg)	12
D (mg)	0
E (mg)	–
Organic acids	
citric (%)	0.1
malic (%)	0.17
oxalic (%)	–
Water (%)	85.5
Digestion time (hrs)	2

zymes and proteins. This bran has a high content of dietary fibre (44 per cent by weight in wheat bran), which forms a ballast which facilitates the passage of food through the digestive tract, and also (again in wheat bran) 14 per cent by weight of protein, and 5 per cent fat.

The **food store** (**endosperm**) is the largest part of the grain. It is made up of mainly carbohydrate, largely in the form of starch, but it also contains 3 per cent fibre, 1 per cent fat and 9 per cent protein. It is this endosperm which is ground up to make conventional white flour. It cannot be digested properly unless it is well mixed with saliva, hence the importance of chewing thoroughly.

The **germ** is much smaller than the starchy part and will grown in the new plant as it absorbs the nutrients in the food store. It tends to be richer in fat, protein and minerals than the endosperm although flour that contains the germ does not store well because the fat quickly becomes rancid – it should be stored in a cool, dark, dry place in a tight container and used within a few months. The exception to this is millet, which will store well for up to two years.

Nutritional and medicinal properties

With all species the protein content of a cereal varies a little according to crop and variety but stays roughly the same. Cereal protein generally lacks the amino-acid lysine which makes it imperfect unless married up to another source of protein rich in this particular essential amino-acid, such as fish and soya-bean products. Twenty-two amino-acids are needed to build protein and of these eight cannot be made by the body but have to be ingested. Vegetable proteins do not supply all eight essential amino-acids but happily the amino-acid in short supply in one food is often available in excess in another.

So pulses like dried beans, peas and lentils which are high in lysine and low in tryptophan make the ideal partner for grains high in tryptophan and low in lysine. Hence the evolution and importance of dishes like beans on toast, hummus with pitta bread, rice or chapatis with dhal, beans and tortillas, rice and bean curd – all of them perfect protein combinations.

To ensure a good protein balance on a vegetarian diet choose 60 per cent grains, 35 per cent pulses or nuts and seeds, and 5 per cent green leafy vegetables, as well as plenty of raw fruit and vegetables to make up the balance of other nutrients.

HAWTHORN

Family: *Rosaceae*
Genus: *Crataegus*
Species: *Crataegus oxyacantha*

This is a perennial thorny shrub or tree with small dark-green leaves which are lightish blue-green underneath and shaped as three irregularly toothed lobes. The tree has fragrant white or red flowers in May or June. In the autumn, it produces a red berry with yellow pulp, which resembles a small apple. The trees have spiny trunks and stems with hard, smooth, ash-grey barks. The hawthorn's hard wood gives it its botanical name, from the Greek *kratos*, meaning strong. Hence the name of the Pilgrim Fathers' boat, *The Mayflower* (hawthorn is sometimes called mayflower).

Hawthorn has been used as a field boundary since Roman times in Britain and Europe. The flowers emit a faint odour of decayed fish as the result of a mixture of coumarin and aminoid compounds. Conse-quently, the tree is avoided by butterflies and bees and is pollinated instead by flies. Hawthorn is a symbol of hope, and is considered sacred by some as it was thought to form Christ's Crown of Thorns. Legends suggest that one should beware of bringing hawthorn into the house as it portends a death in the family.

Nutritional and medicinal properties

Hawthorn is rich in vitamin C, and flavone glycosides. It appears to act as an adaptogenic agent. It is of specific use in hypertension associated with myocardial weakness, arteriosclerosis, paroxysmal tachycardia and angina pectoris. It has a toning effect on the muscles of the vasculature. The twin, almost paradoxical, effects on the heart – first dilating the coronary blood supply, and then slowing down and stabilizing the contraction of heart muscle – mean that it has wide applications for all sorts of heart disturbances. (However, you should of course always go to an experienced practitioner if you have any problems in this area.)

A decoction of the berries is used for treating sore throats, and in India it has been used to relieve kidney complaints, and for nervous conditions, insomnia, giddiness and stress, as well as to treat rheumatism. It is also used to avoid cholesterol build-up.

Haw sauce

This is a rich savoury ketchup which goes well with nut loaves.

1½ lb (750 g) hawthorn berries
⅔ pint (400 ml) apple-cider vinegar
4 oz (100 g) brown sugar
½ oz (15 g) salt
1 heaped teaspoon freshly ground
   black pepper

Strip the hawthorn berries off their sprays, and wash them. Put them in a saucepan, cover with the vinegar and simmer gently for half an hour. Sieve the pulp and return it to the saucepan. Add the sugar and seasonings. Boil hard for 7 minutes, stirring vigorously. Bottle and seal. This will keep at least three months.

HAZELNUT, BARCELONA, COBNUT AND FILBERT

Family: *Corylaceae*
Genus: *Corylus*
Species: *Corylus avellana* (common European); *Corylus americana* (American)

All these nuts are closely related and adapt themselves to their native climates. This alters their individual shape as well as their taste. In Britain, the most common variety is the hazelnut, although most of the nuts growing wild are fodder for squirrels, since our climate does not produce a large enough crop for commercial use. We import a large percentage of our hazelnuts from Europe and the Middle East and many are used in the confectionery industry and in cereals and cakes.

To remove the skins easily, bake in a medium-hot oven for 10–15 minutes. Allow to cool and rub gently between the palms of your hands.

See also: Nuts.

Nutritional and medicinal properties

Most nuts have an alkaline reaction on the digestive system but peanuts, walnuts, hazelnuts, cobnuts, filberts and Barcelonas are all acid-forming and so need to be eaten in moderation. They are good for the teeth and gums and for body-building. Hazelnuts, like hawthorn, are known to improve the heart and prevent hardening of the arteries, but their alleged aphrodisiac virtues may mean that those with shaky hearts had better stay off them.

Nusskuchen (serves 6)

Eating healthily doesn't have to be all sackcloth and ashes. I served this at a house-warming party recently and of the sixteen people there, three asked for the recipe, which I hope speaks volumes.

4 oz (100 g) butter
3 oz (75 g) honey
2 eggs
3 oz (75 g) ground toasted
   hazelnuts
1 tablespoon milk
1 teaspoon chicory coffee, finely
   ground
4 oz (100 g) wheatmeal flour
1 tablespoon baking powder

filling
1½ lb (750 g) Cox's Pippin apples,
peeled, cored and sliced
2 tablespoons Whole Earth
apricot jam
grated rind and juice of ½ lemon

decoration
4 oz (100 g) *unsweetened hazelnut
carob bar, melted*

Soften the butter in a bowl and
work in the honey until well
amalgamated. Separate the yolks
from the whites of the eggs and beat
the yolks into the butter mix. Stir in
the nuts. Warm the milk and soak
the coffee in it, and when the milk is
well flavoured, strain.

Meanwhile, sift the flour with the
baking powder and whisk the egg
whites until stiff. Fold the flour into
the butter and egg mixture,
together with the coffee-flavoured
milk, then gently fold in the egg
whites.

Turn into a greased and floured
8-in (20-cm) sandwich tin and bake
for 25 minutes in an oven preheated
to 37°F (190°C, gas mark 5) until
the cake is shrunk fractionally from
the sides of the tin. Turn out on to a
cake rack and cool.

Meanwhile, cook the apples in a
tightly covered pan with the jam,
and lemon rind and juice until the
apples are soft. Leave to cool.

Split the cake in half and fill with
the cooked apple sauce. Spread the
melted carob with a palette knife
and leave until this has hardened.

HERB TEAS

The word 'tisane' stems from the
Latin *ptisana* and it originally
referred to pearl barley and barley
water, but over the years it has
come to mean an infusion of herbal
leaves in boiling water. Originally
many tisanes were also brewed with
vinegar and were understandably
not very popular.

Plato mentions herb teas in 410
BC and Phiny's *Natural History*
abounds with them. The English
took them to America and the
colonists took to Oswego tea, made
from wild bergamot (*Monarda
didyma*), with alacrity. After the
Boston tea-party American women
drank mint, balm, rosemary and
sage tea. In Britain there was a
resurgence in home-grown herbs
during World War I, when we woke
up to the fact that most of our herbs
were imported from Germany.

Herb teas are now extremely
common in health-conscious America, and are catching on in Britain
and Europe. They are now
marketed in both loose-leaf and
tea-bag form.

How to make an infusion

Infusion are made using the leaves,
flowers or buds of a plant. Warm
the pot. Add 1 dessertspoon or
tablespoon dried herbs to a pint
teapot and pour on 1 pint (600 ml)
boiling water. Cover swiftly to stop
the essential oils evaporating. Leave
for 15 minutes. Stir and strain
before drinking. Add honey, lemon
or spices as desired.

How to make a decoction

A decoction is used to encourage the woody roots of a plant to part with its medicinal properties, while the more delicate and fragile flowers and leaves of a plant will do so readily by infusing.

Add 1 dessertspoon finely chopped roots (or rhizomes) to 1 pint (600 ml) freshly boiled water in a double saucepan and simmer for 20 minutes tightly covered. Strain. The result is very strong tasting and may need to be lightened with concentrated fruit juices.

Always use natural materials when brewing a herb (glass, china, enamel, earthenware) and a strainer made of a natural material like bamboo or silver. Aluminium often blackens the herb and gives it a nasty metallic flavour (and it is poisonous).

Some popular herbal teas are listed below. *See also:* Angelica, Dandelion, Elderflower, Fennel, Ginseng, Hyssop, Parsley, Rosemary, Sage and Thyme.

COMFREY

Family: *Boraginaceae*
Genus: *Symphytum*
Species: *Symphytum officinale*

Many of its country names — knitbone, boneset, bruisewort, gum plant, healing herb — underline the impressive wound-healing properties of comfrey, partly attributable to the allantoin it contains, a chemical which stimulates cell proliferation. The root was once grated and placed as a plaster round broken limbs and strains and worked wonderfully, due variously to a combination of binding mucilage-tannin and allantoin. It is also useful for internal ulceration and its astringency will stem haemorrhages. It will reduce irritation in the chest and help expectoration, and so is good for irritable coughs and bronchitis. It has a reputed anti-cancer action but the presence of hepatotoxic pyrroline alkaloids has recently suggested it may not be entirely safe. Personally I think this is unfounded but to be on the safe side, until the question is finally fully proved or disproved, avoid excessive internal consumption.

Allantoin levels in the roots are highest in the spring and summer, and a decoction tastes rather muddy but for all that not unpleasant. An infusion of the leaves tastes strong and leaves the tongue feeling rather furred.

COWSLIP

Family: *Primulaceae*
Genus: *Primula*
Species: *Primula veris*

These pretty flowers have been overharvested because they were once so popular in tarts, candied and as wine. They were prized for 'cleaning the heart and lungs', and we know now they are an excellent stimulating expectorant and thus useful for congestive bronchitis and coughs. Cowslips are also an excellent generally applicable relaxing sedative remedy, particularly combined with lime blossom. It is best to cultivate a patch of your own, as I do, because they are now so rare in Britain. They will oblige you by self-propagating quite quickly.

The infused flowers taste bland, the wine tastes wonderful, rather like a good medium-sweet sherry.

COUCHGRASS

Family: *Gramineae*
Genus: *Agropyron*
Species: *Agropyron repens*

Rich in minerals, and with anti-microbial properties, couchgrass has a wonderful healing action on the urinary mucosa and so is particularly effective for enuresis and nervous incontinence as well as for urinary infections like cystitis.

Decoct the cut rhizome, which tastes bland and a bit minerally.

GERMAN CHAMOMILE

Family: *Compositae*
Genus: *Matricaria*
Species: *Matricaria recutita*

This is a rather wispy annual, growing up to 2 feet high with erect stems, much branched with very feathery leaves and yellow disc florets forming the central button surrounded by white ligulate florets. The whole plant is strongly aromatic and smells a bit like crushed apples. It is often found growing wild in fields and open ground though it is easily cultivated. I describe it because there are different species of chamomile although in practice there is little difference in their medicinal actions.

Rich in volatile oils, including azulenes, bisabolol, farnesine and other sesquiterpenes, which give it its strong sweetish smell, chamomile is anti-inflammatory and so good for bathing sore eyes, for gingivitis, for sore throats and to accelerate the healing of wounds. It is carminative and so eases flatulence and dyspepsia (*much* better for you at the end of a meal than coffee), and is relaxing – good for soothing anxiety and insomnia. Also, the bitterness in chamomile stimulates digestive secretions and so helps in cases of gastritis.

However, the tea should *never* be infused for more than five minutes, otherwise it causes nausea. Stronger and longer infusions are suitable for external use only.

LIMEFLOWER (or LINDENFLOWER)

Family: *Tiliaceae*
Genus: *Tilia*
Species: *Tilia europaea*

Lime blossom has a long-established reputation as a prophylactic against hypertension and arteriosclerosis and it does indeed have a pronounced healing effect on blood-vessel walls. It is good for nervous, irritable children. (The French herbalist Maurice Mességué recalls an occasion when his father immersed him in a lime-blossom bath to soothe him to sleep). It is also useful for feverish colds because of its diaphoretic and diuretic properties.

If kept longer than a year, the dried flowers can be narcotic and cause nausea and dizziness, so watch your sources. The infused flowers taste slightly sweet and quite strong.

NETTLE

Family: *Urticaceae*
Genus: *Urtica*
Species: *Urtica dioica*

The stinging hairs are high in formic acid and histamine, and the whole plant is rich in minerals, particularly iron and vitamin C. The tea is particularly valuable for infantile and allergic eczema (doubly so when combined with figwort and burdock) and nettles are highly nutritious and encourage the production of breast milk. They also act as a circulatory stimulant, are haemostatic and good for stopping nosebleeds, and are helpful for hypoglycemia.

Certainly not the worst herbal tea I've ever drunk, infused nettle leaves have a positive, strong flavour. It may sound obvious but protect your hands and arms well when harvesting.

RASPBERRY

Family: *Rosaceae*
Genus: *Rubus*
Species: *Rubus idaeus*

Both the fruit and the leaves are high in citrate of iron, which acts as an active alternative blood-making, astringent and contractive agent for the female reproductive area. It has a long history of being drunk regularly throughout a pregnancy to strengthen the tissue of the womb and so assist contractions and check any haemorrhage during labour. It is also helpful for mouth ulcers and bleeding gums, and for conjunctivitis if used externally. (For the latter, the leaves are strained out carefully through coffee filter paper – as you don't want to irritate the eyes still further with particles – and the lukewarm infusion is applied with an eyebath.)

The tea infused from the leaves needs disguising as it tastes bitter and rather strong.

HONEY

Honey is the oldest means of sweetening food. The argument against honey is that it is just another form of sugar. Honey is in fact 98 per cent sugar, a combination of fructose and glucose. The fructose does tend to provide the kind of energy which is sustained and longer flowing and does not cause the very sharp rise in blood sugar that glucose causes. While glucose tends to be a little less sweet than sucrose (ordinary sugar), fructose tends to be a good deal sweeter, especially when tasted in cold foods, which means that honey tastes sweeter and you need less. Honey has a typical 82 calories per ounce compared to 111 calories per ounce for white or brown sugar. The crucial 2 per cent remaining is packed with enzymes, vitamins and minerals. It is this that makes the properties of honey finally defy investigation.

There are quality considerations in selecting honey. Different kinds of blossom produce different flavours and colours. The lighter-coloured honies are mildest in flavour, while the darker ones have more minerals and a stronger, richer flavour. Good honey should be unfiltered and uncooked. Filtering removes the pollen and it is the pollen that gives good honey its cloudiness and valuable nutrients, of which so far only 180 have been identified. Many people believe there are hundreds more undiscovered. Straining through cheesecloth is sufficient to remove extraneous material such as the occasional piece of a bee.

The word 'uncooked' on a honey label would ideally be a clear definition of what temperature was employed during the processing, but unfortunately temperatures up to 145°F (62.7°C) can be used with 'uncooked' still permitted as a description. To be really meaningful the word would have to mean not heated beyond 104°F (40°C), which is just enough to encourage free flow, but not high enough to destroy the vitamins and enzymes. Truly uncooked honey begins to crystallize at room temperature within weeks of bottling. To re-liquify, simple set the jar or can in a pan of hot water.

Honies from a specific source such as orange blossom or clover must be made from nectar mostly or entirely from that plant but it can be a blend of honies from different countries. Two brands of the same type of honey can taste quite different. Beware of cheap brands of honey where the bees are fed by sugar solution outside the hive. This complicates the natural enzyme reaction and vitamins and minerals are missing.

Almost 90 per cent of honey is imported, much of it from Australia, China, New Zealand and South America. British honey is available at a price and its flavour is variable. Our climate tends to mean that supply is never able to keep up with demand.

Propolis is a substance used by bees to glue the hive together. They inject it with enzymes and antibiotics and many claims are made for its medical value. It is available as a liquid, in tablet form or as chewable sweets. As bees collect nectar to make honey they gather **pollen** as their main protein food. This is the fine powder which appears on the stamen of flowers. To collect the pollen, bee-keepers keep a piece of mesh on the floor at the hive entrance and as the bees walk across it, some of the pollen is brushed from the pockets along their legs where they store it and falls through the mesh into the drawer arrangement beneath. The food value of pollen is extraordinary. It contains almost every nutrient known to man and may well contain others we have not recognized in the 3 per cent that no one has as yet successfully been able to analyse. We tend to eat it only in very small amounts in honey but it is available in special pollen supplements.

One Swedish company, Cernelle, has devised a harvesting machine which means that pollen can be collected directly from the flowers. The company then remove the outer casing of pollen, which is mainly made of the substance called sporonine – a form of carbohydrate which, like fibre, the body cannot absorb. This makes the remaining half of the pollen more digestible so that more of its food value can be used by the body. It is wiser to take any pollen product on an empty stomach so that the body has the best possible chance of digesting it.

Royal jelly a mysterious whitish jelly which gets its name because it is the food on which the bees feed their queen. The remarkable fact is that if the queen is killed or lost, the bees can transform an ordinary newborn bee larva into a new queen, who will live for about four years instead of forty-five days, lay millions of eggs instead of being sterile, and grow to about twice a worker bee's size. All this is done simply by feeding it on royal jelly. The bees only produce royal jelly when they want to produce a new queen. The only way to make them make more is to remove the queen's cells they build in which to nurture a new queen so that they will start again. Gathering the jelly is therefore difficult and time-consuming, and it has to be scooped out of each cell by hand in tiny amounts. Royal jelly contains a stunning amount of nutrients including a wide range of proteins, vitamins and minerals. When taken in considerable amounts, it is a very nourishing food and tests have shown that it will help offset the effects of radiation, and correct menopausal disturbances. Royal jelly is available in health-food stores in liquid and capsule form.

Nutritional and medicinal properties

Honey is non-irritating to the digestive tract, is easily and rapidly assimilated, has a gentle laxative effect, and a slight sedative value, is easier for the kidneys to process than any other sugar and – because it is predigested – can go straight into the bloodstream and therefore give a powerful boost of energy. The hygroscopic nature of honey make it a natural healer, since germs need water to breed. It is also an excellent antiseptic and antibiotic, and research in Paris has shown that the bees manufacture several kinds of antibiotics and inject them into the honeycomb and beeswax. Honey can be used for dressing burns – the honey draws moisture away from the burn and encourages healing which is further accelerated by the antiseptic and antibiotic values.

Just because honey is a natural food, it does not mean we should use it without restraint. Bears who come to the hives of wild honey-bees are the only animals in nature with decayed teeth. That should be warning enough. Remember, too, the purpose of honey – it is designed to feed tiny creatures whose wings flap so fast they whine and who exhaust their lives within a year. So, acknowledging its purpose in nature, you can logically assume that eating large quantities of honey would be quite unbalancing to the metabolism.

There have been claims for thousands of years that honey helps rheumatism, arthritis, sleeplessness and bed-wetting, and encourages potency. The minerals in honey are important and include iron, copper, sodium, potassium, manganese, calcium, magnesium and phosphorus, as well as the vitamins B_1, B_3, B_6 and B_{12}, pantothenic acid, biotin and folic acid. There are also large amounts of vitamin C, varying according to the types of nectar. The sugars include dextrose, levulose, sucrose and maltose, and the acids include citric, malic, succinic, formic, butyric, lactic, pyroglutamic and amino. Honey also contains several enzymes.

An excellent cough mixture can be easily made at home by macerating a large chopped onion in 8 oz (225 g) honey for 24 hours, straining through muslin and bottling. Cider vinegar and honey diluted in hot water make a good gargle for ulcerated throats and taken on an empty stomach first thing in the morning will gradually relieve chronic constipation.

Chinese and Japanese reports on the successful treatment of stomach and duodenal ulcers using honey are very impressive.

Warning An unidentified ingredient of raw honey causes a reaction known as 'honey botulism'

100 g HONEY	
Calories	304
Protein (g)	0.3
Carbohydrate (g)	82.3
Cholesterol (g)	0
Fat (g)	0
Fibre (g)	0
Minerals	
calcium (mg)	5
phosphorus (mg)	6
iron (mg)	0.5
sodium (mg)	5
potassium (mg)	51
magnesium (mg)	2.2
zinc (mg)	–
iodine (mg)	–
chlorine (mg)	–
sulphur (mg)	–
silicon (mg)	–
bromine (mg)	–
Vitamins	
A(IU)	0
B_1 (mg)	tr
B_2 (mg)	0.05
B_3 (mg)	0.2
B_5 (mg)	–
B_6 (mg)	0.02
B_{12} (mcg)	0
folic acid (mcg)	–
biotin (mcg)	–
C (mg)	tr
D (mg)	0
E (mg)	–
Organic acids	
citric (%)	–
malic (%)	–
oxalic (%)	–
Water (%)	23
Digestion time (hrs)	–

in babies. This is really a misnomer since botulism is caused by spoiled food, but the severe gastric stress is real enough and raw honey should not be fed to babies until they are at least a year old and then only in tiny amounts.

Honey curd *(makes 1 jar)*

This spread, delicious on oatmeal biscuits, will keep in the refrigerator for up to three months.

4 tablespoons dark honey
2 egg whites
3 egg yolks
the juice and finely grated rind of
    2 lemons
1½ oz (40 g) unsalted butter

Whisk all the ingredients together in a double boiler (or in a bowl over a pan of hot water) and stir the mixture over a low heat until it thickens sufficiently to coat the back of a spoon. This may take about 10 minutes, and certainly won't take longer than 15. Transfer to a sterile, warm jar, and seal when cold.

HORSERADISH

Family: *Cruciferae*
Genus: *Armoracia* or *Cochlearia*
Species: *Armoracia rusticana* or
            Cochlearia armoracia

Horseradish is a hardy perennial of the mustard family and is valued for its large, white root which has a characteristic pungent aroma and a burning taste. Native to eastern Europe, it is commonly cultivated in most northern countries. Once it gets a hold, (as rueful gardeners will know) it is difficult to eradicate and it is now found wild in Britain and North America.

The young leaves are excellent as an addition to salads. When using the roots, they have to be scrubbed clean of soil and any discoloured skin must be removed. Remember that most of the pungency is found on the outer part of the root, and not in the core. Horseradish should be eaten raw and freshly grated – cooking reduces its pungency. It can be preserved by drying or pickling but freezing is definitely not recommended. It is a wonderful decongestant for the sinuses and my long-suffering pharmacist, who prepares it for our patients, normally grates it in a food processor simply because it makes her nose stream and her eyes run. Certainly don't rub your eyes when preparing it.

To dry horseradish, first peel it, cut it into thin strips about 2 inches (5 centimetres) long and spread it on wire cooling racks. Place them in a cool oven (225°F, 110°C, gas mark ¼) and leave until brittle, which will take several hours. Allow to cool, then store in airtight containers. To use, simply crush or crumble the strips, and soak them in cold water for about an hour. Drain off excess liquid, and use as fresh.

To pickle horseradish, peel, coarsely grate and shred 8 ounces (225 grams) horseradish. Place it immediately in 1 pint (600 millilitres) boiling water in which a teaspoon of salt has been dissolved. Leave for 1 minute to blanch and prevent browning. Drain well, then pack it into small warm jars and cover with hot vinegar (ideally apple cider vinegar) and seal with vinegar-proof tops or preserving skins. Drain off excess vinegar before use, take what you need, then re-seal the jar.

Nutritional and medicinal properties

Fresh horseradish contains a glycoside – sinigrin – which is decomposed in the presence of water by the enzyme myrosin, producing mustard oil. It is also extremely rich in vitamin C, and has antiseptic and antibiotic substances, as well as calcium, magnesium, phosphorus, potassium and traces of iron.

It is a strong circulatory stimulant and has an excellent antiseptic action, notably on the lungs and urinary system, acting as a diuretic. It promotes healing, stimulates stomach secretions and is a powerful solvent of excess mucus, especially in the nasal and sinus cavities, and therefore wonderful for colds, coughs, persistent bronchial catarrh and bronchitis. I ask my patients to eat 3 level teaspoons a day before each meal, chewing well, and armed with a large box of tissues. It takes some getting used to, but it works wonderfully.

Applied externally in a muslin poultice, it will stimulate the circulation over inflamed joints or tissues and, like cayenne pepper, is a vital ingredient in formulae which are designed to help poor circulation. It can also be applied as a poultice for pulmonary and urinary infections, urinary stones, and any condition where there is excessive fluid in the body.

Warning Horseradish may cause blisters on some skins (so test on a little patch first), and large internal doses may produce inflammation of the gastrointestinal mucosa, so ensure that you do not exceed 4 grams three times a day. Like all members of the cabbage and mustard family, it tends to depress thyroid function, so it should be avoided where the thyroid levels are sluggish.

100 g HORSERADISH

	Raw	Prepared
Calories	87	38
Protein (g)	3.2	1.3
Carbohydrate (g)	19.7	9.6
Cholesterol (g)	–	–
Fat (g)	0.3	0.2
Fibre (g)	2.4	0.9
Minerals		
calcium (mg)	140	61
phosphorus (mg)	64	32
iron (mg)	1.4	0.9
sodium (mg)	8	96
potassium (mg)	564	290
magnesium (mg)	34	–
zinc (mg)	–	–
iodine (mg)	–	–
chlorine (mg)	818	–
sulphur (mg)	1984	–
silicon (mg)	818	–
bromine (mg)	–	–
Vitamins		
A(IU)	–	–
B_1 (mg)	0.07	–
B_2 (mg)	–	–
B_3 (mg)	–	–
B_5 (mg)	–	–
B_6 (mg)	0.15	–
B_{12} (mcg)	0	–
folic acid (mcg)	–	–
biotin (mcg)	–	–
C (mg)	4	–
D (mg)	0	–
E (mg)	–	–
Organic acids		
citric (%)	–	–
malic (%)	–	–
oxalic (%)	–	–
Water (%)	74.6	87.1
Digestion time (hrs)	4	–

Horseradish sauce

It is always worth while making your own horseradish sauce, because most of those commercially available contain flavourings, preservatives, stabilizers, colourings and sweeteners.

1 teaspoon prepared mustard
1 teaspoon honey
4–5 tablespoons double cream
1½ oz (40 g) grated horseradish
salt and freshly ground pepper to
taste.

Combine the mustard, honey and cream. Stir in the grated horseradish and season to taste. Refrigerate until required and stir well before serving.

HYSSOP

Family: *Labiatae*
Genus: *Hyssopus*
Species: *Hyssopus officinalis*

Hyssop is a very ancient name which can be traced back almost unchanged to the Greek *hussopos* and the Hebrew *esob*. Whether it is the hyssop mentioned in the Bible in the Prayer of David ('Purge me with hyssop and I shall be clean') is questionable. Its common name is 'holy herb' and it was used by the ancient Greeks in purification ceremonies. It was used by Paulus Aegnita in the seventh century as a medicinal plant and by Gerard in the sixteenth century as a cosmetic and strewing herb. It is an aromatic herb, with a bitter, minty flavour which grows into an evergreen shrub with a square, coarse stem and blue flowers. Occasionally the flowers are violet, red, pink or white. The seeds, flowers and leaves all have a strong taste and odour, and hyssop has a mixed fortune as a culinary herb because of its strong flavour. However, it makes an interesting addition to cranberry sauce. Simply add a few fresh sprigs to the sauce as it is cooked initially. Half a teaspoon of the chopped leaves works well in pulse dishes. Hyssop is also used in the distillation of liqueurs like Chartreuse.

Nutritional and medicinal properties

Hyssop is 0.2–1 per cent volatile oil (a flavonoid glycoside, diosmin) and 8 per cent tannin. The leaves account for the aromatic fragrance of the plant because they contain most of the volatile oils. Hyssop acts as a peripheral vasodilator and diaphoretic. It is also relaxing, an expectorant and a carminative. It is a tonic, stomachic, astringent and mild spasmolytic. It is specifically employed in bronchitis and the common cold to improve appetite and stimulate gastric secretions, and as a gargle to soothe sore throats. It actively reduces perspiration and may be applied externally to cuts or bruises round the eye in poultice form. It is particularly effective for coughs, colds and respiratory infections in children, especially those of a nervous or tense disposition. Take it as a tea, drinking 3 cups a day, well sweetened with honey. It has a bitter, rather minty flavour with a musky odour. For treating the common cold, it is most effective mixed in equal parts with elderflower, peppermint and yarrow.

JERUSALEM ARTICHOKE

Family: *Compositae*
Genus: *Helianthus*
Species: *Helianthus tuberosus*

This has nothing to do with the Holy Land. The word comes from a distortion of the Italian *girasole*, or sunflower, to which it is related, hence Jerusalem; and the 'artichoke' part of the name is taken to refer to the slight similarity in flavour between this vegetable and the heart of the globe artichoke.

The plant grows 5–12 feet tall and produces yellow flowers and curious misshapen tuberous growths on the roots – the edible part. They can be lifted any time between October and February and are best left in the ground till needed, as they quickly dry and shrivel. They are not affected by frost as long as they are left in the ground.

The plant is a native of North America, and the explorer Samuel de Champlain noted it in the Indian Gardens of Cape Cod in 1605, and Colonna described it in Italy in 1616. When the plant arrived in England it was initially called Canadian potato.

Jerusalem artichoke has long been cultivated as stock feed in France and is occasionally used in pickles and sauces in the Corn Belt of North America. It has a very individual smoky flavour and is therefore best served alone, not as a second vegetable.

I've always found Jerusalem

100 g JERUSALEM ARTICHOKE (boiled)	
Calories	18
Protein (g)	1.6
Carbohydrate (g)	3.2
Cholesterol (g)	–
Fat (g)	tr
Fibre (g)	–
Minerals	
calcium (mg)	30
phosphorus (mg)	33
iron (mg)	0.4
sodium (mg)	3
potassium (mg)	420
magnesium (mg)	11
zinc (mg)	0.1
iodine (mg)	–
chlorine (mg)	58
sulphur (mg)	22
silicon (mg)	–
bromine (mg)	–
Vitamins	
A(IU)	tr
B_1 (mg)	0.1
B_2 (mg)	tr
B_3 (mg)	–
B_5 (mg)	–
B_6 (mg)	–
B_{12} (mcg)	0
folic acid (mcg)	–
biotin (mcg)	–
C (mg)	2
D (mg)	0
E (mg)	0.2
Organic acids	
citric (%)	–
malic (%)	–
oxalic (%)	–
Water (%)	80.2
Digestion time (hrs)	–

artichokes very difficult to clean. Choose them when they're full and crisp and scrub them under running water. Boil till tender, cool, and peel by rubbing off the spurs.

Nutritional and medicinal properties

Jerusalem artichoke is extremely nourishing, and high in carbohydrates, producing levulose sugars which diabetics can eat. It is a good catarrhal cleanser.

Warning Jerusalem artichokes cause severe flatulence in some people so if in doubt don't serve them at important dinner parties, as I once did.

Fried artichokes

This makes a nice simple lunch dish. Serve with a creamy cheese sauce, offered separately from the vegetable. I love the contrast of the crisp, crunchy coating of Japanese batter masking the meltingly soft, creamy inside.

1 lb (450 g) Jerusalem artichokes
1 egg
¼ pint (150 ml) ice-cold water
4 oz (100 g) rice flour, sieved
freshly ground black pepper, and
* salt if desired*
oil for deep-frying

Parboil the artichokes for about 15 minutes, then peel them when they are cooling. Drop them into the well-seasoned rice flour. Prepare the batter by beating the egg and stirring in the water and flour.

Coat each floured artichoke immediately in the batter and deep-fry in hot oil. Drain on a kitchen towel and serve very hot.

KELP AND OTHER SEA VEGETABLES

Family: *Fucaceae*
Genus: *Fucus*
Species: *Fucus vesiculosis* and others

People have been eating sea vegetables for thousands of years and yet today farming of the sea is the only agricultural frontier, it seems, left on the planet. The Romans, Greeks and Chinese all used seaweeds as a food.

Kelp is a popular name for any of the algae belonging to the *Laminaria* genus of brown seaweeds. It grows deep in the ocean, holding on to the rocks tenaciously with streamers called holdfasts. There are nearly 1000 different species of kelp but the one most often used in tablet form is *Macrocystis pyrifera*. Laver, agaragar, carrageen, and Irish and Icelandic moss are all members of the same group. While at university

in Wales I did occasionally try laver bread but can't say I ever developed a taste for it. I prefer nori grilled and sprinkled into soups, although I should warn beginners that some people are repelled by the smell.

Arami, hiziki, dulse and **wakame** all have similar uses in soups, stews and bean dishes and can be steamed or sautéed, added to salads or eaten with other vegetables. An easy dish for beginners is sautéed carrots, onions and hiziki flavoured with a little garlic and soya sauce. In soups or stews simply add a handful either as it is, or crumbled or torn. Before adding to salads or sautéing, hydrate the sea vegetables in a little water for 20–30 minutes.

Kombu comes in many forms but the most common is sold in thick wide sheets. It is added to soups, stews and beans to improve digestibility. Some people call it the natural monosodium glutamate. **Nori** is cultivated in Japan and gathered wild in Ireland, Scotland and Wales. The Irish call it sloke and the Scots and Welsh call it laver. The Japanese version is cooked and processed into thin purple-black sheets used to wrap rice balls and sushi – a mixture of cooked, vinegared rice and any one of a wide assortment of seafoods or pickled vegetables. Flash-grilled, the sheets turn green and can be used as seasoning in salads and vegetable dishes.

Nutritional and medicinal properties

All sea vegetables absorb nutrients through their entire surface from the sea-water they float in, and since they average 39 per cent salt, other forms of salt should be eliminated or curtailed whenever sea vegetables are used. They are all extremely high in protein, and as sea-water is a solution of all the minerals vital to human health they are an excellent source of minerals. If you decide to harvest them yourself, please take care to choose sites far away from polluted areas.

Kelp is a rich source of organic iodine, helps to correct mineral deficiencies and is a good protector in food, valuable in overcoming poor digestion and goitre, and in rebuilding and maintaining the function of all the glands. It is useful as an adaptogen in thyroid disease of any description.

Arame supplies vitamins A, B_1 and B_2. Hiziki is especially high in calcium and also supplies vitamins A, B_1 and B_{12}, and iron. Wakeme is high in iron, calcium and magnesium and rich in vitamins A, B_1 and B_2. Nori is extremely high in protein, containing 35 per cent, and is high in vitamin A. Dulse is high in protein and vitamin A and supplies vitamins B_6, B_{12}, C and E.

KIDNEY BEAN

Family: *Leguminosae*
Genus: *Phaseolus*
Species: *Phaseolus vulgaris*

Kidney beans have been grown by American Indians for thousands of years. The *Phaseolus vulgaris* species includes many varieties such as black beans, haricot beans, pinto beans, cannellini and flageolet beans as well as the famous red kidney beans associated with the spicy South American chilli dishes. When Columbus discovered the New World he was amazed at the variety of beans growing there. The kidney bean was bought back to Europe in the sixteenth century and its popularity spread rapidly.

See also: Pulses, Sprouted seeds.

Nutritional and medicinal properties

Kidney beans are rich in protein and are particularly high in iron and vitamin A. They produce a gummy substance which helps to slow the passage of sugar through the gut and reduce the cholesterol in the bloodstream.

For a warning about the toxic factor in kidney beans, see under Pulses.

Three bean feast

Chris Fulford cooked this for me when I was too hard-pressed to cook for a guest, transporting it to my clinic from where I moved it to my house. It travels well, and tastes delicious.

2 oz (50 g) each red kidney beans, mung beans and chick-peas, soaked overnight.
6 tablespoons oil
1 tablespoon cumin seeds
1 small piece cinnamon stick
8 oz (225 g) onions, chopped
2 cloves garlic, crushed
14 oz (400 g) can of tomatoes, chopped (or fresh liquidized)
8 oz (225 g) mushrooms, sliced
2 teaspoons coriander seeds

½ teaspoon each of ground
  cummin, turmeric, and cayenne
  pepper
3 tablespoons chopped parsley
freshly ground black pepper

Drain the soaked beans, put

them into a pan with 2 pints (1.25 litres) fresh water, boil rapidly for 10 minutes and then simmer until the beans are slightly under-done.

Heat the oil in a saucepan and sizzle the cummin seeds and cinnamon in it for a few seconds. Add onions and garlic, and stir for a minute or two. Add the tomatoes, mushrooms and remaining spices and herbs. Season to taste. Simmer for 10 minutes.

Add the beans with enough of their cooking liquid just to cover the mixture and simmer gently for 30 minutes. Allow to stand for a while before serving.

100 g KIDNEY BEANS (raw)	Haricot/ navy dried	Red kidney dried
Calories	340	343
Protein (g)	22.5	22.7
Carbohydrate (g)	63.4	59.5
Cholesterol (g)	–	–
Fat (g)	1.6	1.5
Fibre (g)	4.3	4.2
Minerals		
calcium (mg)	146	108
phosphorus (mg)	424	405
iron (mg)	7.8	7
sodium (mg)	19	10.2
potassium (mg)	1220	97.3
magnesium (mg)	180	163
zinc (mg)	2.8	2.8
iodine (mg)	0.005	–
chlorine (mg)	4	–
sulphur (mg)	260	–
silicon (mg)	–	–
bromine (mg)	–	–
Vitamins		
A(IU)	0	22
B_1 (mg)	0.63	0.5
B_2 (mg)	0.2	0.2
B_3 (mg)	2.4	2.3
B_5 (mg)	–	–
B_6 (mg)	0.5	0.4
B_{12} (mcg)	0	0
folic acid (mcg)	–	–
biotin (mcg)	–	–
C (mg)	–	–
D (mg)	–	–
E (mg)	–	–
Organic acids		
citric (%)	–	–
malic (%)	–	–
oxalic (%)	–	–
Water (%)	–	–
Digestion time (hrs)	–	–

KOHLRABI

Family: *Cruciferae*
Genus: *Brassica*
Species: *Brassica caulorapa*

This is a hybrid related to the cabbage but looking rather like a turnip. It is the swelling of the stem near the base which is generally eaten, although the leaves also taste good. Kohlrabi comes in both green and purple varieties and has a rather nutty flavour, a bit like turnip only more delicate. When the vegetable is overripe the flavour can become mustardy and unpleasant.

Better known on the continent than in the UK or the US, kohlrabi can occasionally be found in the shops. It is a biennial and a native to Europe often grown as a substitute for cabbage. It is a fairly recent development (as vegetables go) and

100 g KOHLRABI	
Calories	29
Protein (g)	2
Carbohydrate (g)	6.6
Cholesterol (g)	–
Fat (g)	0.1
Fibre (g)	1
Minerals	
calcium (mg)	41
phosphorus (mg)	51
iron (mg)	0.5
sodium (mg)	8
potassium (mg)	372
magnesium (mg)	37
zinc (mg)	–
iodine (mg)	–
chlorine (mg)	410
sulphur (mg)	735
silicon (mg)	205
bromine (mg)	–
Vitamins	–
A(IU)	20
B_1 (mg)	0.06
B_2 (mg)	0.04
B_3 (mg)	0.3
B_5 (mg)	–
B_6 (mg)	–
B_{12} (mcg)	–
folic acid (mcg)	–
biotin (mcg)	–
C (mg)	66
D (mg)	–
E (mg)	–
Organic acids	
citric (%)	–
malic (%)	–
oxalic (%)	–
Water (%)	90.3
Digestion time (hrs)	3

was first recorded in the sixteenth century as a fodder crop.

Nutritional and medicinal properties

Kohlrabi is rich in potassium, fibre and vitamin C and contains a reasonable amount of carbohydrate.

It has a good reputation as a blood cleanser and is recommended for toxaemia and accompanying poor complexions. It is also useful for dental health, and healthy bone and nail development, as well as for kidney and bowel irritation, especially if eaten raw.

How to cook kohlrabi

Allow one or two kohlrabi per person, slice them and cook them in butter for a few minutes before covering with stock and simmering for half an hour or until tender. The leaves can be chopped and used as a garnish or boiled or steamed separately and added later. Kohlrabi can be made into purées or fritters, or grated and eaten raw in salads. If in doubt treat them as you would do turnips.

LEMON

Family: *Rutaceae*
Genus: *Citrus*
Species: *Citrus limonum*

The exact origin of the lemon is rather obscure, mainly because ancient writings muddle it up with the lime and the citron; and certainly lemons are related to the citron fruit described by Linnaeus and may be a hybrid of the citron and lime. The lemon is thought to be a native of Malaysia and appeared in Europe about the middle of the first century AD. It was introduced further afield by the Crusaders when they found it growing in Palestine and by 1494 lemons were being grown in the Azores and shipped to England.

Today lemons are cultivated all over the world, in appropriate climates, particularly in the Mediterranean and California, and they are available in Britain all the year round. There are many varieties, including wild lemons, and the widespread use of pesticides means they can even be grown in areas with rainy summers, where the dampness encourages the spread of diseases. It also means you need to wash that beautiful, shiny, waxy skin before you grate it, peel it or squeeze it.

Lemons grow on small spiny trees ranging from 10 to 20 feet high and have white and purple flowers and delicate pale green leaves. The yellow skin of a lemon is covered with tiny glands which look like skin pores and contain volatile oils. This is what gives lemon its unique flavour and it can be obtained with a fine grater, or by peeling off wafer thin slices, or by rubbing the skin with a sugar lump. The most aromatic lemons are tree ripened, very oily to the touch and rough skinned. Unfortunately most commercial growers pick them green and many treat them with dyes and sprays, so determine the quality of your fruit by very gently scratching the surface with your nail and sniffing the lemon.

Lemon juice is high in citric acid and so tongue-curling to eat. It is particularly rich in vitamins C, B_1 and B_2 and niacin (B_3). **Citric acid** is a by-product often used as a base for carbonated drinks, as a laxative and as a flavouring in baking. **Pectin** is used in medicine. In World War II the powdered pectin was applied to wounds to stop blood clotting. It was also used for intestinal disorders, as an anti-haemorrhagic and as an antigen. **Volatile oil** from the peel is mostly limonene (85–95 per cent) with aldehydes and esters (5–15 per cent) and it is the latter which are responsible for the flavour and fragrance of the fruit. **Lemon pulp** consists of soluble solids in 'juice' which is largely sugar with citric acid and a touch of malic acid.

Nutritional and medicinal properties

Lemon juice is a wonderful natural antiseptic and destroys bacteria very quickly. It is rich in vitamin C, B-complex vitamins and vitamin P, with calcium, copper, iron, phosphorus, potassium, sulphur and traces of sodium. Lemon juice also contains significant amounts of fructose and citric acid. Note that the calcium content falls signficantly when the peel is removed.

Lemon was used by ships' crews to prevent scurvy and other diseases after the passing of the 1867 Merchant Shipping Act which determined that every vessel visiting a country where lemons could not easily be obtained had to carry enough lemons on board to give 1 oz (25 g) of the juice daily to every crew member.

Heated lemon slices can be applied to boils, and the fresh juice will help acne, eczema, sinus congestion, pyorrhoea and erysipelas if dabbed on externally. It is helpful for dandruff if applied directly to the scalp and included in the rinse-water. Most interesting of all it is an excellent anti-acid as it actually becomes alkaline when it reaches the stomach. It produces potassium carbonate which neutralizes excess acidity in the bodily fluids. It is far more effective than the readily available commercial anti-acid tablets and should be diluted with a little water and sipped before each meal. Lemon juice is also helpful for liver ailments, asthma, colds, fever, headaches, pneumonia, rheumatism, arthritis and neuritis. It also helps to prevent the accumulation

100g LEMON	Peeled	With peel	Juice
Calories	27	20	25
Protein (g)	1.1	1.2	0.5
Carbohydrate (g)	8.2	10.7	8
Cholesterol (g)	–	–	–
Fat (g)	0.3	0.3	0.2
Fibre (g)	0.4	–	tr
Minerals			
calcium (mg)	26	61	7
phosphorus (mg)	16	15	10
iron (mg)	0.6	0.7	0.2
sodium (mg)	2	3	1
potassium (mg)	138	145	141
magnesium (mg)	0.6	–	8
zinc (mg)	–	tr	–
iodine (mg)	–	–	0.005
chlorine (mg)	16	–	–
sulphur (mg)	125	–	–
silicon (mg)	31	–	–
bromine (mg)	–	–	–
Vitamins			
A(IU)	20	30	20
B_1 (mg)	0.04	0.05	0.03
B_2 (mg)	0.02	0.04	0.01
B_3 (mg)	0.1	0.2	1
B_5 (mg)	–	0.23	0.1
B_6 (mg)	–	0.11	0.05
B_{12} (mcg)	0	0	–
folic acid (mcg)	–	–	7
biotin (mcg)	–	0.5	0.3
C (mg)	53	77	46
D (mg)	–	0	–
E (mg)	–	–	–
Organic acids			
citric (%)	3.84	–	6.08
malic (%)	tr	–	0.29
oxalic (%)	–	–	0
Water (%)	90.1	87.4	91
Digestion time (hrs)	1½	–	–

of fatty deposits, so is useful if you are trying to lose weight.

Canned or frozen unsweetened lemon juice is similar in nutrients to the fresh lemon, except that it has much less vitamin C, but is light years away in taste. Concentrated lemon juice has five times the strength of fresh. Lemonade concentrate has more carbohydrate and very little of anything else worth while.

Real lemonade

When I worked as a cook in Cannes, I used to look forward to sipping my *citron pressé* in the afternoon sun while watching the crowds stroll along the Croisette. It was simply made – fresh lemon juice with water and white sugar offered separately so you could mix it to taste. In those days I was astonishingly ignorant about the 'pure white and deadly' aspects of sugar. This is a more virtuous version of *citron pressé*.

3 lemons, unpeeled
3 tablespoons honey
2 pints (1.2 litres) boiling water
ice
sprigs of mint
2 extra slices of lemon

Wipe the lemons well and dice, catching the juice. Put the pieces and juice into a strong glazed jug (not a glass one). In a separate bowl dissolve the honey in a little of the boiling water. Add this to the lemons and then pour the remaining boiling water over them. Leave for 15–30 minutes (check from time to time that the taste is not becoming bitter). Strain. Pour the lemonade over the ice cubes in a glass jug. Add the mint and fresh lemon slices. Chill and leave to stand an hour before serving.

LEMON BALM

Family: *Labiatae*
Genus: *Melissa*
Species: *Melissa officinalis*

This is a hardy perennial with a short root, squarish stem and joint pairs of toothed heart-shaped or oval leaves, sprouting on either side of the stem. The flowers are small and white and grow along the stem, giving off a lovely lemony smell when crushed. The plant grows about 2 feet high.

It is a native to southern Europe and was first introduced to Britain by the Romans. Balm is a symbol of sympathy and gentleness. Linnaeus named it *Melissa* after the Greek for bee, because of the bees' attraction to it. The Greeks grew lemon balm by behives thinking it enhanced the honey, and John Gerard mentions, in the sixteenth century, that the leaves were rubbed on to the hives to keep the bees happy.

The leaves themselves taste pleasantly lemony and are used for flavouring. Dried, they retain their scent and are used in pot-pourri. However, when dried they do not make a satisfactory tea but fresh they taste sensational. The fresh leaves also complement cooked apple, marrow jam and summer cups, and go nicely with rice and raisin dishes and in omelettes.

The famous Melissa Cordial, *Eau de Melisse de Carmes* or Carmellite Water is used in Europe to flavour several liqueurs. It is basically a mixture of lemon balm, angelica root and lemon peel, spiced with nutmeg, although often other ingredients are added. Taken by itself, it was believed to 'renew vigour, strengthen the memory and chase away melancholy'.

In Spain, fresh lemon balm is used in soups and green salads and also to flavour milk.

Nutritional and medicinal properties

The fresh plant contains 0.1 per cent essential oil, 5 per cent tannin, a bitter principle, resin and a succinic acid. The Arabs introduced it as a medicinal plant especially of benefit in anxiety and depression, and it has been used as a sedative and tonic tea ever since.

It is a particular favourite of mine for treating all sorts of children's illness. One reason for this is the helpful fact that it tastes quite acceptable and goes down easily. Normally I advise parents to administer it, well sweetened with honey, in copious amounts at the first signs of colds, flus and fevers. I also suggest they soak the child in a hot bath containing an infusion of lemon balm. He or she is then taken out of the bath, rubbed down vigorously, wrapped in several warm, woollen blankets and allowed to sweat it out.

Lemon balm is used in conjunction with other remedies to treat nervous tachycardia and restlessness. It has some hypoten-sive action and is useful for the sort of people who find themselves in place and life situations they are not ready to accept, and who consequently become dispirited.

The fresh leaf rubbed on to a bite will soothe it. The Ancients thought that the tea would ensure long life, and Prince Llewellyn of Wales was believed to have lived to be 115 years old simply by drinking several cups of it a day!

Lemon balm sauce

This is not a herb you often think of cooking with, but it complements custards and rice pudding beautifully, and marries well with certain vegetables.

6 lemon balm leaves
¼ pint (150 ml) milk
½ oz (12 g) butter
½ oz (12 g) cornflour
freshly ground white pepper
a few extra lemon balm leaves

Simmer the leaves in the milk for 15–20 minutes, then take out the leaves. Melt the butter and cook the flour in it for a couple of minutes. Add the flavoured milk, and stir to make a sauce. Put in the merest hint of pepper and a few finely shredded lemon balm leaves. Pour the sauce over vegetables like beans and broccoli which particularly appreciate this treatment.

LENTIL

Family: *Leguminosae*
Genus: *Lens*
Species: *Lens esculenta*

The beauty of lentils is that they do not require soaking before cooking. Two main types are widely available here: Chinese, which vary from whitish to green; and Indian, which vary from pink to red. Generally speaking red lentils have more protein than the others.

The chief exporters of lentils are Chile, the USA, Argentina, India, Pakistan and the countries of the Middle East. Russia grows lentils but does not export any.

See also: Pulses, Sprouted seeds.

Nutritional and medicinal properties

Lentils lose much of their essential amino-acid content during cooking. Nevertheless they are a valuable source of protein in poor Third World countries. They are generally made into a complete protein by being served with rice or chapatis. They are about 25 per cent protein and 54 per cent carbohydrate, and contain some vitamin A and B together with good traces of iron and calcium. Because lentils are so high in calories they are extremely good nourishment and are helpful for low blood pressure and anaemia. In parts of the Middle East lentil soup is used for ulcerated stomachs and any ulceration in the digestive tract.

Simple dahl

I begged Ruth van Velsen for this recipe. It's so simple that she couldn't believe I wanted it, but that's one of the reasons I wanted it. The other was it tastes wonderful. If you find red lentils a bore to pick over, use brown ones instead.

8 oz (225 g) red lentils
2 large onions
several cloves garlic, sliced
2 teaspoons curry powder
12 oz (325 g) tomatoes, fresh or tinned
1 bay leaf

Cook the lentils until soft in boiling water with the bay leaf. (The time this takes varies, so keep checking.) Meanwhile fry the onions and garlic until golden. Stir in the curry powder and cook for 1 minute. Add the tomatoes, and cook for another 5 minutes. Beat this mixture into the cooked lentils. Add salt to taste.

LETTUCE

Family: *Compositae*
Genus: *Lactuca*
Species: *Lactuca sativa*

Lettuce originated in the Middle East and very good use they make of it there too. I ate lettuce which tasted like ambrosia in a marvellous fish restaurant by the Bosphorus. It was April and the lettuce was a Romaine, each crisp leaf meticulously washed and simply presented in a tall glass full of fresh lemon juice – some used salt, I didn't need to. The best part was the long crisp core which tasted superbly sweet and juicy. Trying to repeat the experience back home in London was a disaster as the core tasted horribly bitter, presumably the result of chemical sprays.

The Kings of Persia ate lettuce in 550 BC and by the fifth century its cultivation had spread to China. Columbus took it with him to the New World and by the sixteenth century it was common in England. The expressed bitter white juice of wild lettuce was dried on plates, formed into cakes and used as one of the oldest soporifics. It was given, with poppy seed, to patients before and after operations, and *Lactuca virosa* is still used to soothe muscular pain, manic states, anxiety and insomnia. Its cultivated cousin contains only a fraction of lactucarium, yet Maurice Mességué, France's most famous herbalist, successfully treated an American millionairess for insomnia with the simple prescription of three braised lettuces for supper. He also observed that it allays physical desire and was consequently called 'the herb of eunuchs'.

Cabbage (or head) lettuce (*Lactuca sativa* var. *capitata*) is a cultivated form of the wild lettuce originating in the southern Caucasus. It was popular in sixteenth-century Britain served as a cooked vegetable. Varieties include Avon Defiance, Boston (or Butterhead) and Webb's Wonderful. These are available all year round, some being imported from Holland. Iceberg lettuce is an American variety so called because it used to be stored under layers of crushed ice. It is available all year round but supplies are less regular in the summer. Grown extensively in the USA it is now cultivated on a smaller scale in Europe. Look for a well-formed, round head with green under-leaves and avoid heavy white heads which indicate age and bitterness.

Cos lettuce (*Lactuca sativa* var. *longifolia*) (called Romaine lettuce in the USA) is thought to have originated in ancient Egypt. It has long, smooth, crisp leaves forming an elongated head. It is available from early October to early February and though the UK grows its own it also imports a lot from Israel. Varieties include Paris White, Little Gem (which has a nice crisp heart), and Salad Bowl (which has lots of leaves and no heart).

Asparagus lettuce (*Lactuca sativa* var. *angustare*) has narrow leaves and a thick, edible stem. **Leaf and curled lettuce** (*Lactuca sativa* var. *crispa*) sport rosettes of curled leaves, edged like oak leaves.

Lamb's lettuce (*Valerianella locusta*) comes from the fact that the leaves are greenest and most flavoursome when lambing begins. Known also as corn-salad this was originally cultivated by the Romans and spread to England 400 years ago. Its main season is from mid-October to the end of April but it is available all year and Britain tends to grow its own and import a little from Europe.

Nutritional and medicinal properties

Cos lettuce has slightly more calories, protein, carbohydrates and fibre than Iceberg as well as more calcium, phosphorus, iron, potassium and vitamins A and C. Boston (or Butterhead) lettuce has half the vitamin A of, and less vitamin C than, Cos (or Romaine). The latter contains a substantial amount of vitamin E. Because all lettuce is high in iron it is recommended for anaemia as well as urinary infections, constipation, obesity, rheumatism and arthritis and – if taken in heroic doses – for insomnia.

100 g LETTUCE

	Boston (or Butterhead)	Cos (or Romaine)	Iceberg
Calories	14	18	13
Protein (g)	1.2	1.3	0.9
Carbohydrate (g)	2.5	3.5	2.9
Cholesterol (g)	–	–	–
Fat (g)	0.2	0.3	0.1
Fibre (g)	0.5	0.7	0.5
Minerals			
calcium (mg)	35	68	20
phosphorus (mg)	26	25	22
iron (mg)	2	1.4	0.5
sodium (mg)	9	9	9
potassium (mg)	264	264	175
magnesium (mg)	–	–	11
zinc (mg)	0.2	–	–
iodine (mg)	–	–	–
chlorine (mg)	570	740	1382
sulphur (mg)	580	690	687
silicon (mg)	2400	530	1464
bromine (mg)	1.9	–	–
Vitamins			
A(IU)	970	330	1900
B_1 (mg)	0.06	0.05	0.06
B_2 (mg)	0.06	0.08	0.06
B_3 (mg)	0.3	0.4	0.3
B_5 (mg)	0.2	–	–
B_6 (mg)	0.07	–	0.005
B_{12} (mcg)	0	–	0
folic acid (mcg)	34	–	10.3
biotin (mcg)	0.7	–	–
C (mg)	8	18	6
D (mg)	–	–	0
E (mg)	0.5	–	0.5
Organic acids			
citric (%)	–	–	0.02
malic (%)	–	–	0.17
oxalic (%)	–	–	0.0071
Water (%)	95.1	94	95.5
Digestion time (hrs)	–	2¼	2¼

Caesar Salad

I ate a version of this at Joe Allen's restaurant in London and thought it could be improved, so worked out my own variation. If you use fresh horseradish root, grating it will make your eyes water while you prepare and clear your sinuses beautifully.

1 good-sized Romaine lettuce

dressing
4 tablespoons olive oil
2 tablespoons sunflower oil
1 clove garlic, crushed
1 tablespoon grainy mustard
1 tablespoon Worcester sauce
½ teaspoon grated horseradish root, freshly grated or bought prepared
1 egg
4 tablespoons fresh lemon juice
4 tablespoons grated parmesan cheese

croutons
3 slices slightly stale Granary bread
a little olive oil

Cut off the base of the lettuce with a steel knife so that the leaves don't bruise and wash each leaf separately under cold running water. Then spin them in a salad spinner until absolutely dry (wet lettuce doesn't take kindly to dressing). Cover the lettuce with a damp tea towel and crisp up in the deep freeze while you stir the croutons but no longer.

Make the dressing in a large, deep, wooden salad bowl. Mix the oils and garlic with a fork, then slowly add the remaining ingre-dients except the cheese, beating vigorously until frothy. Finally, add the cheese.

To make the croutons, first brush both sides of each slice of bread with olive oil. Then cube them and stir the cubes in a heavy frying pan under a watchful eye for 5 minutes.

To serve, toss the lettuce in the dressing, ensuring it gets well coated. Add the croutons last and serve immediately. Offer the peppermill so that those who want it spicier can add freshly ground black pepper.

LIMA BEAN

Family: *Leguminosae*
Genus: *Phaseolus*
Species: *Phaseolus lunatus*

Lima beans are native to Lima in Peru. By the seventeenth century they were growing in tropical areas all over the world and are still the most widely cultivated bean crop in Africa.

They are also known as butter beans, and are available canned, dried or frozen. The beans vary in colour, but are usually white. The raw bean contains a toxic substance and must be soaked overnight and cooked.

See also: Pulses, Sprouted seeds.

Nutritional and medicinal properties

Lima beans are particularly rich in iron and so excellent for treating anaemia. Being high in protein they are good for body-building and in

South America are given to people suffering from haemorrhoids.

Lima bean salad

This is simplicity itself once the beans have been soaked and cooked.

4 sticks celery, diced
½ cucumber, diced
12 oz (325 g) cooked Lima beans
4 tablespoons French dressing
1 tablespoon chives, chopped

Mix the celery and cucumber with the beans. Moisten with the dressing and add the chives.

LINSEED

Family: *Linaceae*
Genus: *Linum*
Species: *Linum usitatissimum*
          (fibre and seed flax)

Linseed is the seed of a variety of the common flax plant. The oil is used commercially in the production of paints, inks, linoleum, varnishes and oils, particularly the oil used to coat cricket bats and lacrosse sticks. The oil is a mixture of glyceride of linoleic, linolenic, oleic, stearic and palmitic acid. Its high iodine content is due mainly to the linoleic and linolenic acid components.

Linseed oil is golden yellow, amber or brown and is classified as a drying oil because it thickens and hardens when exposed to the air, which makes it good for varnish etc. It has a low melting point and is more viscous than most vegetable oils. There are several commercial qualities of linseed oil.

See also: Oils.

Nutritional and medicinal properties

Linseed oil was used as a food by the Greeks and Romans and continues to be used in this way in Central Europe. Its flavour deteriorates on exposure to the air, but if it is refined and deodorized it is palatable and a good source of protein (33 per cent) as well as being high in minerals, such as phosphorus and calcium. It is also an extremely useful poultice and a good chest rub. Used in this way it is locally drawing, soothing and healing. It can be applied to boils and furuncles and to ease chest pains of a bronchitic or pulmonary origin.

The seeds themselves, which are rich in mucilage, act as a gentle bulk laxative and are useful as a tonic for spastic constipation if taken with plenty of liquid. Take up to 6 grams of crushed seed, three times a day. They contain a cyanogenic glycoside called linamarase but there is no fear of poisoning because it breaks up in the stomach only partially. Linseed has the dual ability to expand in the gut so exciting peristalsis, while at the same time reducing irritation and blocking reabsorption. Linseed also deodorizes the bowel by the slow release of tiny amounts of hydro-cyanide.

LOVAGE

Family: *Umbelliferae*
Genus: *Ligusticum*
Species: *Ligusticum scoticum*

This is a large perennial which grows up to 7 feet high. It has mid-green leaves and produces small yellow-white flowers at midsummer. Its stem is thick and hollow, like angelica, but it is more translucent and succulent. Both the leaves and the stems taste rather like peppery celery, with just a hint of parsley.

It was much used by the Greeks and Romans and was taken to America by the settlers. Unhappily, it has now largely fallen out of culinary use. However, it was once popular in Scotland where it was known as shunis, and the North American Indians ate it. Because it is abundant in vitamin C, it was popular with sailors and fishermen suffering from scurvy, and one of its country names is sea parsley. Lovage is also called the Magi herb, because of its association with the Three Wise Men, who sought the plant on their search for the Messiah.

Lovage is grown from seed and is planted in the spring or autumn in rich, moist soil in sun, or in partial sun, but do bear in mind that it grows very tall, so give it plenty of space. It may also be grown more quickly from root division. All parts of the plant are useful and make an interesting alternative to celery. The chopped leaves go particularly well with tomatoes and potatoes. The stems can, at a pinch, be candied like angelica and the seeds used on bread or biscuits. In ancient times, they were used in confectionery and pickled, like capers.

Nutritional and medicinal properties

Lovage is rich in an essential oil (umbelliferone), as well as starch, a variety of resins, and vitamin C. An infusion, which is quite tasty when included in soup, will act as a tonic and diuretic and is mildly stimulating. It was once used as an emmenagogue to induce menstruation. Lovage is strongly antiseptic and acts as a good natural deodorant if added as an infusion to bath water.

Lovage soup *(serves 6)*

Lovage has a rather exotic taste – a cross between celery and pepper, with a hint of curry. This soup goes particularly well with corn bread (see page 137).

2 onions, sliced
2 cloves garlic, sliced
1 oz (25 g) butter
2 tablespoons chopped lovage leaves
1 oz (25 g) cornflour
½ pumpkin, cut into chunks
2 pints (1.25 litres) vegetable stock
a little salt
½ pint (300 ml) milk
2 tablespoons chopped parsley

Sauté the onions and garlic in the butter. Add the lovage and flour, and cook the roux for a few minutes. Add the pumpkin and stock, and a pinch of salt. Stir until it comes to the boil, then simmer until the pumpkin is soft. Add the milk and liquidize. Reheat. Add the parsley.

MAIZE (OR CORN)

Family: *Gramineae*
Genus: *Zea*
Species: *Zea mays* var. *indenta*
(dent corn); *Zea mays*
var. *rugosa* (sweet-corn)

Corn (or maize, as the British call the plant) originates from the cross-breeding of at least three American wild grasses and has been subjected to such radical genetic manipulation that it now grows 10 feet tall with huge cobs (compared to its dwarfish ancestral fruit).

Corn is a native of both the Americas. It was used 10,000 years ago and in Mexico there have been found fossilized pollen grains from corn 60,000 years old. Magellan took it with him to the East Indies and in the sixteenth century it was taken by other explorers to Africa, India, Japan and China, but even then it was scorned as nutritionally inferior to wheat and rye – which indeed it is because it lacks the amino-acids lysine and tryptophan and is deficient in niacin so that people who are dependent on it have been subject to pellagra. However, maize flour is the staple food of the Piedmontese whose stone-masons and navvies are renowned for their toughness and endurance. Corn is classified according to the texture of the kernels.

Dent corn is so called because of its appearance, resulting from the hard and soft starch in the kernel drying unevenly and forming a dent in the top of the grain. This is the most popular type in the USA and cornflour and meal are ground from it, although it is not as nutritious as other varieties.

Sweet-corn (or corn on the cob) is too sweet to use as flour but is a valuable source of energy because its carbohydrate content is so easily transformed into sugar. It is rich in vitamins A and C. It is now available in an astonishing variety of colours, including jet black, and is delicious eaten raw while still very young and milky, or boiled and rubbed with a little butter and salt or, best of all I think, the way I've eaten it in Turkey – roasted in its protective leaves over charcoal.

Flintcorn is so called because it has such a hard endosperm which is difficult to grind. It is now mainly used as animal feed. The kernels store particularly well. **Flourcorn** has a very thin endosperm and kernels of soft starch which are easy to grind, and it is this that is generally used in South America. But the kernels are soaked in lime water before grinding, which frees the niacin content so that it can be absorbed by the body, making pellagra unknown in Latin America.

Popcorn comes from a bullet-like endosperm which when heated causes the moisture inside to expand as steam so that it explodes into the familiar fluffy popcorn. Other corns will crack or pouch but will not explode. Popcorn has the lowest nutritional value of all the corn varieties. There is now a microwave variety available in the US. **Podcorn** has a separate covering round each kernel which makes it unique among corns. This may be the original type from which the plant evolved but nowadays it is seldom used as the hard husks around the kernel make it difficult to grind.

Maize has been pressed for its **oil** ever since the Peruvians began to cultivate it thousands of years ago. It is now widely used as a substitute for the traditional olive oil. Although its flavour is bland it makes a good general cooking oil but some find it too heavy for use in salad dressings. It is very high in linoleic acid containing up to 53 per cent and it also contains traces of oleic, linolenic and arachidic acids. Corn oil is an excellent source of phosphorus and fat-soluble vitamins A, D and E.

See also: Flours, Grains, Oils.

Nutritional and medicinal properties

Sweet-corn is best eaten as fresh as possible as the older it gets the more the vitamins C, A and B are depleted (in that order). It needs to be particularly well chewed to be properly digested and is believed to help anaemia and constipation. It depresses the action of the thyroid gland and so is best suited for those who live in hot climates.

The extravagant tassles that grow from the top of the cob itself, which are the stigmas of the female flowers, make an excellent soothing diuretic. Gather just before pollination using them fresh and infuse 1 oz (25 g) to 1 pint (600 ml) for 15 minutes. Drink three cups daily.

Cornbread

This is an American recipe which I particularly like because it is so easily made. It accompanies a bean soup wonderfully and married up like this is soundly nutritional. The quantities here make one loaf 9 inches (23 centimetres) square.

8 oz (225 g) cornmeal
5 oz (150 g) wholewheat flour
1 tablespoon baking powder
1 teaspoon sea salt
2 eggs
4 tablespoons honey
2 tablespoons black strap molasses
12 fl oz (300 ml) buttermilk

Mix the dry ingredients in a large bowl and carve out a dent in the middle into which the eggs are broken and beaten with a fork. Spoon the honey and molasses into the egg (it helps if the spoon is dipped into very hot water first) and beat well. Add the buttermilk, stirring well, then gradually crumple the walls of the well by drawing in the dry ingredients, and mix until well blended, but don't over-do it.

Pour the mixture into a lightly oiled loaf tin 9 in (23 cm) square and bake in a preheated oven at 350°F (180°C, gas mark 4) for 30–35 minutes until the bread is well puffed up and a lovely golden brown. It should be firm to touch and eaten warm.

100 g MAIZE

	Sweetcorn	Corn oil	Cornflour
Calories	96	884	354
Protein (g)	3.5	0	0.6
Carbohydrate (g)	22.1	0	92
Cholesterol (g)	0	–	–
Fat (g)	1	100	0.7
Fibre (g)	0.7	0	–
Minerals			
calcium (mg)	3	0	15
phosphorus (mg)	111	–	39
iron (mg)	0.7	0	1.4
sodium (mg)	tr	0	52
potassium (mg)	280	0	61
magnesium (mg)	48	–	7
zinc (mg)	1.0	–	tr
iodine (mg)	0.005	–	–
chlorine (mg)	112	0	71
sulphur (mg)	368	–	1
silicon (mg)	50	–	–
bromine (mg)	0.31	–	–
Vitamins			
A(IU)	400	–	–
B_1 (mg)	0.15	0	tr
B_2 (mg)	0.12	0	tr
B_3 (mg)	1.7	0	–
B_5 (mg)	–	–	tr
B_6 (mg)	–	–	tr
B_{12} (mcg)	–	–	0
folic acid (mcg)	–	–	tr
biotin (mcg)	–	–	tr
C (mg)	12	0	0
D (mg)	–	–	0
E (mg)	–	–	–
Organic acids			
citric (%)	–	–	–
malic (%)	–	–	–
oxalic (%)	–	–	–
Water (%)	72.7	0	12.5
Digestion time (hrs)	3	3½	–

MARGARINE

This is a commercially manufactured substitute for butter. It is legally defined as 'plasticised emulsion of edible oils and fats with water and skimmed milk, with or without the addition of vitamins A and D, sodium chloride, sugars and other minor ingredients and permitted additives'.

The composition of margarine is controlled. There has to be a minimum of 80 per cent fat, of which not more than one tenth may be milk fat. The level of water must not exceed 16 per cent. Because butter contains fat-soluble vitamins A and D naturally, margarine has to be fortified with vitamins A and D. Margarine needs emulsifiers to prevent it from separating and stabilizers may also be used. Anti-oxidants are added to prevent the oil from oxidizing and going rancid. Colours may also be added, including carotenoids, which are yellow-red colourings naturally derived from plants. The use of flavourings, however, is not currently controlled in Britain. There may be other miscellaneous additives including salt. Preservatives and artificial sweeteners are not permitted.

Nutritional and medicinal properties

Ever since margarine came on the market there has been noticeable rivalry between butter and margarine manufacturers and not surprisingly the average person is confused as to what he or she should eat. Personally I come down very heavily in favour of unsalted and preferably home-made butter. Vegetables oils used to make margarine have first to be solidified by a process called hydrogenation. They are then mixed with skimmed milk and reworked to add salt and remove excess water. The solidification process used frequently turns the unsaturated fats into saturated fats, so raising the cholesterol content of the product. Since 1960 many margarine producers have claimed to have solved this problem and now produce a low-cholesterol margarine made with polyunsaturated fats. However, before we get too excited about this perhaps we ought to take a look at how margarine is made. Hydrogenation is the next step after refining – hydrogen gas is introduced to liquid oil in the presence of a metallic catalyst, usually nickel or cadmium. This succeeds in bonding hydrogen ions on to the oil molecules, saturating them and transforming them from a liquid to a solid. The resulting hydrogenated oil actually has the same molecular structure as plastic when examined under a microscope. You will find that no microbes will attack it, nor will it grow mould in the normal way. In other words it is an entirely dead product.

The other problem I have with margarine is one of labelling. Any label that states 'high in polyunsaturates' plays down the fact that hydrogenation is in itself a saturation process. What this really means is that the oil was high in polyunsaturates before it was hydrogenated so that margarine could be made from it.

Butter is saturated and has cholesterol but it is at least a real food. Margarine has approximately the same amount of calories as butter and normally it has added vitamin A and D. United States government regulations specify the minimum amount of vitamin A (1500 IU) which must be added to a pound of margarine. Margarine in tubs is likely to have more polyunsaturated fats than margarine in stick forms because it may not be solidified. Low-calorie margarines contain more water and half the amount of fats than their polyunsaturated sister. These margarines though usable for spreads cannot be used for cooking.

See also: Butter.

MARJORAM

Family: *Labiatae*
Genus: *Origanum*
Species: *Origanum Majorana* (sweet or knotted marjoram); *Origanum onites* (pot marjoram); *Origanum vulgare* (wild marjoram or oregano)

This is a herbaceous plant belonging to the mint family. It grows wild in the Mediterranean and Asia and the most popular variety is **sweet (or knotted) marjoram,** which is cultivated as a biennial or perennial. It tends to die in winter in cooler climates. It has a square, downy stem, with short-stemmed, elliptical, velvety green-grey leaves. Clusters of pale lilac or white flowers appears on spikes at the end of the branches from July to September, giving it a knotted appearance.

Sweet marjoram is native to North Africa, the Middle East and parts of India, but it has been introduced and naturalized in south-west Africa, the Mediterranean coast, Central Europe and North America. It enjoys a well-drained rich soil and craves sun. It has a delicate sweet fragrance which the Greeks believed came from the touch of Aphrodite, who first cultivated the flower. It was favoured by Pliny, Gerard, Culpepper and Parkinson, both for its culinary and medicinal values. It used to be woven into bridal garlands as a symbol of happiness, and planted on top of graves to ensure eternal bliss for the departed. In the Middle Ages, it was used as a magic charm against witchcraft.

The flavour of sweet marjoram is a bit like thyme but it is much sweeter and more scented. The scent becomes very strong when the herb is dried. Consequently, dried marjoram was strewn on the floors of halls and cottages in the Middle Ages, and was an ingredient in Elizabethan 'swete' bags. The Elizabethans also used muslin bags of dried marjoram in bath water to soothe aching limbs.

Sweet marjoram is used to flavour soups and goes well with some of the more robust vegetables. It marries well with cheese and with bread and scones, acting in a double role, as it is a useful aid for digestion.

Wild marjoram has a much stronger flavour and is often called oregano. It is much used in the Mediterranean to complement savoury sauces, particularly tomato ones, and liberally sprinkled over pizzas. It has rose-purple flowers and was known as 'Joy of the Mountains' by the Greeks and the Romans, because they thought it brought happiness. They used it as a preservative and for dyeing wool.

Sweet marjoram perishes easily in the cold, so **pot marjoram** is often grown in its place. It is hardier and has a less sweet flavour. Indeed, sometimes it can be quite bitter. It too is a Mediterranean plant and grows a foot high, with white flowers. It is used in exactly the same way as sweet marjoram, although it really shouldn't be, because of its stronger flavour. It goes particularly well in vegetable dishes which include garlic or wine.

Nutritional and medicinal properties

Sweet marjoram contains 2 per cent essential oil, as well as mucilage, bitter substances and tannic acid. The chemical constitutents of pot marjoram are much the same but oregano contains only 0.5 per cent essential oil, of which 15 per cent is thymol.

Marjoram is a weak expectorant and anti-spasmodic, carminative, aromatic, a weak hypertensive, antiseptic and diaphoretic. It accelerates the healing process by increasing the white blood cells so that there are more of them to fight infection. It is very useful in most simple gastrointestinal disorders, and a weak tea is an excellent digestive aid. It is particularly useful for children's colic.

Beetroot and marjoram

This recipe also works well with raw grated celeriac, or with a mixture of celeriac and beetroot.

2 lb (1 kg) beetroot
1½ oz (40 g) butter
juice of 1 lemon
1 teaspoon marjoram
salt
freshly grated black pepper.

Bake the beetroot in its skin until tender. Peel it and while it cools, melt the butter and stir in the remaining ingredients. Dice the beetroot and mix it into the butter sauce. Eat hot with sautéed potatoes.

MILK

Milk has been used as a food since time immemorial. Human milk is less than 2 per cent protein, but that is because babies take four months to double their birth-weight whereas newborn reindeer have to double their birth-weight within a few weeks in order to survive the winter, so their mother's milk contains approximately 10 per cent protein and 20 per cent fat. Ewe's milk, which is becoming increasingly popular in Britain, is 5 per cent protein and 6 per cent fat; goat's and cow's milk contain some 2 per cent less of each; and mare's milk is closer to human's at 2 per cent protein and 1 per cent fat. Horse's milk may seem an odd thing to drink but the Russians keep more than 250,000 milch mares.

Cow's milk is 88 per cent water but ranks higher than meat as a quality protein. The fat is 60 per cent saturated and 40 per cent unsaturated (very little is polyunsaturated) and is held in separate droplets to form an emulsion, while the proteins are held both in suspension and solution. The protein in milk is altered even at temperatures as low as room temperature, and when added to hot drinks like tea and coffee it increases its allergic properties as much as a hundred-fold and remains resistant to hydrochloric acid and the enzyme trypsin which breaks down protein during digestion. The body even produces antibodies in response to the 'foreign' protein. Eczema, asthma and migraine are often symptoms of allergy to cow's milk, especially in children, and recently it has been discovered that chronic constipation may also be an allergic reaction to milk. Milk allergies may be due to the way milk is heat-treated and so changes its protein structure. Some studies have suggested a direct link between heat-treated mik and the risk of heart disease, but unpasteurized or 'raw' milk is increasingly difficult to obtain and government regulations concerning its sale are under review. It contains bacteria which will turn it into soured milk or yoghurt if left alone, and these bacteria actively facilitate digestion. Dairy herds are commonly treated for mastitis with antibiotics and there is growing concern that their presence may result in allergic responses in humans drinking the cow's milk as well as a build-up of immunity to certain bacteria, making increasingly strong doses of antibiotics necessary when prescribed to humans.

Pasteurized milk is heat-treated to 161°F (72°C) for 15 seconds and then cooled rapidly to 50°F (10°C). Sometimes it is also **homogenized,** a process where the milk is forced under extreme pressure through a tiny valve which breaks up the clusters of fat globules to a uniform size and distributes them throughout the milk so there is no cream layer. Pasteurization destroys some of the vitamins, calcium and antibodies in milk.

Ultra Heat Treatment (UHT) is similar to pasteurization but the milk is heated to a much higher temperature 270°F (132°C) for 1 second and then packed in sterile cartons. This process destroys even more of the vitamins, calcium and antibodies than pasteurization does, notably vitamins B_6 and B_{12}, folic acid and vitamin C. It will keep for several months without refrigeration, though if left in a warm place for a few days it will not sour but will be colonized by harmful bacteria that give it an unpleasant smell and distinctly odd taste.

Sterilized milk is homogenized

milk poured into bottles and hermetically sealed and then heated to 230°F (110°C). The high heat gives the milk a thick creamy appearance and a cooked flavour. It will keep indefinitely without refrigeration.

To make **filled milk**, the cream is removed and replaced by another fat, usually vegetable. It is cheaper than full-cream milk.

Most **dried milk powders** are low fat because they are spray-dried **skimmed milk** made as a by-product of the butter process. Some have added vegetable fat to give a richer taste, and extra fat may also have been added if the product has been enriched with vitamins A and D, because they are fat-soluble. The drying process reduces the B, C, A and D vitamins and though this milk is valued by slimmers it is not suitable for babies.

Canned concentrated milk was first used during the American Civil War. **Evaporated milk** is milk with half the water content evaporated which can be diluted and put into cans. It can be made at home using a pressure cooker. **Condensed milk** is processed in the same way but has sugar added.

Buttermilk is produced either as a by-product of butter-making or by adding a culture to skimmed milk. The latter version is marketed as 'cultured buttermilk'. Buttermilk has very little fat left in it and proportionately ten times the protein, so that it is ideal for those on low-fat diets.

Goat's milk has smaller fatty globules evenly distributed throughout the milk, and this natural homogenization makes it easier to digest than cow's milk. It is also available dried and powdered.

Nutritional and medicinal properties

Milk contains a reasonable spectrum of vitamins except for E and C. Its strong point is minerals, particularly phosphorus and calcium, and it is a good emergency food for people whose diets are obviously deficient but not in specific ways that can be easily identified or corrected (provided they are not milk-intolerant). But for most of us on a reasonably rich and balanced diet milk should be used modestly particularly as it encourages heavy catarrhal secretion.

Milk left on the doorstep in glass bottles can lose up to 80 per cent of its vitamin A and 9 per cent of its riboflavin, but the greatest loss of nutrients occurs in plastic containers. Milk packed in these and left under supermarket fluorescent lights can lose up to 14 per cent of its riboflavin within 24 hours. Waxed cartons, on the other hand, block out most of the destructive light. Milk heated in an open saucepan loses 7 per cent of its riboflavin and boiling reduces the vitamin C content by 22 per cent.

The vitamin content of milk varies according to the seasons. Vitamin A can vary from 235 IU in winter to 350 IU in summer and likewise the B vitamins fall in winter and rise in summer.

How to make buttermilk, sour cream and cottage cheese

These can all be made simultaneously using fresh unpasteurized milk. Assemble a shallow ladle for skimming, a small bowl, a very large one capable of holding 1 gall (4.5 litres) or two bowls capable of holding ½ gall (2.25 litres), some pieces of cheesecloth or muslin and ¼ cup of yoghurt.

100 g MILK	Fresh whole milk (pasteurized)	Fresh whole Channel Island milk	Fresh skimmed milk	UHT longlife milk	Condensed milk
Calories	63	76	33	65	322
Protein (g)	3.3	3.6	3.4	3.3	8.3
Carbohydrate (g)	4.7	4.7	5.0	4.7	55.5
Cholesterol (g)	13.5	–	3	–	–
Fat (g)	3.8	4.8	0.1	3.8	9
Fibre (g)	–	–	–	–	–
Minerals					
calcium (mg)	120	120	130	120	280
phosphorus (mg)	95	95	100	95	220
iron (mg)	0.05	0.05	0.05	0.05	0.2
sodium (mg)	50	50	52	50	130
potassium (mg)	150	140	150	140	390
magnesium (mg)	12	12	12	12	27
zinc (mg)	0.35	0.35	0.36	0.35	1
iodine (mg)	–	–	–	–	–
chlorine (mg)	95	100	100	100	260
sulphur (mg)	30	30	31	30	81
silicon (mg)	–	–	–	–	–
bromine (mg)	–	–	–	–	–
Vitamins					
A(IU)	128	–	tr	–	–
B_1 (mg)	0.04	0.04	0.04	0.04	0.08
B_2 (mg)	0.19	0.19	0.2	0.19	0.48
B_3 (mg)	0.086	–	–	–	–
B_5 (mg)	0.35	0.35	0.36	0.35	0.85
B_6 (mg)	0.04	0.04	0.04	0.04	0.02
B_{12} (mcg)	0.3	0.3	0.3	0.02	0.5
folic acid (mcg)	5	5	5	5	8
biotin (mcg)	2	2	2	2	3
C (mg)	1.5	1.5	1.6	1.5	2
D (mg)	0.03	0.018	tr	0.022	0.088
E (mg)	0.1	0.09	tr	0.09	0.42
Organic acids					
citric (%)	–	–	–	–	–
malic (%)	–	–	–	–	–
oxalic (%)	–	–	–	–	–
Water (%)	87.6	86.3	90.9	87.6	25.8
Digestion time (hrs)	–	–	–	–	–

1. Let 1 gall (4.5 litres) milk stand undisturbed at room temperature for about 4 hours to allow the cream to rise to the top.
2. Skim the cream off into a small bowl. Stir in half the yoghurt and cover the bowl with cheesecloth.
3. Stir the rest of the yoghurt into the skimmed milk in the small bowl and cover with cheesecloth. The cheesecloth will stop foreign matter dropping in and allow the free circulation of air round the product.

100 g MILK (continued)

	Evaporated milk (unsweetened)	Dried skimmed-milk powder	Sterilized milk cow's	Goat's milk	Buttermilk (cultured skim)
Calories	158	355	65	71	36
Protein (g)	8.6	36.4	3.3	3.3	3.6
Carbohydrate (g)	11.3	52.8	4.7	4.6	4.9
Cholesterol (g)	–	–	–	–	–
Fat (g)	9	1.3	3.8	4.5	0.08
Fibre (g)	–	–	–	–	0
Minerals					
calcium (mg)	280	1190	120	130	122
phosphorus (mg)	250	950	95	110	93.9
iron (mg)	0.2	0.4	0.05	0.04	0.04
sodium (mg)	180	550	50	40	131
potassium (mg)	390	1650	140	180	138.8
magnesium (mg)	28	117	12	20	–
zinc (mg)	1.1	4.1	0.35	0.3	–
iodine (mg)	–	–	–	–	–
chlorine (mg)	350	1100	100	130	–
sulphur (mg)	84	320	30	–	–
silicon (mg)	–	–	–	–	–
bromine (mg)	–	–	–	–	–
Vitamins					
A(IU)	–	30	–	–	4.1
B_1 (mg)	0.06	0.42	0.03	0.04	0.04
B_2 (mg)	0.51	1.6	0.19	0.15	0.18
B_3 (mg)	–	–	–	–	0.09
B_5 (mg)	0.85	3.5	0.35	0.34	–
B_6 (mg)	0.04	0.25	0.03	0.04	0.04
B_{12} (mcg)	tr	3	0.2	tr	0.22
folic acid (mcg)	7	21	4	1	–
biotin (mcg)	3	16	2	2	–
C (mg)	1	6	0.8	–	0.8
D (mg)	0.088	0	0.022	0.06	–
E (mg)	0.56	tr	0.09	–	–
Organic acids					
citric (%)	–	–	–	–	–
malic (%)	–	–	–	–	–
oxalic (%)	–	–	–	–	–
Water (%)	68.6	4.1	87.69	87	90.5
Digestion time (hrs)	–	–	–	–	–

4. Leave for 24 hours in a warm place.
5. Remove the cheesecloth drapes and put solid covers on the sour cream (in the small bowl) and drinking buttermilk (in the larger one) and refrigerate. The sour cream and buttermilk should have a lovely clear flavour but do not expect them to be as smooth as their shop-bought counterparts.
6. To make cottage cheese heat the buttermilk to between 105°F and 115°F (40°C and 46°C) for about half an hour, stirring from time to time.
7. Pour the result (curds and whey) into a straining container or a colander lined with cheesecloth and leave over a bowl to catch the dripping whey. Let the curds drain until reasonably dry and decant and refrigerate. If you wish, add ¼ teaspoon salt to every pint (600 ml) cheese.

MILLET

Family: *Gramineae*
Genus: *Pennisetum* (bulrush millet); *Panicum* (common millet); *Setaria* (foxtail millet)
Species: *Pennisetum typhoideum* (bulrush millet); *Panicum* (common millet); *Setaria italica* (foxtail millet)

The term 'millet' covers a hotchpotch of grasses which can withstand drought, and on which one third of the world depends. I remember eating **finger millet** (*Elensine coracana*) as a child in East Africa. The trick was to scoop it from the pot, fashion it into a ball, dent it and scoop up beans into the hole deftly closing it before popping it into the mouth – all with the fingers of one hand. I spent some happy hours mastering the art. (It was also made into a fermented beer but I was never allowed to sample it.)

In the US millet is grown mainly for cattle feed and for the syrup that some varieties yield from their stems. **Bulrush millet** (Pennisetum typhoideum) is also a native of Africa and is a vital staple along the southern fringes of the Sahara, but it also thrives in India and Pakistan. Broom corn (or prosso millet) grows in the USSR, Manchuria and China, where it is used for chicken feed, but in Asia and Eastern Europe it is appreciated as food. And so it should be. It has a lovely fresh buttery taste, is extremely easy to prepare, looks attractive and nutritionally is valuable.

See also: Flours, Grains.

Nutritional and medicinal properties

As well as being a good source of high-quality protein, millet has a high silicic acid content (good for hair, nails and teeth). It is richer in iron than any other cereal, with a well-spread balance of amino-acids. It is, however, deficient in vitamins C, A and B_{12}, and so is best served as they do in Japan with rice, which does have these vitamins. Mix one part of millet to two of rice. The tiny grain swells hugely when cooked and needs five parts of water to one of millet and 25 minutes of very gentle simmering in a closely covered pot.

Normandy millet

This is a simple French recipe with a subtle contrast of textures.

```
100 g MILLET
(raw)

Calories                327
Protein (g)             9.9
Carbohydrate (g)        72.9
Cholesterol (g)         –
Fat (g)                 2.9
Fibre (g)               3.2
Minerals
  calcium (mg)          20
  phosphorus (mg)       311
  iron (mg)             6.8
  sodium (mg)           –
  potassium (mg)        430
  magnesium (mg)        162
  zinc (mg)             –
  iodine (mg)           –
  chlorine (mg)         –
  sulphur (mg)          –
  silicon (mg)          160
  bromine (mg)          0.38
Vitamins
  A(IU)                 0
  B₁ (mg)               0.73
  B₂ (mg)               0.38
  B₃ (mg)               2.3
  B₅ (mg)               –
  B₆ (mg)               –
  B₁₂ (mcg)             –
  folic acid (mcg)      –
  biotin (mcg)          –
  C (mg)                0
  D (mg)                –
  E (mg)                –
Organic acids
  citric (%)            –
  malic (%)             –
  oxalic (%)            –
Water (%)               11.8
Digestion time (hrs)    3¼
```

1 cup millet
5 cups water
1 tablespoon sunflower oil
2 carrots, sliced
1 shallot, finely chopped
1 tablespoon arrowroot, blended
* in a little water*
a pinch of sea salt
thyme to taste

Cook the millet as previously described and while it simmers fry the vegetables in the oil. Once softened add the other ingredients and stir to make a smooth sauce. Place the fluffy cooked millet in a serving dish, spoon the sauce over it and serve immediately.

MINT

Family: *Labiatae*
Genus: *Mentha*
Species: *Mentha viridis* (garden mint or spearmint); *Mentha piperita* (peppermint)

Mint embraces a whole family of plants. The twenty-five species include balm, hyssop, lavender, marjoram, rosemary, sage and thyme as well as the *Mentha* species. About thirty varieties of the latter exist in temperate climates of the world and these include peppermint, spearmint, orangemint, applemint, pineapplemint, and eau de Cologne mint.

Mint plants are strongly scented and are cultivated for their aromatic oil. They originate from the Mediterranean and from western Asia though they are now grown in most temperate and sub-tropical climates. The classification of species has proved a headache because they easily cross and hybridize. Even the familiar peppermint is a hybrid and not a distinct species.

Mints are perennials with square, branching stems and oblong, serrated or scalloped dark green leaves. The stems are topped by leafy spikes of white and violet flowers which blossom between July and September. They grow from 18 inches to 4 feet high.

Mint was said to have been brought to England by the Romans who called it *mentha* after a mythological nymph who was found in the arms of Pluto by his wife Persephone, who crushed her underfoot in jealousy. However, the unfortunate Mentha turned into a sweet-smelling plant, which smells sweeter the more she is crushed.

The ancient Hebrews used to strew synagogue floors with mint and it was one of the bitter herbs eaten at the Passover. Athletes perfumed their bodies with mint to give them strength. The Romans appreciated the digestive qualities of mint, and in the Middle Ages it flourished in monastic gardens as a cure for many ailments. In the Middle East, mint is still fed to stallions, in the belief that it is strengthening and an aphrodisiac.

Mint blends well with garlic and cucumber in cheese and yoghurt dishes, and is wonderful chopped in salads, particularly fruit salads, and in summer drinks. It has a cleanly refreshing, delicately fruity aromatic taste.

Spearmint (*Mentha viridis*) is one of the most common garden varieties native to the Mediterranean and was probably the variety introduced to Britain by the Romans, who incidentally also introduced mint sauce. Many varieties of spearmint exist, varying in the colour of leaf and stem, and in hairiness, leaf shape and flavour. There are also decorative and curly types.

Gerard and Parkinson extolled its virtues and Culpepper mentioned remedies incorporating mint for forty ailments, ranging from sore throat to dandruff. Spearmint is useful for all minor ailments including colds, flus, fevers, indigestion, gas, cramps and spasms. It has the same herbal properties as peppermint except that it is less stimulating. The menthol found in this mint is a stimulating diaphoretic, and a mixture of elderflowers and mint makes an excellent tea for sweating therapy.

Peppermint (*Mentha piperita*) is a hybrid of spearmint and water mint, with several cultivated varieties including black peppermint and white peppermint, depending on the stem colour. White peppermint certainly has the best flavour.

The Greeks and Romans crowned their victors with peppermint, adorned tables with it and used it to flavour wine and sauces. There is some evidence that it was used by the ancient Egyptians and it appears in thirteenth-century

Icelandic herbals. However, it was not used in Western Europe until the seventeenth century.

Peppermint acts as a carminative and anti-spasmodic with a noticeable action on the lower bowel. It is an aromatic and stimulant and is useful for frayed nerves. It is a peripheral vasodilator and diaphoretic with a paradoxical cooling effect and therefore particularly good for managing fevers in the hot stages, where the patient feels restless and agitated. It is also excellent for calming digestive upsets and will still a tendency to vomit. It is useful for morning sickness. An infusion of the leaves has a clear strongly minty flavour, as you would expect, and cools in hot weather and warms in cold temperatures.

Pennyroyal (*Mentha pulegium*) is a native of the Middle East and is cultivated in Europe and the United States. It has a strong pungent odour and makes a good mosquito and flea repellant. The Greeks used pennyroyal in potions given to prospective candidates for initiation into the mysteries of Demeter, the goddess of nature. It is believed to have been the first mint to be deliberately cultivated. Pliny, Dioscorides, the Magicians of Wales and the Anglo-Saxon leeches (healers) all valued it.

Pennyroyal contains the essential oil pulegium, which is a powerful aromatic and is used as a diaphoretic, aromatic, emmenagogue and stimulant. It is an excellent herb for fevers and lung infections because it induces sweating and assists the circulation. It is also good for the treatment of nervous headaches.

It is useful in the regulation of the menstrual flow and for relieving cramps. It should not be used by those who have a tendency towards excessive blood loss.

Water mint (*Mentha aquatica*) is the most common wild mint and enjoys damp places, as its name suggests. The flavour tends to be too rank for cooking. Corn (or field) mint (*Mentha arvensis*) grows commonly in dry conditions and is a cross with water mint. Like its close cousin, it is not good for cooking. Horse mint (*Mentha longifolia*) is not widespread in Britain and is supposed to be the biblical mint. It is cultivated in the East.

Round-leaved mint (*Mentha rotundifolia*) grows wild in Britain and its better-known cultivated varieties include applemint, Bowles mint, and pineapplemint. All of them are among the best culinary mints. Applemint has a delicate flavour and is good in a fruit salad. For cooking, I prefer it to spearmint. Eau de Cologne mint, orange mint, bergamot mint and lavender mint (*Mentha citrata*) belong to a species of mint mostly valued for its fragrant orange flavour, which goes wonderfully in ice-creams and fruit sauces.

Nutritional and medicinal properties

The mints all contain similar chemical constituents though there are considerable variations in the relative proportions of these compounds among them. They all contain a volatile oil, ranging from about 0.3–0.4 per cent in peppermint, through 0.7 per cent in spearmint, to 1–2 per cent in corn mint. Among dozens of aroma chemicals present in the volatile oil are menthol, methone and carvone. In addition to volatile oils, mints also contain numerous biologically active constituents including flavonoids such as rutin, resins, tannin and azulene, among others.

Warning Menthol may cause allergic reactions in some sensitive people and these reactions may include flushing, contact dermatitis and headache. Small babies may not react well to a menthol ointment applied to their nostrils to treat cold symptoms and some have been known to collapse. Since peppermint and corn mint both contain sizeable amounts of menthol, be cautious when using these mints on children and babies and be particularly cautious when using their oils. Menthol applied locally in its oil form to adults, however, has been reported to stop headache, neuralgia and itching. Pennyroyal oil is an abortificant and should not be used.

Fried eggs with mint

This is a quick, simple supper dish.

1 small red chilli-pepper
2 tablespoons corn oil
8 oz (225 g) mushrooms,
    preferably big flat ones, sliced
1 tablespoon chopped fresh mint
a squeeze of lemon juice
freshly ground black pepper
4 eggs

Slice the chilli very finely, wearing gloves, and wash the gloves well afterwards. If you do it with bare hands and rub your eyes afterwards, you're in trouble.

Fry the chilli gently in the oil for a minute and add the mushrooms, mint, lemon juice and seasoning. Cover the pan and let the mushrooms sweat. Decant into a hot dish, and keep warm. Fry the eggs briskly in the same pan (you may need to add a little more oil). Slide them out of the pan on to the mushrooms and serve.

MUESLI

Muesli was first issued as a prescription by Dr Bircher-Benner at his clinic in Zurich seventy years ago. He revived an old Swiss dish by serving a kind of fruit porridge to his patients which encouraged mastication but was easily digested and left a satisfying feeling of fullness to discourage overeating. It met with such approval that it rapidly spread round the world. Henry Ford loved it and the English christened it 'Swiss Breakfast'.

Today's commercially available muesli is too cereal-orientated. Muesli began as a dish primarily of fresh unpeeled fruit, was made up only as needed, and most importantly was always served at the beginning of a meal, thereby ensuring that the raw fruit triggered off the correct working of the digestive enzymes. It was never served as a dessert. The liquid content ranged from top-of-the-milk, through cream, yoghurt or unsweetened condensed milk, to nut cream or almond purée. Dr Bircher-Benner particularly recommended yoghurt because the bacteria in it has a beneficial effect on the intestines and digestive tract.

Nutritional and medicinal properties

This dish is a complete food, perfectly balanced, rich in calcium, phosphorus and other trace minerals and abundant in all the vitamins.

Muesli *(serves 6)*

Making your own muesli is not only cheaper, it allows you to ring the changes so that you never tire of it.

4 tablespoons raw oats
1 tablespoon cracked wheat
1 tablespoon cracked rye
1 tablespoon millet
6 ripe eating apples
2 tablespoons dried fruit (apple rings, prunes, apricots, pears)
juice of 1 lemon
juice of 1 orange
½ pint (300 ml) plain yoghurt
honey (optional)
nuts (optional)
1 tablespoon linseed or Linusit Gold

Toast all the cereals except the linseed in a heavy-bottomed pan to bring out their nutty flavour. Chop the apples, including the skin and cores, finely. Mix all the ingredients

except the honey, nuts and linseed well and keep covered in a cool place overnight to macerate. The next morning stir in the linseed (rich in essential fatty acid) and add honey and nuts if desired. Take advantage of fresh fruit in season and add this too if it appeals.

100 g MUESLI	
Calories	368
Protein (g)	12.9
Carbohydrate (g)	66.2
Cholesterol (g)	–
Fat (g)	7.5
Fibre (g)	7.4
Minerals	
calcium (mg)	200
phosphorus (mg)	380
iron (mg)	4.6
sodium (mg)	180
potassium (mg)	600
magnesium (mg)	100
zinc (mg)	2.2
iodine (mg)	–
chlorine (mg)	330
sulphur (mg)	–
silicon (mg)	–
bromine (mg)	–
Vitamins	
A(IU)	150
B_1 (mg)	0.33
B_2 (mg)	0.27
B_3 (mg)	2.7
B_5 (mg)	–
B_6 (mg)	0.14
B_{12} (mcg)	0
folic acid (mcg)	48
biotin (mcg)	–
C (mg)	tr
D (mg)	0
E (mg)	3.2
Organic acids	
citric (%)	–
malic (%)	–
oxalic (%)	–
Water (%)	5.8
Digestion time (hrs)	–

MUNG BEAN

Family: *Leguminosae*
Genus: *Phaseolus*
Species: *Phaseolus mungo*

You can buy sprouted mung beans (called bean sprouts) in sophisticated greengrocers, but they are much nicer grown at home and eaten at their very tender, first stages. They are also excellent to cook with.

Cultivation of the bean began in India and gradually spread throughout Asia. There are several varieties, from green through to yellow or golden and black. The black mung bean or black gram, is the rarest and the most important in Indian cultures.

See also: Pulses, Sprouted seeds.

Nutritional and medicinal properties

Mung beans are rich in vitamins A, C and E and contain calcium, phosphorus and iron.

Mung dhal

This is usually scooped up in chapatis, the chapatis acting as cutlery.

1 lb (450 g) mung beans
2 onions
3 cloves garlic
1 in (2.5 cm) fresh ginger root
4 tablespoons corn oil
1½ teaspoons ground turmeric
½ teaspoon chilli powder
2 teaspoons ground coriander
a pinch of salt
1½ teaspoons ground cummin
*a handful of chopped fresh
    coriander leaves*

Soak the beans for an hour, drain them, put them in a saucepan with just enough fresh water to cover them and simmer for 45 minutes. Meanwhile chop the onions, garlic and ginger, and fry in the oil. Add the turmeric and chilli when the onion is well softened, and the coriander and cummin nearer the end when the onion has almost dissolved. Cook for 3 minutes, stirring.

Turn this mixture into the dhal just as the mung beans are nearing perfection. Add a pinch of salt. Garnish with the coriander.

MUSHROOM

Mushrooms belong to many families of the division *Thallophyta*.

Field Mushrooms
Family: *Agaricaceae*
Genus: *Agaricus*
Species: *Agaricus campestris*

As spore-bearing plants, mushrooms are the oldest plants in the world and feature in legends and fairy tales. The Greeks and Romans were familiar with them and the Emperor Claudius was poisoned with inedible mushrooms by his wife. There are many mushrooms that will cause nausea (like *Psalliota xanthoderm* which looks like a horse mushroom but when cut shows a clear yellow surface) and others which are extremely poisonous like the famous Death Cap mushroom *Amanita phallordes* with its cold, clammy, white gills and the glutinous volva which may easily be found by digging down to the base of the stem. So children need to be taught to examine fungi right down to the roots by experienced adults. There is also an abundance of hallucinogenic mushrooms in Central and South America which were and are regarded as sacred and used only in religious ceremonies. The Aztecs called them *Teonanacall* meaning divine flesh.

Mushrooms multiply not by seeds but by minute spores. That they should have been cultivated – not by introducing spores as one would expect but by planting bits of the thread like underground roots – was an enormous technological leap forward which began in France in the seventeenth century, pioneered by market gardeners who inoculated the used hotbeds in which they had cultivated melons.

The bulk of the fungus is a mass of hyphae which probe rather in the manner of roots and worms through organic material. When conditions are perfect a bunch of massed hyphae pushes through the surface to form a fruiting body. Underneath the cap of this body are gills fused together to produce a series of pores. The spores are formed on the gills and are scattered by the elements to give rise to new mycelia.

There are over 250 varieties of edible mushrooms and their consumption is accelerating by 10 per cent a year. Commonly cultivated mushrooms include **button, cup,** and **flat** mushrooms, all of which are grown in the UK, although Taiwanese, Belgian and French imports are fairly common. The Chinese have been cultivating **Volvariella volvacea** on paddy straw for centuries and use these dried as well as fresh. The Japanese grow the **shitaze,** *Lentinus edobes,* in holes drilled in hardwood tree trunks.

The famous *Boletus edulis,* the **cap,** or *porcini* as they are called in Italy, rank with **morels** and **girolles** in superlative flavour and are widely available (at a price!) in Europe. Even the **truffles,** *Tuber melanosporum* and *Tuber marquiatum,* are now being engineered for cultivation, instead of being sought out deep among the roots of oaks by sniffing pigs or dogs specially trained for the purpose. They have an inimitable taste and aroma, rather like liver paté, and a tiny sliver goes a long way.

The interesting thing about mushrooms is that though they have a muscular chewy texture and flavour quite close to meat (and their protein is rich in lysine which cereals tend to lack, so they complement them beautifully) and though they appear firm and dry, they are in fact about 90 per cent water. So they make an excellent garnish, and a wonderful sponge for surrounding juices, are lovely eaten raw with the simplest of dressings and appear unembarrassed in any vegetable culinary context.

Nutritional and medicinal properties

There are no special benefits for health except the ordinary benefits derived from eating them as a food. Certain naturopaths forbid their cancer patients to eat them; I don't as I feel that the suggestion that they may encourage tumours is unproven, but I do advise patients suffering from thrush not to eat them or any other yeast-carrying foods.

Champignons à la Provençale

This is a deliciously simple lunch-time dish – abundant reward for all that early-morning labour picking the mushrooms.

½ lb (225 g) fresh field mushrooms
4 tablespoons olive oil (no other will do)
freshly ground black pepper
sea salt
1 clove garlic, crushed
4 tablespoons chopped fresh parsley
grated rind, and juice, of ½ lemon

Wash the mushrooms, and slice them leaving the stalks on. Heat the oil in a deep frying pan and sauté the mushrooms over a gentle heat for 5 minutes. Add the rest of the ingredients and cook for 3 more minutes.

Serve cool with plenty of bread to mop up the juices but taste again before the dish reaches the table and adjust the seasoning – its intensity changes as the temperature drops.

100 g MUSHROOMS	Raw	Fried
Calories	28	210
Protein (g)	2.7	2.2
Carbohydrate (g)	4.4	0
Cholesterol (g)	0	–
Fat (g)	0.3	22.3
Fibre (g)	0.8	4
Minerals		
calcium (mg)	6	4
phosphorus (mg)	116	170
iron (mg)	0.8	1.3
sodium (mg)	15	11
potassium (mg)	414	570
magnesium (mg)	13	16
zinc (mg)	0.1	0.1
iodine (mg)	–	–
chlorine (mg)	57	100
sulphur (mg)	250	74
silicon (mg)	65	–
bromine (mg)	1.9	–
Vitamins		
A(IU)	tr	–
B_1 (mg)	0.1	0.07
B_2 (mg)	0.46	0.35
B_3 (mg)	4.2	–
B_5 (mg)	2	1.4
B_6 (mg)	0.1	0.06
B_{12} (mcg)	0	0
folic acid (mcg)	23	20
biotin (mcg)	–	–
C (mg)	3	1
D (mg)	0	0
E (mg)	0.1	tr
Organic acids		
citric (%)	0	–
malic (%)	0.14	–
oxalic (%)	–	–
Water (%)	90.4	64.2
Digestion time (hrs)	2½	–

MUSTARD

Family: *Cruciferae*
Genus: *Brassica*
Species: *Brassica hirta* or *alba* (white mustard); *Brassica nigra* (black mustard); *Brassica juncea* (mustard greens)

The name 'mustard' is applied to three plants of the cabbage family, two of which are closely related. These two have small, round, dark-coloured seeds and are known as black or brown mustard, while the third, called white mustard, has large ochre-yellow seeds. However, all three mustards are substantially different in character.

Mustard originated in the Middle East and around the Mediterranean, and has been cultivated for more than 2000 years. In 1634, the mustard and vinegar makers of Dijon in France were given the exclusive right to make mustard and in return swore to wear 'clean and sober clothes' and also to keep only one shop in the town so that there could be no argument about any poor mustard and its origins. They were also required to put their names on casks and stone jars. Since 1937, Dijon mustard has become an appellation controlled by French law, and today Dijon still produces a large proportion of the world's mustard. The use of mustard was probably introduced to Britain by the Romans. In Shakespeare's time, Tewkesbury was the famous centre for mustard in England. Eventually the English were also forced to legislate to ensure consistent quality of mustard.

The pungency of mustard is the result of an essential oil which is absent in the living seed and in the dried milled powder and only forms when the crushed seed is mixed with water. An enzyme then causes a glucoside to react with the water and the inimitable taste of mustard comes to the fore. So when mixing mustard with water you must give it time for a reaction to take place, if you want a really strong taste. If you do anything to upset the enzyme, you not only discourage the development of the pungency, but you also finish up with an unconverted glucoside which is bitter-tasting. The enzyme is inhibited by salt or vinegar and killed by boiling water so powdered mustard should always be mixed with cold water and allowed to macerate for some time before using. However, once the essential oils have had time to develop, they will not later be degraded by adding salt or vinegar, or even by heating although as the oils are volatile they can be easily lost altogether if heated too quickly. So to preserve mustard's pungency in cooked food, add it late and cook it very gently.

While the white 'alba' mustard seeds are not as strongly flavoured as their black cousins, the enzymes are not as easily damaged. White mustard is also strongly preservative and discourages moulds and bacterias and helps emulsification which is useful when making mayonnaise.

English white mustard is grown

in Cambridgeshire and Essex, while the black is occasionally to be found in Lincolnshire and Yorkshire. In the early nineteenth century, a young miller from Norwich, Jeremiah Colman, began taking an interest in mustard and by the middle of the century had set up a factory devoted entirely to its preparation. Today his family name is virtually synonymous with **English mustard** and it is still ground mechanically on the same site in Norwich and grown by East Anglian farmers from seed which is still selected by the company.

At one time, good English mustards were made from a judicious mixture of 37 per cent brown and 50 per cent white mustard flour, and about 10 per cent rice flour, together with spices such as pepper, chilli pepper and even ginger. Today a dash of turmeric is added for colour, and wheatflour, which improves the character of the powder by absorbing some of the oiliness natural to mustard seed, is used instead of rice flour.

The odd thing is that English mustards are popular in France while Britain imports large quantities of less ferocious **French mustards**. The two main types of mustard used in France are the pale Dijon or white mustard, and a darker Bordeaux mustard. Bordeaux mustard is dark because it contains the seed coat, and is sour-sweet, with vinegar and sugar heavily flavoured with tarragon and other herbs and spices. It is ideally suited for eating with foods where it needs to enhance, not

mask, the taste. It therefore does very well in salad dressings. Dijon mustard is sharp and salty with a strong, hot taste (but not as strong as English mustard), and has a more dominating effect on the dish in which it is used.

Düsseldorf is the great **German mustard** centre, producing a Bordeaux-type dark, sweet-sour mustard flavoured with herbs and spices. It also produces a type of mixed mustard which is very popular in the United States, mild and thick.

Nutritional and medicinal properties

The pungent taste and tear-producing properties of mustard seeds are due to nitrogen and sulphur-containing compounds called isothiocyanates. These are formed from two glucosides, called sinigrin (which is present in brown mustard) and sinalbin (which is present in white mustard). These are normally found in ground mustard seeds when the seeds are dried and it is only when they are wet that special enzymes like myrosin break down these glucosides to form isothiocyanates. Apart from the varying amounts of sinigrin and sinalbin, all the mustards have similar chemical constituents. They contain 25–37 per cent fat, with protein and mucilage and numerous other biologically active compounds. Brown mustard yields a volatile oil (about 1 per cent) composed almost exclusively of allyl isothiocyanate which is formed from the breakdown of sinigrin.

Both brown and white mustard seeds are used in treating rheumatism, arthritis, sciatica, lumbago and neuralgia, and they are also used in emetics, diuretics, stimulants, appetizers and rubefacients. In China, a 10–20 per cent solution made from white mustard

100 g MUSTARD (greens)	
Calories	31
Protein (g)	3.0
Carbohydrate (g)	5.6
Cholesterol (g)	–
Fat (g)	0.5
Fibre (g)	1.1
Minerals	
calcium (mg)	183
phosphorus (mg)	50
iron (mg)	3
sodium (mg)	32
potassium (mg)	377
magnesium (mg)	27
zinc (mg)	–
iodine (mg)	0.043
chlorine (mg)	–
sulphur (mg)	–
silicon (mg)	–
bromine (mg)	–
Vitamins	
A(IU)	7000
B_1 (mg)	0.11
B_2 (mg)	0.22
B_3 (mg)	0.8
B_5 (mg)	–
B_6 (mg)	–
B_{12} (mcg)	–
folic acid (mcg)	–
biotin (mcg)	–
C (mg)	97
D (mg)	–
E (mg)	–
Organic acids	
citric (%)	–
malic (%)	–
oxalic (%)	0.0077
Water (%)	89.5
Digestion time (hrs)	3½

seeds has been successfully injected into various acupoints of people suffering from chronic bronchitis. Plasters made of white mustard can be applied to painful joints. The application is continually renewed until just before blisters are raised. Black mustard can be added to hot water as a footbath to ease chilblains. It should be taken sparingly internally because it can cause inflammation.

Mustard greens are recommended as a tonic for anaemia, constipation, rheumatism, arthritis, acidity, kidney and bladder ailments, and bronchial inflammation and are recommended particularly for pregnant women and nursing mothers, to rid the system of accumulated poisons. Mustard greens are rich in vitamins A, B and C and contain bulk fibre which produces a mildly laxative effect. A wonderful all-round reviver is a hot mustard footbath taken simultaneously with iced compresses applied to the head. A tea made from the seeds and used as a gargle loosens mucus congestion.

French mustard with herbs

This is adapted from Bee Nilson's *Herb Cookery* (Pelham Books, 1985), a classic cook-book in my opinion. Instead of the anchovy essence she uses, I double up on the mushroom ketchup.

6 tablespoons dry mustard
1 teaspoon sugar (I would use brown)

1 tablespoon olive oil
1 teaspoon sea salt
2 teaspoons tarragon vinegar
2 teaspoons mushroom ketchup
a generous pinch of powdered
  marjoram

Put the mustard in a basin and mix to a stiff paste with cold water. Add all the other ingredients to the paste and stir well, diluting with a little more vinegar if it feels too stiff. Store in a covered jar.

This has a lovely mild flavour, and is particularly good with rarebit.

NUTS

This is the name given to any seed or fruit consisting of a soft – usually edible kernel surrounded by a hard woody shell. To most people nuts are something to nibble with drinks in the pub or to fill up the time between gargantuan meals at Christmas, but they ought to be more highly regarded as an important alternative source of protein. Nuts contain far more protein than vegetables.

Nuts and seeds in their shells keep for about a year and are roughly half the price of shelled nuts. All shelled nuts should be kept in an airtight container in a cool, dry, dark place to prevent the fats becoming rancid, and stored in this way will last for about four months.

Nuts are twice as nourishing in the raw form as when roasted because heat denatures the protein and fat. Once denatured the fat is much more subject to rancidity which leads to free-radical formation, now known to be damaging to the circulatory system. Commercial processes are capable of disguising rancidity by roasting and flavouring. Since stability and food value are decreased by roasting but the calories remain the same I would advise restraint as far as roasted nuts are concerned – admittedly a bit of a challenge as roasting makes them tastier and crunchier.

The healthiest method of roasting is dry-roasting at home in *small* batches. This can be done on a baking sheet in the oven whilst baking something else or in a heavy-bottomed frying-pan with a lot of stirring using a wooden spoon. They are 'done' when they taste the way you like them. If you really must add salt, then add a little oil towards the end of the cooking, stirring vigorously to get all the nuts covered by a thin film of hot oil, then sprinkle in the salt and stir again.

An increasingly popular alternative to roasted-and-salted nuts is tamari-roasted nuts. For tamari-roasting no oil is needed. Simply dribble soya sauce on to the hot nuts and seeds and stir to coat them lightly. Then roast them until they become dry again. Do this in a frying pan, as if you use the oven you'll find you squander too much soya sauce.

See also: Almond, Brazil nut, Cashew-nut, Chestnut, Coconut, Hazelnut, Peanut, Pecan, Pine nut, Pistachio, Walnut.

Nutritional and medicinal properties

Nuts are a concentrated storehouse of food – low in water and high in unsaturated fat, as well as protein which sees the developing plant through the first few days of its life. They need to be combined with other vegetable proteins in the same way as grains and beans in order to make a complete protein contain-

100 g NUTS

	Almonds	Beechnuts	Brazil nuts	Cashews	Hazelnuts and filberts
Calories	598	568	654	561	634
Protein (g)	18.6	19.4	14.3	17.2	12.6
Carbohydrate (g)	19.5	20.3	10.9	29.3	16.7
Cholesterol (g)	–	–	–	–	–
Fat (g)	54.2	50	66.9	45.7	62.4
Fibre (g)	2.6	3.7	3.1	1.4	3
Minerals					
calcium (mg)	234	–	186	38	209
phosphorus (mg)	504	–	693	373	337
iron (mg)	4.7	–	3.4	3.8	3.4
sodium (mg)	4	–	1	15	2
potassium (mg)	773	–	715	464	704
magnesium (mg)	270	–	225	267	184
zinc (mg)	–	–	–	–	–
iodine (mg)	0.002	–	–	–	0.002
chlorine (mg)	6	103	–	–	60
sulphur (mg)	96	103	433	–	446
silicon (mg)	4	113	–	–	–
bromine (mg)	–	–	–	–	–
Vitamins					
A(IU)	0	–	tr	100	–
B_1 (mg)	0.24	–	0.96	0.43	0.46
B_2 (mg)	0.92	–	0.12	0.25	–
B_3 (mg)	3.5	–	1.6	1.8	0.9
B_5 (mg)	–	–	–	–	–
B_6 (mg)	0.1	–	0.1	–	0.56
B_{12} (mcg)	0	–	0	0	0
folic acid (mcg)	0	–	–	–	62.1
biotin (mcg)	–	–	–	–	–
C (mg)	tr	–	–	–	tr
D (mg)	0	–	0	0	0
E (mg)	7.3	1	21	5.91	28.1
Organic acids					
citric (%)	–	–	–	–	–
malic (%)	–	–	–	–	–
oxalic (%)	0.41	–	–	0.32	–
Water (%)	4.7	6.6	4.6	5.2	5.8
Digestion time (hrs)	2½	3	–	3¼	3

ing all eight amino-acids including isoleucine and lysine which nuts lack. Nuts are thought to be very fattening and are avoided by slimmers. However, if chewed thoroughly, they are very filling and an excellent source of energy, so a quantity containing not too many calories can be very satisfying.

Nuts are a good source of B vitamins, unsaturated fatty acids, lecithin and minerals. The B

100 g NUTS (continued)

	Pinenuts	Pistachios	Fresh sweet chestnut	Walnuts (black)	Walnuts (English)	Pecan
Calories	552	594	194	628	651	687
Protein (g)	31.1	19.3	2.9	20.5	14.8	9.2
Carbohydrate (g)	11.6	19	42.1	14.8	15.8	14.6
Cholesterol (g)	–	–	–	–	–	0
Fat (g)	47.4	53.7	1.5	59.3	64	71.2
Fibre (g)	0.9	1.9	1.1	1.7	2.1	2.3
Minerals						
calcium (mg)	–	131	27	tr	99	73
phosphorus (mg)	–	500	88	570	380	289
iron (mg)	–	7.3	1.7	6	3.1	2.4
sodium (mg)	–	–	6	3	2	tr
potassium (mg)	–	972	454	460	450	603
magnesium (mg)	–	158	41	190	131	142
zinc (mg)	–	–	–	–	–	–
iodine (mg)	–	–	0.002	–	0.003	–
chlorine (mg)	–	–	–	–	12	–
sulphur (mg)	–	–	–	–	22	–
silicon (mg)	–	–	–	–	12	–
bromine (mg)	–	–	–	–	–	–
Vitamins						
A(IU)	–	230	–	300	30	130
B_1 (mg)	0.62	0.67	0.22	0.22	0.33	0.86
B_2 (mg)	–	–	0.22	0.11	0.13	0.13
B_3 (mg)	–	1.4	0.6	0.7	0.9	0.9
B_5 (mg)	–	–	–	–	0.58	–
B_6 (mg)	–	–	–	–	0.7	–
B_{12} (mcg)	–	–	–	–	0	–
folic acid (mcg)	–	–	–	–	77	–
biotin (mcg)	–	–	–	–	1.3	–
C (mg)	–	0	–	–	4	2
D (mg)	–	0	–	–	–	–
E (mg)	–	5.2	–	–	21	–
Organic acids						
citric (%)	–	–	–	–	–	–
malic (%)	–	–	–	–	–	–
oxalic (%)	–	–	–	–	–	–
Water (%)	5.6	5.3	52.5	3.1	3.5	3.4
Digestion time (hrs)	2¾	–	2¾	3	3	2¾

vitamins include folic acid, which is destroyed in the body by some drugs and by processing or heat-treating food. This vitamin is essential for proper growth. Nuts

also contain niacin, for healthy nerves, and thiamin needed for the conversion of glucose to energy. A good source of thiamin is the red skins around peanuts. (However, strictly speaking, the peanut is not a nut – it is a bean, a member of the legume family.) The only nut to contain any vitamin C is the coconut, which contains traces in its flesh and milk.

Fat-soluble vitamin E is also present in nuts which have not been heat-treated. Vitamin E acts as a natural anti-oxidant and prevents the essential fatty acids in the nut and other foods from being destroyed by oxygen. The vitamin E is carried in the essential fatty acids in the nut. Nuts also contain lecithin, a natural emulsifier which allows fat to be broken down in particles small enough to pass through arterial walls – rather than being deposited and so promoting arteriosclerosis.

Nuts contain many valuable minerals, including magnesium for healthy nerves, potassium for regulization of fats, and zinc for reproductive health. They also contain some dietary fibre, but not as much as grains and beans. Coconuts and almonds have more fibre than other nuts. Technically Brazil nuts are seeds and almonds are fruit.

Fresh nut butter

Excellent nut butter can be made with all the following: almonds (raw or roasted); hazelnuts (roasted are best); walnuts (I prefer raw); Brazil nuts (best left crunchy, and

100 g NUTS (continued)	Chinese water chestnut	Hazelnuts and cobnuts (kernel only)
Calories	79	380
Protein (g)	1.4	7.6
Carbohydrate (g)	19	6.8
Cholesterol (g)	–	–
Fat (g)	–	36
Fibre (g)	0.8	6.1
Minerals		
calcium (mg)	4	44
phosphorus (mg)	65	230
iron (mg)	0.6	1.1
sodium (mg)	20	1
potassium (mg)	500	350
magnesium (mg)	12	56
zinc (mg)	–	2.4
iodine (mg)	–	–
chlorine (mg)	15	6
sulphur (mg)	45	75
silicon (mg)	–	–
bromine (mg)	–	–
Vitamins		
A(IU)	0	–
B_1 (mg)	0.14	0.4
B_2 (mg)	0.2	–
B_3 (mg)	1	–
B_5 (mg)	–	–
B_6 (mg)	–	0.55
B_{12} (mcg)	–	0
folic acid (mcg)	–	72
biotin (mcg)	–	–
C (mg)	4	tr
D (mg)	–	–
E (mg)	–	21
Organic acids		
citric (%)	–	–
malic (%)	–	–
oxalic (%)	–	–
Water (%)	78.3	41.1
Digestion time (hrs)	–	–

Brazil nut butter makes an interesting frosting mixed with milk and honey); cashews (raw or roasted, except that they are never really raw – they are steamed before leaving the country of origin); and coconut (very rich and creamy – a dollop in a vegetable curry sauce raises it to new heights). Spread it on wholemeal bread or oatcakes for a nourishing snack.

¾ pint (450 ml) oil (sesame is
*   compatible with all kinds of*
*   nuts and seeds)*
4 oz (100 g) shelled fresh nuts
sea salt

Pour most of the oil into a liquidizer and add the nuts. If you hold just a little back it will save you making a mixture which is too runny. Much depends on how oily the fresh nuts you choose are to begin with.

Blend to a paste stopping every few seconds to scrape down the sides of the container with a plastic or rubber spatula. You can stop when the paste still has fragments of nuts to give it a crunchy texture, if this is the way you like it, or continue blending till it is completely smooth.

Season lightly with salt, stir well, then pack the butter in screw-top glass jars and store in the fridge.

OATS

Family: *Gramineae*
Genus: *Avena*
Species: *Avena sativa*

Oats will grow in almost any climate and type of soil. They are a very popular crop in Scotland and are used in many recipes, including porridge, puddings, cakes and biscuits. The wild oat (*Avena fatua*) is sometimes grown for animal food.

Whole grain oats (or groats) are grains from which the husks have been removed by heating, which reduces the risk of rancidity and does not significantly damage the nutrients. They can be used in soups and casseroles or in place of rice. Sprouted groats have a sweet taste and are an excellent addition to salads. **Oatbran** is a vital source of fibre which helps to control the levels of cholesterol in the body. It contains the oatgerm and is more nutritious than wheat bran. **Instant oatmeal** has tiny flakes and has been precooked, and so has lost much of its nutritional value. **Steelcut oats** have a higher nutritional value than rolled oats, which are subjected to high temperatures during processing. This destroys some of the nutrients. **Hulled (or gritted) oatmeal** is not heated at all during processing, so is also nutritionally superior. **Rolled oats** are quicker cooking and have been heated.

See also: Grains.

Nutritional and medicinal properties

Oats have almost the same protein content as wheat but 8 per cent more fat, which is largely polyunsaturated. They are higher in essential amino-acids than any other cereal. They contain B vitamins, especially inositol, which is important for nourishing brain cells and for good eyesight. They also contain vitamin E and are rich in minerals, particularly potassium, calcium and phosphorus.

Healthy granola

So called because most homemade-granola recipes call for a fairly heavy syrup of oil and honey to be poured over the dry ingredients, which is delicious but horrendously calorific. This version gives a lovely deep-roasted flavour to the ingredients and stores well in a screw-topped glass jar.

4 oz (100 g) sesame seeds
4 oz (100 g) sunflower seeds
4 oz (100 g) pumpkin seeds
1 lb (450 g) raw rolled oats
4 oz (100 g) desiccated coconut

4 oz (100 g) ground flax seed or
  Linusit Gold
4 oz (100 g) raisins
½ teaspoon ground anise seed
4 oz (100 g) muscovado sugar
1½ teaspoons sea salt

100 g OATMEAL

	Raw	Porridge*
Calories	401	44
Protein (g)	12.4	1.4
Carbohydrate (g)	72.8	8.2
Cholesterol (g)	–	–
Fat (g)	8.7	0.9
Fibre (g)	7	0.8
Minerals		
calcium (mg)	55	6
phosphorus (mg)	380	43
iron (mg)	4.1	0.5
sodium (mg)	33	580
potassium (mg)	370	42
magnesium (mg)	110	13
zinc (mg)	3	0.3
iodine (mg)	–	–
chlorine (mg)	73	890
sulphur (mg)	160	18
silicon (mg)	–	–
bromine (mg)	–	–
Vitamins		
A(IU)	–	–
B_1 (mg)	0.5	0.05
B_2 (mg)	0.1	0.01
B_3 (mg)	–	–
B_5 (mg)	1	0.1
B_6 (mg)	0.12	0.01
B_{12} (mcg)	0	0
folic acid (mcg)	60	6
biotin (mcg)	20	2
C (mg)	0	0
D (mg)	0	–
E (mg)	0.8	0.1
Organic acids		
citric (%)	–	–
malic (%)	–	–
oxalic (%)	–	–
Water (%)	8.9	89.1
Digestion time (hrs)	–	–

* Made with 60 g oatmeal and 2 level
teaspoons salt per 500 ml water

Use a heavy cast-iron pan and roast the seeds and oats in it by cooking over a medium heat for 5 minutes, stirring constantly. Add all the other ingredients except the salt and sugar, and stir over the same heat for 10 minutes more. Now sprinkle in the sugar and salt, and stir for 2 minutes or until every morsel is covered with them. Cool. Store in a glass jar tightly stoppered. Serve with fresh fruit and milk, plain yoghurt or nut milk.

OILS

Virtually all oils sold for culinary purposes come from the seeds or fruits of plants (including nuts, beans and grains). The kind of oil or fat used in cooking makes a vital contribution to both the character and flavour of any dish. Some oils have very little flavour of their own, while others have their own inimitable flavour evoking the feel of a particular country or region.

Fats and oils are made of fatty acids and glycerol, which are chemically linked. Saturated fats contain their full quota of hydrogen atoms and generally harden at room temperature. Animal fats like butter are highly saturated whereas fish oils are relatively unsaturated. Most vegetable oils (except for palm and coconut oils which are not recommended for cooking), are also relatively unsaturated.

It also matters whether the fatty acids in oils are 'essential' or not. The body needs to consume certain fatty acids, just as it may be provided with vitamins, because it cannot make them intrinsically. These fatty acids are derived from linoleic acid, which is essential for the production of prostaglandins which help the blood to clot and prevent thrombosis. Linoleic acid is vital for the formation of nervous tissue.

The term 'cold-pressed' is very deceptive. What it really means is that the oil concerned was cold-processed, that is, chilled and filtered, *not* that it is unrefined. Some of these oils are solvent-extracted and all are chemically refined. There are no legal definitions for this mechanically extracted oil, resulting in labelling imprecision. However, the terminology that indicates a genuine alternative to refined oils includes the words 'pressed' or 'expeller-pressed', and should be accompanied by the clear wording 'no preservatives'. The words 'crude' or 'unrefined' can describe a mixture of pressed and solvent-extracted oil and do not guarantee the pure alternative. The clearest labelling will say something like 'Unrefined almond oil, 100 per cent expeller-pressed'. Unrefined pressed oil is dark in colour, and sediment will accumulate on the bottom of the bottle. Both the odour and flavour will be strong and distinctive.

The word 'virgin' is bandied around a lot as far as olive oil is concerned and it is another term with no legal definition. The term originated when small-scale hydraulic pressing was the only extraction method in use and 'virgin' referred to the first pressing, meaning that which came most easily. This first or virgin pressing was darker and more aromatic and full of flavour than subsequent pressings (which were sometimes aided by heat), and therefore the most desirable as far as cooking was concerned. The word 'pure' as far as olive oil is concerned may mean that it has some virgin mixed in to it (probably 5–20 per cent) to improve the flavour, but generally refers to second pressings extracted at high temperatures, and perhaps even solvent-extracted. Olive oil and sesame oil are really the only two kinds that can be genuinely cold-pressed on any sort of commercial scale.

Refined oils will usually keep a year or more but will lose some of their vitamins A and D, iodine, minerals and volatile acids, and in some cases their vitamin E. Refining and removing all particles of seed and juice reduces the chance of the oil becoming rancid. A rancid oil is one which has been acted on by oxygen. Oxidation leads to the formation of free radicles. The vitamin E present in unrefined oil prevents both oxidation and the formation of free radicles. Vitamin E and other natural anti-oxidants are in unrefined oil simply because they have not been subjected to mistreatment with lye, caustic soda and filtration. Unrefined oils will keep for six months or longer at 65°F (18°C), even longer at lower temperatures. Rancid oil has an unmistakable bitter flavour and a rank smell. However, fractionally rancid oil is impossible to detect so it is wise to take precautions to deter the process. Heat encourages rancidity, so keep your refined oil cold before and after opening. Light accelerates rancidity, so keep it in the dark.

The potential for rancidity is also related to the amount of unsaturated fat naturally found in the oil. Unsaturated fatty acids are fairly unstable and polyunsaturated fatty acids are quite volatile. Thus an oil such as safflower oil, which nowadays is touted widely because it is the highest in polyunsaturates, is undesirable in the sense that it is the hardest to keep fresh. It is in fact advantageous to use the whole range of vegetable oils because this provides the body with a complete variety of fatty acids and so reduces the burden placed on the body by an unbalanced supply. Another factor often mentioned as affecting the stability of vegetable oils is the heat used to extract them. High heat affects the molecular structure, denaturing it and making it more unstable and more prone to oxidation.

But it is not possible to say what oils are produced at which temperatures because different producers follow different procedures and the same producer will vary from one week, month or season to the next. It is, however, safe to assume that expeller-pressed oils have not had their stability impaired by pressing temperatures. Certainly sesame and olive oils are not cooked at all before pressing.

Several of the most important oils are covered under separate entries – *see* **Linseed, Maize, Olive,**
Peanut, Poppy, Sesame, Soya, Sunflower, Walnut.

Rapeseed oil, known commercially as colza oil, is extracted from the seeds of bright yellow rape, which so many fondly mistake for mustard. Until recently the high levels of an indigestible substance called eurcic acid in rapeseed oil meant it could only be used in limited quantities. However, new varieties are now available which contain little eurcic acid and this, coupled with generous EEC subsidies, has meant that the use of this oil is now increasing. It is certainly a good source of linoleic acid and polyunsaturates and is used extensively in Indian cookery, mainly for frying.

Cotton seed oil is mainly used to make up margarines and cooking fats. People in the Middle East and Far East appreciate it for its distinctive flavour. It is rich in linoleic acid and other polyunsaturates.

Safflower oil is made from the yellow flowered member of the thistle family widely cultivated in India and the Middle East. It is strongly flavoured and some people do not find it particularly pleasant.

Many people tend to confuse safflower with sunflower oil and regard them as one and the same but the plants are quite different although they do share the common denominator of the *Compositae* family. Safflower oil is the richest in linoleic acid of all the oils, containing up to 80 per cent, and hard on its heels follows sunflower oil containing 65 per cent.

Recent research has shown that

all oils high in linoleic acid will effectively lower cholesterol in the blood but these have to be coupled with B and E vitamins to be effective.

Palm oil comes from the fruits of the oil palm which is a different species from the coconut palm and is widely used in West Africa. Besides the fact that it is difficult to get hold of, it is not recommended from the health point of view because it is rather high in saturated fats. However, it is often used in manufactured foods, so keep your eyes peeled when reading labels.

100 g OIL

	Corn	Olive	Safflower	Sunflower	Peanut	Soyabean	Vegetable
Calories	884	884	884	884	884	884	899
Protein (g)	0	–	–	–	–	–	tr
Carbohydrate (g)	0	0	–	–	–	–	0
Cholesterol (g)	–	–	–	–	–	–	–
Fat (g)	100	100	100	100	100	100	99.9
Fibre (g)	0	0	–	–	–	–	–
Minerals							
calcium (mg)	0	0	–	–	–	–	tr
phosphorus (mg)	0	0	–	–	–	–	tr
iron (mg)	0	0	–	–	–	–	tr
sodium (mg)	0	0	–	–	–	–	tr
potassium (mg)	0	0	–	–	–	–	tr
magnesium (mg)	0	0	–	–	–	–	tr
zinc (mg)	–	–	–	–	–	–	tr
iodine (mg)	–	–	–	–	–	–	–
chlorine (mg)	–	–	–	–	–	–	tr
sulphur (mg)	–	–	–	–	–	–	tr
silicon (mg)	–	–	–	–	–	–	–
bromine (mg)	–	–	–	–	–	–	–
Vitamins							
A(IU)	–	–	–	–	–	–	tr
B_1 (mg)	0	0	–	–	–	–	tr
B_2 (mg)	0	0	–	–	–	–	tr
B_3 (mg)	0	0	–	–	–	–	tr
B_5 (mg)	–	–	–	–	–	–	–
B_6 (mg)	–	–	–	–	–	–	tr
B_{12} (mcg)	–	–	–	–	–	–	0
folic acid (mcg)	–	–	–	–	–	–	tr
biotin (mcg)	–	–	–	–	–	–	tr
C (mg)	0	0	–	–	–	–	0
D (mg)	–	–	–	–	–	–	0
E (mg)	–	–	–	–	–	–	–
Organic acids							
citric (%)	–	–	–	–	–	–	–
malic (%)	–	–	–	–	–	–	–
oxalic (%)	–	–	–	–	–	–	–
Water (%)	0	0	–	–	–	–	tr
Digestion time (hrs)	3½	3½	3½	3½	3½	3½	–

OKRA

Family: *Malvaceae*
Genus: *Hibiscus*
Species: *Hibiscus esculentus*

This is one of the oldest vegetables in the world and was originally grown by the Abyssinians and the Bantu tribes in Africa. It was brought to the Caribbean by African slaves and from there it spread to America where it became known as gumbo. Also known as lady's fingers, today it is important in the cooking of the Balkans, eastern Mediterranean and South America. It is also popular in the USA and the West Indies and its native Africa.

The young pods are pale green and grow to a finger length in size (hence one of the popular names). They harbour soft, white, seeded flesh, which exudes a sticky juice during cooking. The flavour is neutral to slightly bitter, and very mild. Okra is available in the UK, generally imported from Kenya, and its season runs from summer to the early autumn. Canned okra is available in most Greek and Indian food shops and keeps its flavour quite well – one of the few tinned products I don't mind using. Because of its glutinous texture when cooked, it is widely used to thicken and flavour stews.

Nutritional and medicinal properties

Okra is extremely high in calcium and low in calories and because of the mucilage, is useful for stomach ulcers as well as sore throats, pleurisy and colitis. Current research suggests it may also be useful for the treatment of diabetes. West Indians eat it when trying to lose weight.

100 g OKRA	
Calories	36
Protein (g)	2.4
Carbohydrate (g)	7.6
Cholesterol (g)	–
Fat (g)	0.3
Fibre (g)	1
Minerals	
calcium (mg)	92
phosphorus (mg)	51
iron (mg)	0.6
sodium (mg)	3
potassium (mg)	249
magnesium (mg)	41
zinc (mg)	–
iodine (mg)	0.022
chlorine (mg)	–
sulphur (mg)	710
silicon (mg)	–
bromine (mg)	–
Vitamins	
A(IU)	520
B_1 (mg)	0.17
B_2 (mg)	0.21
B_3 (mg)	1
B_5 (mg)	–
B_6 (mg)	–
B_{12} (mcg)	–
folic acid (mcg)	–
biotin (mcg)	–
C (mg)	31
D (mg)	–
E (mg)	–
Organic acids	
citric (%)	0.02
malic (%)	0.12
oxalic (%)	0.048
Water (%)	88.9
Digestion time (hrs)	2½

Okra (Coo-coo)

This is a popular Arabic dish generally served cold, but is just as good hot with pilaf or as one of a choice of vegetables for a main course. I always though okra was used only in Mediterranean and Middle Eastern cookery until my West Indian patients began to give me recipes for it. This is one of them and has the lovely name of coo-coo. Any that is left is served sliced and fried with grilled tomatoes and eggs.

12 small, fresh young okra
2½ pints (1.5 litres) water
pinch of sea salt
8 oz (225 g) yellow cornmeal
1½ oz (40 g) butter

Wash and scrub the okra. Cut off any hard stems and cut across into ¼ inch (6 millimetre) slices. Add the okra to the boiling salted water, and boil, covered, for 10 minutes. Then slowly pour the cornmeal into the pan, stirring hard. Cook at a rolling boil for 5 minutes, stirring vigorously until the mixture is thick and smooth. Turn the mixture into a greased bowl to mould it and then turn it out on to a warmed serving plate with a little butter melted on the top. It goes well with ratatouille.

OLIVE

Family: *Oleaceae*
Genus: *Olea*
Species: *Olea europaea*

Olives are said to have been first cultivated 6000 years ago and we have confirmation that they were used in ancient Egypt 4000 years ago. The gnarled trees grow to a great old age – some olive trees in Palestine date back to the Christian era. They are chiefly cultivated around the Mediterranean, and in California, South America and Asia.

There are two main types of olive in the shops. **Green olives** are picked unripe and pickled while immature, while **black olives** are allowed to ripen and become dark on the tree. Crude olives taste intensely bitter and are inedible. The bitterness has to be washed out by many changes of water or by pickling in brine for some months. Even then, some varieties of olives do not succumb to this treatment and, although they will produce oil, will never be palatable.

The most important product from the olive is **olive oil**. It is the most deliciously flavoured oil but has become prohibitively expensive, so it is now frequently mixed with other vegetable oils such as sunflower. It is low in polyunsaturates and so is very stable.

See also: Oils.

Nutritional and medicinal properties

Ripened black olives contain very little vitamin A, but have slightly more carbohydrate, fat and calories than green olives. All olives are high in minerals, especially sodium, calcium and potassium. They are fairly high in fat and fibre. Greek olives, or at least the ones we find in Britain, are generally black, salted and preserved in oil. Therefore they are saltier and richer than most other olives and consequently have more calories, protein, fat, carbohydrate and sodium.

The rich oleic content (80 per cent) of olive oil makes it completely digestible, and increases the absorption of the fat-soluble vitamins A, D, E, and K. It is low in linoleic acid, so some nutritionists advise combining olive oil with another which is high in this acid – such as safflower oil – to provide a really well-balanced salad oil.

Olives are demulcent, mildly purgative, antiseptic and weakly astringent. The oil is used as a laxative for chronic constipation, and as it reduces the flow of gastric secretions, it is still occasionally used to treat peptic ulcers. The leaves can be made into a strong decoction for wound treatment. In the old days they were used as an antipyretic and valued for their hypotensive activity. The oil stimulates bile secretion, facilitating the dumping of gallstones and I have had excellent results using copious amounts with patients on a liver cleanse, but because the process is quite strenuous I do recommend it be supervised by a professional medical herbalist or naturopath.

Olive bread (Zeytin ekmegi)

This is a regional speciality from Antalya in Turkey. It is also prepared by the Greeks and Armenians belonging to the Eastern Orthodox Church and was traditionally eaten during the forty days of Lent to expand a diet temporarily without meat, eggs or dairy produce. It is extremely tasty. I have modified it only by substituting wholewheat flour.

dough
½ oz (12 g) fresh yeast or ¼ oz (6 g) dried yeast
1 teaspoon brown sugar
½ pint (300 ml) tepid water

100 g GREEN OLIVES IN BRINE	
Calories	116
Protein (g)	1.4
Carbohydrate (g)	1.3
Cholesterol (g)	0
Fat (g)	12.7
Fibre (g)	1.3
Minerals	
calcium (mg)	61
phosphorus (mg)	17
iron (mg)	1.6
sodium (mg)	2400
potassium (mg)	55
magnesium (mg)	22
zinc (mg)	–
iodine (mg)	–
chlorine (mg)	–
sulphur (mg)	–
silicon (mg)	–
bromine (mg)	–
Vitamins	
A(IU)	300
B$_1$ (mg)	–
B$_2$ (mg)	–
B$_3$ (mg)	–
B$_5$ (mg)	0.02
B$_6$ (mg)	0.02
B$_{12}$ (mcg)	0
folic acid (mcg)	–
biotin (mcg)	tr
C (mg)	0
D (mg)	–
E (mg)	–
Organic acids	
citric (%)	–
malic (%)	–
oxalic (%)	–
Water (%)	78.2
Digestion time (hrs)	–

1 lb (450 g) wholewheat flour
½ teaspoon salt

filling
1 tablespoon olive oil
1 onion, finely diced
20 olives, halved and stoned
oil for glazing

Put the yeast and sugar in a bowl, add a few spoonfuls of warm water, mix until the yeast is dissolved, and leave for 10 minutes till the mixture begins to froth. Sift the flour and salt into a large bowl. Make a well in the centre of the flour and pour the yeast mixture into it. Add enough of the warm water to make a firm dough. Knead on a floured surface for 10–15 minutes till the dough becomes soft and elastic.

Having washed and dried your mixing bowl, oil it lightly. Roll the dough in it until the surface of the dough is greased all over – this will prevent it going crusty and cracking as it rises. Cover the bowl with a damp cotton cloth and put in a warm place for at least 2 hours till it has doubled in size. Then transfer the dough back to a working surface, punch down and knead for a few minutes. Cut it into two even pieces and roll each one to form a smooth ball. Roll each ball out into a rectangle 8×16 in (20×40 cm) and ¼ in (6 mm) thick. Set these aside, covered with a damp cloth, while you prepare the filling.

Heat the oil in a small saucepan, add the onion and fry till soft – do not let it brown. Stir in the olives and leave to cool. Then spread half the mixture over one of the rectangles of dough, staying well clear of the edges. Roll up each

rectangle, beginning from one of the longer sides; punch the edges so that they are sealed. Place the two loaves on a greased baking sheet with the joins underneath.

Slash the top of each loaf with three diagonal cuts. Cover them with a cloth and leave to prove in a warm place for 30 minutes. Brush the tops with oil and bake in an oven preheated to 375°F (190°C, gas mark 5) for 40 minutes till golden. Serve warm if you can.

ONION

Family: *Amaryllidaceae*
Genus: *Allium*
Species: *Allium cepa*; *Allium fistulosum* (green onion)

The onion is a hardy bulbous plant belonging to the lily family. The onion has been in cultivation for so long that its country of origin is uncertain. It is rarely, if ever, found wild.

The **common onion** is medium sized and round in shape, with a brown outer casing. The **spring onion (scallion)** is a very young onion, with a fine skin and a long green stalk, excellent in salads – both the bulb and the stalks are used. The **pickling onion (pearl onion)** comes from the first picking of the mature onion and is used for pickling or whole in stews, etc. The **Spanish onion** has many varieties, all of which are large and mild flavoured. These onions are often stuffed and cooked whole.

Nutritional and medicinal properties

The onion contains vitamins B, C and E, carotene, calcium, iron, phosphorus, potassium, sodium, sulphur and traces of copper. It is also rich in anti-microbial substances, fibre, glycosides, hormones similar to insulin, and volatile oil. In fact its constituents are similar to those of garlic and like garlic it contains a naturally antiseptic oil, allyl disulphate, and cycloallin.

Research at the Royal Victoria Infirmary, Newcastle, showed that cycloallin helps the walls of blood vessels to dissolve clots which form from inside. It seems that frying or boiling onions does not affect its efficacy in this area. The onion is reputed to be helpful for heart disorders and arthritis. The cycloallin also dissolves fibrin, which forms in inflamed joints as part of the inflammation process. Onions actively reduce the blood pressure and the blood sugar level. They are said to increase the flow of urine, to be slightly laxative and antiseptic, and to relieve sinus conditions. Used externally as a local stimulant, the juice can be applied to cuts, and used to treat acne and promote hair growth. Onions are also helpful for nails, hair and eyes. Crushed onion applied to the chest as a poultice relieves inflammation of the lungs and put between gauze bandages and applied over the ears, will relieve earache (although admittedly it looks very strange)!

Boiled onions lose some of their calories and carbohydrates as well as a very small portion of their minerals. As one would expect, fried onions are high in calories (355 to 100 g); they increase in mineral content, and their vitamin content rises a little also. Spring onions contain traces of protein, carbohydrate, fibre and very little fat. They have more calcium and

100 g ONIONS	
Calories	38
Protein (g)	1.5
Carbohydrate (g)	9
Cholesterol (g)	0
Fat (g)	0.1
Fibre (g)	0.6
Minerals	
calcium (mg)	27
phosphorus (mg)	36
iron (mg)	0.5
sodium (mg)	10
potassium (mg)	157
magnesium (mg)	12
zinc (mg)	0.1
iodine (mg)	–
chlorine (mg)	–
sulphur (mg)	–
silicon (mg)	–
bromine (mg)	–
Vitamins	
A(IU)	40
B_1 (mg)	0.03
B_2 (mg)	0.04
B_3 (mg)	0.2
B_5 (mg)	0.14
B_6 (mg)	0.1
B_{12} (mcg)	0
folic acid (mcg)	10
biotin (mcg)	0.9
C (mg)	10
D (mg)	0
E (mg)	0.3
Organic acids	
citric (%)	–
malic (%)	–
oxalic (%)	–
Water (%)	89.4
Digestion time (hrs)	–

potassium and vitamin C than raw ordinary onions. They also have half the amount of sodium and just a trace of vitamin A.

Roast onions

These are unbelievably simple to make but delicious, low in calories and very good for cleansing the bloodstream. My housekeeper Rose remembers her mother putting onions in the embers of a coal fire, testing them with a skewer and hauling them out with tongs.

They were then served just as they were or occasionally a little cheese was sprinkled on the inside.

Put medium-sized onions, unpeeled, into a roasting pan. Cook them at 350°F (180°C, gas mark 4) in the same way as a baked potato, for 2–2½ hours. The skins then come off easily, and the onion inside is delicious, soft and full of flavour. Serve hot with seasoning and butter or cold with a little oil dressing poured over.

PARSLEY

Family: *Umbelliferae*
Genus: *Petroselinum*
Species: *Petroselinum crispum*

This is a familiar biennial kitchen herb closely related to caraway and producing a low-growing noisette of curled and crumpled leaves. However, there are a large number of different varieties, some of them plain-leaved. In the UK and the USA the curly-leaved variety is grown almost exclusively, but in the Middle East the plain-leaved variety dominates.

Do not confuse curly parsley with the poisonous fool's parsley which is a common garden weed. The leaves of fool's parsley are darker and give out an unpleasant smell when broken.

Nutritional and medicinal properties

Parsley is a power-house of vitamins and minerals and particularly high in vitamins E, B and C, the digestive enzyme apiin and iron, potassium, copper and magnesium. It is easily digested (in only 1¼ hours) and readily assimilated.

All parts of the plant can be used but the leaves are used for bladder infections, especially combined with equal parts of echinacea and marshmallow. Don't administer parsley if there is acute inflammation, particularly if it is in the kidneys. The root is particularly useful for treating chronic diseases and ailments of the liver and gall-bladder. It can be used with a small amount of liquorice and marshmallow for the treatment of jaundice, asthma and coughs, and to relieve water retention. The leaves will cheer up depressed gastric digestive performance and relieve visceral and vascular spasms. Eating plenty of the fresh leaves will promote lactation, but heavy consumption of the herb, or ingestion of any of the seeds, must be avoided during pregnancy.

The tea infused from the leaves tastes very bland – I prefer to eat lots of them fresh.

Fried parsley

This tastes rather like the elegant fried seaweed one gets in Chinese restaurants, and it looks amazing.

Take very fresh parsley and divide it into sprigs. If absolutely necessary wash and dry it well on a soft cloth. Have a deep pan of oil (a combination of peanut and sunflower oil lends a nice flavour), and heat to 325°F (163°C) – no hotter or the parsley will shrivel.

Drop a few of the sprigs in at a time, and cook for 2 minutes, turning with a slotted spoon. Drain well.

The parsley will emerge bright emerald and very crisp. It is excellent served with stir-fried vegetables.

100 g PARSLEY	
Calories	44
Protein (g)	3.6
Carbohydrate (g)	8.5
Cholesterol (g)	–
Fat (g)	0.6
Fibre (g)	1.5
Minerals	
calcium (mg)	203
phosphorus (mg)	63
iron (mg)	6.2
sodium (mg)	45
potassium (mg)	727
magnesium (mg)	41
zinc (mg)	–
iodine (mg)	–
chlorine (mg)	–
sulphur (mg)	–
silicon (mg)	–
bromine (mg)	–
Vitamins	
A(IU)	8500
B_1 (mg)	0.12
B_2 (mg)	0.26
B_3 (mg)	1.26
B_5 (mg)	–
B_6 (mg)	–
B_{12} (mcg)	–
folic acid (mcg)	–
biotin (mcg)	–
C (mg)	172
D (mg)	–
E (mg)	–
Organic acids	
citric (%)	–
malic (%)	–
oxalic (%)	0.19
Water (%)	85.1
Digestion time (hrs)	1¼

PARSNIP

Family: *Umbelliferae*
Genus: *Pastinaca*
Species: *Pastinaca sativa*

Parsnips probably originated in the Rhine valley and have been cultivated since Roman times. The poor particularly relished the sweet taste of parsnips because they could not afford expensive sugar, and the Elizabethan nobles enjoyed parsnips in a batter fried with honey or sugar. The sweet taste comes from the conversion of starch to sugar in the root. This happens after the first frost, so parsnips are one of the few vegetables best left in the ground during the winter and certainly not uprooted until after some initial frost.

The parsnip was so relished in England that the potato came into favour mainy because it was sweet 'like a parsnip' (the first potatoes being sweet potatoes). The green tops were fed to cows as late as the nineteenth century and were reputed to make good milk. Parsnips were taken to America in the seventeenth century and have since remained popular there even though they seem to have fallen from grace in Britain.

Parsnip is a biennial root vegetable with a thick, knobbly, tapering, yellow root and deeply and finely lobed leaves. It likes deep, rich soils which should be marked in some way (the speedily growing radish is the favourite). Neglected parsnips can become troublesome weeds.

Parsnips are in season from September to February and Britain grows all it needs. Choose small or medium-sized ones, as the large ones are too woody. Parsnips marry well with potatoes, carrots and turnips.

Nutritional and medicinal properties

Parsnips are a good source of vitamins A and C, carbohydrate, potassium, calcium and fibre. They are said to be useful to relieve the kidney of stones, as a diuretic, for various types of inflammation (gout, colitis, stomach ulcers) and for soothing diarrhoea.

Parsnip pie

My initial introduction to parsnips was unfortunate. I was fourteen and had just come from abroad to boarding school in England where we were served great plates of sloppy, plainly boiled parsnip. Happily I later discovered the delights of puréed parsnips, roasted parsnips and raw grated parsnip in salad.

12 oz (350 g) parsnips, pared
  thinly and cut into chunks
knob of butter
1 tablespoon honey
½ teaspoon ginger
¼ teaspoon mixed spice
grated rind, and juice, of
  2 lemons
1 egg, separated
a little sugar

pastry
6 oz (175 g) wholemeal flour
pinch of sea salt

3 oz (90 g) butter
1 egg yolk

Simmer the parsnips in a covered pot until the pieces are tender when pierced by a skewer (about 20–30 minutes). Drain well and dry over gentle heat. Add a knob of butter and purée in a liquidizer. Add the other ingredients (except those for

100g PARSNIP	
Calories	76
Protein (g)	1.7
Carbohydrate (g)	17.5
Cholesterol (g)	–
Fat (g)	0.5
Fibre (g)	2
Minerals	
calcium (mg)	50
phosphorus (mg)	77
iron (mg)	0.7
sodium (mg)	12
potassium (mg)	541
magnesium (mg)	32
zinc (mg)	0.1
iodine (mg)	–
chlorine (mg)	1040
sulphur (mg)	960
silicon (mg)	800
bromine (mg)	1.3
Vitamins	
A(IU)	30
B_1 (mg)	0.08
B_2 (mg)	0.09
B_3 (mg)	0.2
B_5 (mg)	0.5
B_6 (mg)	–
B_{12} (mcg)	–
folic acid (mcg)	67
biotin (mcg)	0.1
C (mg)	–
D (mg)	–
E (mg)	–
Organic acids	
citric (%)	0.13
malic (%)	0.35
oxalic (%)	0.01
Water (%)	79.1
Digestion time (hrs)	3½

the pastry, and keeping back a little lemon rind) and liquidize again.

Make the pastry, and line a flan dish with two-thirds of it, thinly rolled. Fill the pastry case with the purée. Make a lattice top with the remainder of the pastry and cook in an oven preheated to 400°F (200°C, gas mark 6) until this is golden brown (30–40 minutes). Pile the beaten white of an egg, sweetened with a touch of sugar and flavoured with a little lemon rind round the edge, and return the pie to a switched-off oven for 10 minutes to set. Remove. Cool. Garnish the windows of the lattice with bright yellow primroses and serve. It's a wonderful looking dish, a great golden sunburst particularly welcome in dismal March.

PEA

Family: *Leguminosae*
Genus: *Pisum*
Species: *Pisum sativum* (garden pea); *Pisum sativum* var. *arvense* (dried pea)

Peas belong to the pea and pod family (*Papilonaceae*) which includes beans, alfalfa, and clover. They are an extremely nourishing food. Some varieties are eaten with the pod – for example mangetout peas (or snowpeas), which are popular in the Orient and Europe rather than in the United States. Other varieties are cultivated for their beautiful flowers. The garden peas with which we are familiar with today were developed in the fifteenth century by a French gardener and arrived in England in Tudor times. At that time they were very expensive and a status symbol. Peas were taken to America in 1800.

There are three main types of pea available in Britain: the round-seeded pea, which has tough pods and round, smooth seeds and is good for drying; the wrinkle-seeded or marrowfat pea, which wrinkles when mature and needs to be served fresh as it is not suitable for drying; snowpeas (or mangetout peas), which are eaten pod and all. Peas are really just immature seeds, and the less mature they are the better and sweeter they taste.

Dried peas include whole marrowfat blue peas, and skinless yellow or green split peas which are generally used in purées.

The UK is the major producer and exporter of peas. They are at their best in June and July although their season continues into early Autumn during mild weather. The gardener will always have an advantage over the shopper as regards peas, because they are a good example of a vegetable that is incomparably finer when picked really young and cooked shortly afterwards. Peas are available dried, canned and frozen all the year round.

See also: Pulses.

Nutritional and medicinal properties

Young peas are high in protein, carbohydrates and vitamins B and E, whereas dried peas are also rich in phosphorus, calcium, sodium and vitamin A and are a particularly valuable source of the B-complex vitamins. Weight for weight, peas contain as much protein as meat. Fresh peas are extremely nourishing and body-building. They help anaemia, low blood pressure and emaciation. They contain nicotinic acid, which is believed to reduce cholesterol in the blood.

100 g PEAS

	Raw green	Boiled mangetouts	Boiled fresh	Canned cooked (drained)	Frozen
Calories	84	43	71	88	68
Protein (g)	6.3	2.9	5	4.7	5
Carbohydrate (g)	14.4	9.5	12	16.8	12
Cholesterol (g)	0	0	–	–	–
Fat (g)	0.4	0.2	–	–	–
Fibre (g)	2	1.2	–	2.3	1.9
Minerals					
calcium (mg)	26	56	23	26	19
phosphorus (mg)	116	76	99	76	86
iron (mg)	1.9	0.5	–	1.9	1.9
sodium (mg)	2	0	1	236	115
potassium (mg)	316	119	196	96	135
magnesium (mg)	35	–	–	–	–
zinc (mg)	0.7	–	–	–	–
iodine (mg)	–	–	–	–	–
chlorine (mg)	–	–	–	–	–
sulphur (mg)	50	–	–	–	–
silicon (mg)	–	–	–	–	–
bromine (mg)	–	–	–	–	–
Vitamins					
A(IU)	640	610	540	690	600
B_1 (mg)	0.35	0.22	0.28	0.09	0.27
B_2 (mg)	0.14	0.11	0.11	0.06	0.09
B_3 (mg)	2.9	–	2.3	0.8	1.7
B_5 (mg)	0.75	–	–	–	–
B_6 (mg)	0.16	–	–	–	–
B_{12} (mcg)	0	–	0	–	0
folic acid (mcg)	35.5	–	–	–	–
biotin (mcg)	0.5	–	–	–	–
C (mg)	27	14	20	8	13
D (mg)	0	–	–	–	–
E (mg)	2.1	–	–	–	–
Organic acids					
citric (%)	–	–	–	–	–
malic (%)	–	–	–	–	–
oxalic (%)	–	–	–	–	–
Water (%)	83.3	–	86.6	77	82.1
Digestion time (hrs)	–	–	–	–	–

Split pea soup
(serves 6)

This is a rib-sticking soup suitable for winter and a meal in itself with bread.

1 lb (450 g) green split peas, soaked overnight
3 oz (75 g) pearl barley
2 teaspoon salt
2 bay leaves
4 pints (2.3 litres) water
2 tablespoons olive oil
1 onion, finely chopped
1 carrot, finely chopped
2 cloves garlic, peeled and crushed in a little salt
2 teaspoons chopped fresh thyme (or 1 teaspoon dried thyme)

Bring the peas, barley, salt and bay leaves to the boil in the water, and then reduce the heat to simmer for an hour, stirring from time to time to ensure that the bottom doesn't catch and scorch.

Heat the oil in a saucepan and sauté the onion, carrot, garlic and thyme until the carrot is tender. Add this mixture to the peas and barley and simmer for 30–45 minutes. Fish out the bay leaves. Adjust the seasoning and serve very hot.

PEANUT

Family: *Leguminosae*
Genus: *Arachis*
Species: *Arachis hypogaea*

The peanut is also known as the ground-nut, monkey nut, goober, goober pea, ground pea and pinda.

Peanuts are an annual legume, native to South America, and grow in almost every warm country of the world. The cultivation in South America can be traced back more than 1000 years. Peanuts are cultivated in the United States, India, China and West Africa, and in the United States half the crop is used to make **peanut butter**. Unhappily most commercial peanut butter nowadays is hydrogenated, in order to stop it becoming rancid. This process renders the butter useless as far as essential fatty acid is concerned. It is much better therefore to make your own (follow the recipe for fresh nut butter given under Nuts). Peanut butter contains more protein, weight for weight, than steak.

From peanuts is expressed an important oil called **arachis (or groundnut) oil**. When purified this is virtually tasteless and is one of the finest commercial cooking oils, often used as a substitute for olive oil, particularly by the French who appreciate it more than the alternative – inferior olive oil. After the oil has been removed, nuts are used as high-protein fodder.

See also: Nuts, Oils.

Nutritional and medicinal properties

Peanuts are highly nutritious but also very calorific. They contain tryptophan and methionine in low amounts and for this reason some nutritionalists advise against eating peanuts as a complete protein. Average peanut butter is usually only 70 per cent peanuts, the remaining 30 per cent being hydrogenated fat and refined sugar in the form of dextrose. Buy peanut butter which is 100 per cent peanuts and put it on wholegrain bread to be assured of a complete protein. Peanuts are rich in linoleic acid, which reduces the risk of cholesterol deposits in the arteries. They provide a higher proportion of pantothenic acid than any food except liver. Under certain conditions some substances in

100 g PEANUTS

	With skin	Without skin	Oil	Roasted with skin	Roasted salted	Peanut butter
Calories	564	568	884	582	589	581
Protein (g)	26	26.3	–	26.4	25.6	27.9
Carbohydrate (g)	18.6	17.6	–	20.8	22.2	17.1
Cholesterol (g)	–	–	–	–	–	–
Fat (g)	47.5	48.4	100	50	50	50.4
Fibre (g)	2.4	1.9	–	2.7	2.2	1.9
Minerals						
calcium (mg)	69	59	0	69.4	77.8	62
phosphorus (mg)	401	409	0	410	400	488
iron (mg)	2.1	2.1	0	2.2	2.2	2
sodium (mg)	5	5	0	4.9	422	620
potassium (mg)	674	674	0	694.4	677.7	659
magnesium (mg)	206	206	0	–	–	–
zinc (mg)	–	–	–	–	–	–
iodine (mg)	0.02	–	–	–	–	–
chlorine (mg)	23	–	–	–	–	–
sulphur (mg)	45	–	–	–	–	–
silicon (mg)	5	–	–	–	–	–
bromine (mg)	–	–	–	–	–	–
Vitamins						
A(IU)	–	0	–	–	–	–
B_1 (mg)	1.14	0.99	0	0.32	0.3	0.13
B_2 (mg)	0.13	0.13	0	0.13	0.1	0.13
B_3 (mg)	17.2	15.8	0	17.4	16.7	15.5
B_5 (mg)	–	–	–	–	–	–
B_6 (mg)	–	–	–	0.4	0.4	0.33
B_{12} (mcg)	–	–	–	0	0	0
folic acid (mcg)	–	–	–	–	–	–
biotin (mcg)	–	–	–	–	–	–
C (mg)	0	0	–	0	0	0
D (mg)	–	–	–	–	–	–
E (mg)	–	–	–	–	–	–
Organic acids						
citric (%)	–	–	–	–	–	–
malic (%)	–	–	–	–	–	–
oxalic (%)	–	–	–	–	–	–
Water (%)	5.6	5.4	–	–	–	–
Digestion time (hrs)	3¼	–	3½	–	–	–

peanuts can combine with iodine and act as a blocker so that it cannot reach the blood. So eat peanuts cautiously, certainly not daily and not in huge quantities.

Experiments with animals have found that peanut oil causes atheroma, and although it does not automatically follow that this happens in man, a question mark remains over it. However, when unrefined, it is a good source of linoleic acid and other polyunsaturates.

Peanut butter sauce

This is delicious poured over hot tofu (soya-bean curd) and served with a side salad, or over vegetables and grains.

½ cup peanut butter, preferably home-made
1 onion, grated
1 clove garlic, crushed
2½ tablespoons skimmed milk powder
¼ teaspoon honey
4 tablespoons fresh lemon juice
4 tablespoons soy sauce

Mix all the ingredients together and add just enough hot water to make a heavy cream. If you want a smoother sauce, purée the mixture before adding the water.

PECAN

Family: *Juglandacea*
Genus: *Carya*
Species: *Carya olivaeformis*

The pecan and other American hickory nuts are related to walnuts and have a somewhat similar flavour. They look rather like elongated walnuts but are fleshier, with thinner shells which can be easily cracked. The shell itself is red-brown and of the many varieties of pecan the 'paper-skin' is most popular because these shells can be cracked with the fingers.

Pecan trees grow naturally along the Mississippi from Iowa southwards to the river valleys of Oklahoma, Texas and north Mexico. Orchards are located as far north as Virginia and California. Pecans have been introduced to other countries but the United States and Mexico produce most.

When choosing pecans look for dry, smooth shells and hold the nuts in your hand to ensure they feel heavy. The nut itself should appear to be dry but prove to be crisp, moist and smooth to eat. The nuts are popular in pies and flans, particularly in America, and can be treated in exactly the same way as walnuts.

See also: Nuts.

Nutritional and medicinal properties

Pecans can absorb up to 75 per cent of their own weight in oil. They are a good nutritious food, recommended for people suffering from low blood pressure and emaciation, and help to build healthy teeth.

Pecan mushroom sauce

This is good with pasta or as a filling for baked potatoes.

4 tablespoons olive oil

1 *large onion, diced*
2 *cloves garlic, finely sliced*
2 *teaspoons allspice*
1 *teaspoon finely grated fresh
    root ginger*
8 *oz (225 g) mushrooms, sliced
    thinly*
1 *lb (450 g) tomatoes, skinned
    and roughly chopped*
1 *tablespoon tomato purée*
freshly ground black pepper
4 *oz (100 g) shelled pecans,
    chopped*
2 *heaped tablespoons finely
    chopped fresh parsley*

Heat 1 tablespoon of the oil and gently fry the onion, garlic and spices for 4–6 minutes until the onion is soft and transparent. Add the mushrooms, cover and cook gently for 10 minutes, stirring from time to time. Add the tomatoes and tomato purée and season. Cook on for 10 more minutes.

In a separate pan, heat the remaining oil and fry the chopped pecans for 4–5 minutes until lightly burned. Stir half the nuts into the sauce and add the parsley, stirring briefly. Sprinkle the rest over the pasta or potato and cover with the sauce. Serve hot.

PEPPER

Family: *Piperaceae*
Genus: *Piper*
Species: *Piper nigrum* (black, or
            true, pepper)

Black and white pepper comes from the same plant – a vine which comes from the tropical forests of monsoon Asia. It is grown in most tropical countries which have a suitable warm, wet climate, including India, Indonesia, Sri Lanka, Madagascar and Brazil. Pepper has been an important caravan import into Europe since the days of the ancient Greeks and Romans. It has been used not just for flavouring but for barter, tribute and ransom.

To obtain black peppercorns, unripe berries from the pepper plant are dried in the sun so that the skin turns black and wrinkled. To obtain white peppercorns, ripe red berries are soaked in water, and dried, and then the hulls are removed. White pepper has a milder flavour than black pepper. All pepper is best bought unground because ground pepper is often adulterated with such substances as powdered date-stones and inferior spices. Also, the fragrance of pepper is very illusive and, once ground, peppercorns easily lose part of their flavour.

There are many distinct varieties of pepper which vary in both aroma and pungency as well as size and colour of the corn. When choosing black peppercorns make sure they cannot be crushed between the fingernails and that they are free of attachments like stalks as well as dust. They should be even in size. Store them in a sealed glass jar and they will keep almost indefinitely.

Pepper contains the alkaloid piperine which is a stimulant. This causes a flow of saliva and gastric juices and so is an aid to digestion. However, it can be an irritant if it is added at the beginning of cooking a dish, so it is best to grind pepper into a dish only minutes before it is due to be served.

Nutritional and medicinal properties

Pepper is used medicinally to stimulate appetite and promote perspiration. It is useful for atonic

100 g PEPPER	
Calories	308
Protein (g)	8.8
Carbohydrate (g)	68
Cholesterol (g)	–
Fat (g)	6.5
Fibre (g)	–
Minerals	
calcium (mg)	130
phosphorus (mg)	130
iron (mg)	10.2
sodium (mg)	7
potassium (mg)	42
magnesium (mg)	45
zinc (mg)	1.8
iodine (mg)	–
chlorine (mg)	60
sulphur (mg)	99
silicon (mg)	–
bromine (mg)	–
Vitamins	
A(IU)	–
B_1 (mg)	–
B_2 (mg)	–
B_3 (mg)	–
B_5 (mg)	–
B_6 (mg)	–
B_{12} (mcg)	0
folic acid (mcg)	–
biotin (mcg)	–
C (mg)	0
D (mg)	0
E (mg)	–
Organic acids	
citric (%)	–
malic (%)	–
oxalic (%)	–
Water (%)	–
Digestion time (hrs)	–

dyspepsia. It also stimulates the mucous membranes and the nervous system and raises the body temperature. It is therefore excellent at the beginning of a cold, but don't be timid about its use – chew at least sixteen black peppercorns, one at a time and one immediately after another, if necessary with a glass of iced water on standby. It may be used as a gargle and externally as a rubefacient. In East Africa it is used as an abortifacient. My ayah always told me that the body odour resulting from eating peppercorns repelled mosquitoes, and as I was constantly prone to being bitten, she tried to encourage me to eat them.

PEPPER (CAPSICUM)

Family: *Solanaceae*
Genus: *Capsicum*
Species: *Capsicum frutescens* and *Capsicum annuum*

Known as the sweet pepper, or bell pepper, the capsicum was originally a shrubby perennial plant native to South America and unable to withstand the cold. Recent developments have produced a more hardy variety which can be grown with care in Britain, and most states in the USA, but it almost always needs some artificial heat to start growing. Botanists class the fruit of the pepper as a berry. Many seeds are contained within its walls and the pungent flavour comes from capsaicin, a compound found in the walls of the fruit.

Peppers were discovered in South America by Columbus and taken to Spain, but did not reach Hungary, the main area of cultivation, until the sixteenth century. They are now widely grown in Mediterranean countries, particularly Spain, southern France, Italy and North Africa and are extremely popular in Hungary.

Sweet (or bell) pepper is the most common type. It is medium sized and bell shaped with a slightly sweet, mild taste. It may be used unripe (when it is green), or ripe (when it is red or yellow). A special variety of red pepper (or pimiento), pointed in shape but free from the pungency of chilli, is dried and ground to make the spice **paprika**, also known as Hungarian pepper. In order to reduce the pungency of this bright red powder even more, the core and seeds are usually removed, so paprika is simply the powdered dried flesh. Unfortunately, there are many inferior paprikas sold although they are no longer adulterated with red lead as was the case in the old days. Good paprika should have a brilliant red colour although the Spanish *pimentón* often turns towards vermilion in colour. If it is a dirty brown, it is almost certainly stale. Good paprika should taste mild and sweet and should be used in generous quantities, particularly as it is high in vitamin C. Use it liberally in goulashes made from vegetable ingredients and Spanish vegetarian recipes.

Chilli peppers are a pungent variety of capsicum, cultivated in hot countries throughout the world. They vary greatly in shape and size, ranging from tiny round chillis about the length of a little finger to giant varieties almost a foot long, and in pungency from mild to positively explosive. When ripe they are usually red, but may be yellow, cream or even purple-black. Taken in moderate quantities, they act as a digestive stimulant, and they are rich in vitamin C, but hot chillis can cause blisters and inflammation as well as painful swelling of the throat and tongue, so do be careful. In particular seeds or bits of chilli can be harmful, and in the countries where they are much eaten are usually carefully ground or pulverized. Habitual chilli-eaters seem soon to acquire immunity and you can observe babies being given chillis almost as comforters, as one would give a child a dummy to suck.

The fresh, green, unripe chillis are now readily available in Britain and the United States, particularly from West Indian and Indian shops. Choose those that are firm and not wilted, and either green or beginning to change colour. Be careful, because they may be very pungent or mild in flavour – either way they will usually have a delicious capsicum flavour in addition to their hotness. Green chillis are preferable to dried in most pickles, and one particularly good use of them is to grind them to a paste with creamed coconut and green coriander, seasoned with a little salt and lemon juice.

This makes a delicious Indian chutney.

Always remember, when processing chillis, not to touch your face or your eyes because the powerful volatile oils can cause itching and burning. If you want a reasonably mild flavour, remove the seeds first.

Fresh ripe chillis should have been ripened on the bush. Ripe chillis dry very easily in the sun or in a warm oven. When whole they are used in pickles or put into dishes to add pungency. They are not eaten, and need to be removed if the desired pungency is reached before the dish is ready. These are the chillis from which chilli sauce or paste is made and Tabasco sauce is the commercial variety readily available. Home-made chilli sauce is infinitely superior and simple to make. Cook fresh red chillis with salt, vinegar, brown sugar, garlic and spices to your own individual taste and rub the pulp through a sieve to remove the skins and seeds.

Chilli powder is an easy way to introduce this powerful flavour to cooking. It can be strong or slight and of varying fierceness and should not be confused with paprika. The best chilli powder is home-ground. The dried chillis should first be slightly roasted by stirring them in a heavy-bottomed frying pan until they turn dark red and fume slightly (stand well back because this may make the eyes smart). Take care not to burn them. After cooking, cool them, and grind them in a blender mill, then sieve them. Note that commercial chilli powders are often mixtures containing oregano, chocolate, cumin and other adulterants. Strictly speaking, it is incorrect to call these mixtures chilli.

Cayenne pepper is a particular type of ground red chilli which is supposed to have come originally from Cayenne in French Guyana, although it is much more likely that the name came from Tupi, the lingua franca of the Amazon Basin and the South American coast. Passed-down recipes suggest that the seeds were removed from red hot chillis and the pods ground up with a little flour and salt into a paste. The paste was then dried in small cakes and lightly baked before being ground into powder. The usual distinction, if any, between cayenne and chilli powder is that the latter is much coarser.

If you get burnt by chilli, apply some aloe vera gel fresh from the growing plant leaf if you have it, but failing this apply milk or yoghurt to soothe the burn.

Nutritional and medicinal properties

Bell peppers are most nutritious if eaten raw, and are valuable for liver disorders, obesity, constipation, high blood pressure and acidosis.

I could write a poem about the wide and various therapeutic uses of cayenne pepper, and it is probably the herb I use most in my own herbal pharmacy. Used externally on severe cuts or grazes and taken internally as a tea, it should stop bleeding almost instantaneously by going immediately into the bloodstream and adjusting the blood pressure so that it is equalized throughout the body.

This takes the high pressure which causes rapid bleeding away from the wound and clotting starts immediately. Cayenne is a great food for the circulatory system because it feeds the necessary elements into the cell structure of the arteries, veins and capillaries so that these regain the elasticity of youth, and the blood pressure adjusts itself to normal. It rebuilds the tissue in the stomach and heals stomach and intestinal ulcers (astonishing though this may seem

100 g SWEET PEPPERS (raw)

	Sweet green	Hot green	Hot red	Hot red (dry)	Sweet red
Calories	22	37	93	321	31
Protein (g)	1.2	1.3	3.7	12.9	1.4
Carbohydrate (g)	4.8	9.1	18.1	59.8	7.1
Cholesterol (g)	0	–	–	–	–
Fat (g)	0.2	0.2	2.3	9.1	0.3
Fibre (g)	1.4	1.8	9	26.2	1.7
Minerals					
calcium (mg)	9	10	29	130	13
phosphorus (mg)	22	25	78	240	30
iron (mg)	9	0.7	1.2	7.8	0.6
sodium (mg)	13	–	–	373	–
potassium (mg)	213	–	–	1201	–
magnesium (mg)	–	–	–	–	–
zinc (mg)	–	–	–	–	–
iodine (mg)	0.019	–	–	–	–
chlorine (mg)	–	–	–	–	–
sulphur (mg)	–	–	–	–	–
silicon (mg)	–	–	–	–	–
bromine (mg)	–	–	–	–	–
Vitamins					
A(IU)	420	770	21600	77000	4450
B_1 (mg)	0.08	0.09	0.22	0.23	0.08
B_2 (mg)	0.08	0.06	0.36	1.33	0.08
B_3 (mg)	0.5	1.7	4.4	10.5	0.5
B_5 (mg)	0.23	–	–	–	–
B_6 (mg)	0.26	–	–	–	–
B_{12} (mcg)	0	–	–	–	–
folic acid (mcg)	9.8	–	–	–	–
biotin (mcg)	–	–	–	–	–
C (mg)	128	235	369	12	204
D (mg)	0	–	–	–	–
E (mg)	0.7	–	–	–	–
Organic acids					
citric (%)	–	–	–	–	–
malic (%)	–	–	–	–	–
oxalic (%)	0.016	–	–	–	–
Water (%)	93.4	88.8	74.3	12.6	90.7
Digestion time (hrs)	3¼	–	–	–	–

to the timid). It stimulates the peristaltic motion of the intestines and aids in assimilation and elimination. It is an excellent stimulant as well and can be used in plasters, poultices and ointments as a rubefacient where quick relief, as in the case of arthritis, rheumatism and sore muscles, is required.

I usually administer cayenne pepper in the form of infusions, rather than decoctions, because some value is lost when cayenne is simmered for any length of time. Administered as an infusion, I advise patients to take quarter a teaspoon three times a day, and after three days to increase to half a teaspoon three times daily, and then add a quarter of a teaspoon each day thereafter until the maximum recommended dose of 1 teaspoon three times a day is reached. To stop a haemorrhage like nosebleed, I administer 1 teaspoon of the powder in a cup of hot water to be drunk as quickly as possible.

Green sweet peppers are rich in fibre, potassium, folic acid, and vitamins C, B_1 and B_2, and are low in calories. Cayenne pepper is high in a variety of trace minerals and vitamin C.

Stuffed peppers

This recipe was given to me by Joan Blythe who is an excellent and imaginative cook and here found a way to use soya mince so that it tasted interesting (and not, as it generally does, of shredded cardboard).

4 large green peppers
1 large onion
1½ tablespoons olive oil
2 cloves garlic, crushed
2 oz (50 g) brown rice, cooked
6 oz (175 g) soya mince
2 tomatoes
2 level dessertspoons chopped parsley
salt (optional)

Wash and dry the peppers, cut the stalk ends off with a sharp knife, with a small circle of pepper attached to each. Set the stalks aside and remove the seeds and ribs from the peppers, without breaking the skins. Scald the peppers for 5 minutes in a pan of boiling water, then lift them out and drain them upside down.

Peel the onion and cook it lightly in the oil, with the garlic, then add the rice, soya mince, tomatoes and parsley. Add just enough water to cover and simmer until all the ingredients are soft. Then remove from the heat, fill the peppers with this rice and soya filling, and put the tops back on. Place the peppers in a greased oven-proof dish, brush the skins with a little olive oil, and put about 2–3 tablespoons water in the bottom of the dish. Cover the dish with a tight-fitting lid and bake in a preheated oven at 375°F (190°C, gas mark 5) for 30 minutes or until tender.

Serve with brown French breadsticks and a tomato sauce flavoured with paprika and soured cream.

PINE NUT

Family: *Pinaceae*
Genus: *Pinus*
Species: *Pinus pinea*

This is the edible seed of the stone pine found on the northern coasts of the Mediterranean, as well as on the southern Atlantic coast of Spain and Portugal in the West and on the coasts of the Black Sea in the East.

The cones are harvested during the winter from November onwards and they are then stored until the summer when they are spread in the sun to open. The seeds can then be shaken out and cracked and the kernels extracted. Their flavour is very delicate and may have a slight hint of turpentine, which will dissipate after storage and on heating. They taste deliciously nutty and are used in a wide variety of Italian dishes, including the famous *pesto Genovese*. One can find them in recipes originating from countries as far apart as Spain and Egypt but particularly the Lebanon.

See also: Nuts.

Nutritional and medicinal properties

Pine nuts are a good source of protein, fats and carbohydrate and therefore excellent for body-building.

Strawberry pignolia

Periodically I invite a few of my patients who are making heavy weather of their new way of eating round for lunch. When I served this to someone who couldn't imagine civilized life without pastry, sugar and cream, it cheered him up considerably. When I told him it took only a few minutes to make, his delight turned to ecstasy.

*8 oz (225 g) fresh, hulled
   strawberries
2 oz (50 g) pine nuts
1 tablespoon raw honeycomb
4 bananas
4 tablespoons granola*

Liquidize the strawberries, pine nuts and honeycomb to a smooth purée. Chill. Just before serving, pour this mixture into glass dishes, layered alternately with the bananas and granola. You can omit the granola and use any fresh fruit in season instead of the bananas.

PISTACHIO

Family: *Anarcardiaceae*
Genus: *Pistacia*
Species: *Pistacia vera*

The fruits of which the pistachio nut is the kernel grow in clusters on small trees believed to have originated in the mountains of South Turkestan. They have been cultivated in the Mediterranean and the Middle East for 3000–4000 years. They also grow in Iran, Afghanistan and the south-western parts of the United States.

There are many cultivated varieties and separate male and female trees. The kernel of the pistachio nut is covered with thin brown-red skin but the flesh of kernel is bright green. In general the greener the colour the better the quality.

Pistachio nuts taste deliciously delicate and extracts and essences are made with fresh good-quality nuts. I first encountered them in Turkey, their shells gaping open like little dry mussels to reveal the bright green kernels. Unhappily pistachios are not at all well known outside the countries in which they grow, probably because they are rather expensive compared to other more common nuts.

See also: Nuts.

Nutritional and medicinal properties

Pistachio nuts are a good source of protein and contain several vitamins including A and B_1. They are fairly rich in potassium and phosphorus and have small amounts of iron and calcium.

Pistachio ice cream

Every time I grace my favourite London restaurant, I have this for dessert. Once they'd run out, and I nearly never went back!

3 eggs, separated
5 dessertspoons soft light brown sugar
4 oz (100 g) unsalted and shelled pistachios
½ pint (300 ml) double cream
a few drops green colouring (optional)

Mix the egg yolks with half the sugar until pale and creamy, using an electric beater. Transfer the mixture to a double boiler and cook until the sugar is absolutely dissolved, and the whole mix has a toffee-like consistency. Cool in the refrigerator. Chop the pistachios finely (a food mill accelerates the process). Beat the egg whites in a bowl until stiff, and fold in the remaining sugar. Whip the cream in another bowl until stiff.

Place the egg yolk mixture in a big bowl and fold in first the cream, then the egg whites and three-quarters of the nuts. Add a few drops of colouring at this stage (just enough to turn it a pale green), if you want to. Sprinkle the rest of the nuts into the bottom of a large plastic container and pour the mixture over the top. Freeze. Serve scooped into tall glasses.

POPPY

Family: *Papaveraceae*
Genus: *Papaver*
Species: *Papaver somniferum* (opium poppy); *Papaver rhoeas* (corn poppy); *Papaver nudicaule* (Iceland poppy); *Papaver orientale* (oriental poppy)

Many kinds of poppy are grown for ornament and although the leaves of the common cornfield poppy we see in this country can be boiled like spinach (and incidentally are slightly narcotic) and the stems of the blue poppy taste rather like lettuce stems, it is really only the opium poppy that has real culinary importance.

The opium poppy is a native of the Middle East and opium was well known to the Egyptians, Greeks and Romans. Its cultivation probably stretches back to AD 800 in China, whence it spread into India and Iran. Opium is the gummy latex which oozes from the green, unripe seed pods when they are slit. It contains some twenty-four different alkaloids which I hope would be of no interest to the cook. Yet interestingly the seeds of the opium poppy when ripe contain no alkaloids at all, and both the seeds and oil are used as important foods.

There are many varieties of opium poppy and there are two quite distinctive types of poppy seed. The sort commonly available in Europe looks like blue-grey shot, but the seed used in India is much smaller and creamy yellow. The Indian variety is sweeter in flavour. Poppy seeds are used in cookery in Europe to give added taste and texture, and in the Middle East are used mainly in confectionery. The flavour when baked is pleasantly nutty.

Poppy seed is also an important source of oils. The first cold pressing (*see* Oils) produces a clear edible oil which the French call olivette. The second pressing produces a red oil which is then decolourized and used for paints and industrial purposes.

Nutritional and medicinal properties

Although the part of the poppy most used for medicinal purposes is the petals of the corn (or red) poppy and the capsules of the opium poppy, the seeds have been used to treat intestinal disorders and to keep bowel movements regular. The doctor and herbalist Dioscorides, who lived in the first century AD said of poppy seeds, 'It doth soften the belly gently', and they have been used in various sleep potions in the past, although their action is very mild and have little effect on true insomniacs.

POTATO

Family: *Solanaceae*
Genus: *Solanum*
Species: *Solanum tuberosum*

Potatoes are the underground tubers of a family that embraces tomatoes, aubergines, red peppers, tobacco and the deadly nightshade and have not always been regarded as the good, safe, non-fattening, nourishing food they really are. (Happily the suggestion that they might be implicated in spina bifida has now been disproved.) Potato berries are poisonous, as are potatoes that have been exposed to light and have turned green; and the wild, distorted, pocked tubers the Incas ate were sometimes poisonous too. It was impossible to grow wheat or corn in such a climate, so potatoes were cultivated, crushed, dried in the hot, rarified air and turned into flour, *Chino*, which did not spoil.

The first potatoes brought back to Europe, in 1537, were erroneously assumed to be truffles. They didn't catch on very fast because of their original strange, threatening appearance and sweet potatoes were initially preferred. In 1580 Sir Francis Drake introduced a boat-load of potatoes from Colombia via Virginia (hence the misconception that potatoes first came from North America). He was enthusiastic about their virtues: 'These potatoes be the most delicate root that may be eaten and doe farre exceed our pareseneps or carats . . . the inside eateth like an apple but is more delicious than any sweet apple, sugred.' Judging from his description he was probably talking about the sweet potato.

Initially potatoes were a luxury fetching £300 a pound and were regarded as a food with special properties, including that of being an aphrodisiac. There are records of them being served in hospitals in Seville in 1573.

The Italians were the first European nation to grow potatoes on a large scale. The Irish became economically dependent on potato-growing. In the early nineteenth century many of the Irish poor lived virtually exclusively on potatoes, consuming a heroic 3½ kilograms (nearly 8 pounds) a day to meet their daily energy requirements. The potato blight of 1845 and 1846 caused mass death and encouraged huge migration to the USA. Redcliffe Salaman in his *History and Social Influences of the Potato* (1949) shows how it came to be used to exploit the poor. Landowners fed labourers on it at very little cost like cattle, effectively keeping them in abject poverty and

using it as a substitute for meat and bread.

Today potatoes grow prolifically in northern temperate climates and to a lesser extent in subtropical climates, where they yield less. Given plenty of moisture and feeding and provided they are earthed up to give the tubers room to grow, they will yield 20–40 tonnes a hectare, containing some 280 kilograms of protein. Only soya (with its amazing 380 kilograms per hectare) outyields potatoes in protein content.

There are numerous varieties of potatoes, with each producer country growing both early and main-crop varieties, which ensures year-long supplies. Russia is the world's biggest producer, followed by China, West Germany, Poland, the USA, Czechoslovakia, East Germany, Britain, France and Spain.

The tendency today is to breed only for yield, disease resistance and the high sugar content required by crisp manufacturers. Sadly the old varieties are dying out, although scientists at the Scottish Plant Breeding Station in Edinburgh are trying to stem this tide by reintroducing indigenous wild and primitive cultivated potato types from South America in order to widen the breeding stock and so increase the variety of flavours.

Pride of Bute is long, blue skinned and floury, an ideal baking potato – though you don't often see it around. **Sefton Wonder** is firmly waxy and makes delicious potato salads. **Desiree**, red, and rosy, is an ideal boiler. **King Edwards** are floury and so make good mash, as do **Pentland Hawk** and **Pentland Ivory**. **Maris Piper** is a fine baker and **Maris Peer**, **Wilja** and **Estima** are early main-crop varieties especially useful for salads. Newer introductions to the market include **Cara**, a good baking potato and **Romanov**, rather similar to Desiree.

Britain imports her early spring potatoes from Cyprus and Egypt and her main-crop ones from Holland and Italy. When choosing avoid green, damaged or wrinkled potatoes. Choose floury ones for mashing, waxy types for salads and firm, waxy ones for chips.

Nutritional and medicinal properties

Contrary to public myth, potatoes need be neither boring nor fattening. Indeed I try and encourage my patients to eat a baked potato most days. They are superabundant in potassium and vitamin C (although this falls rapidly by spring if a potato is stored all winter). They are 80 per cent water, 2 per cent protein, wonderfully fibrous, and if the skins are left on, also very filling, and only 24 calories an ounce. It's the oil, milk or butter used to dress them that makes them so lethal for calorie-counters.

Because potatoes are floury and moist and contain only a tenth of 1 per cent of fat they guzzle fat as readily as spongy muffins and the modest amount of fat people usually put in mashed potatoes makes the calories rocket by 50 per cent. The chip is three times more calorific than the boiled potato. Potato crisps are seven times more calorific, weight for weight. Only by spooning neat butter straight into your mouth could you ingest more calories.

Surprisingly, thickly cut chips made as is common in the UK are easily defended as nourishing food. They contain 250–290 calories per 100 grams, less than the same weight of dried toast (300 calories), water-biscuits (440 calories) and starched-reduced crispbread (380 calories). So you may be stunned to realize you are actually far better off eating a reasonable portion of chips, if you are weight-watching, than seemingly virtuous cheese and water biscuits. The only problem here is one of greed, as they taste so good.

Baking a potato is the least calorific and most nourishing way to serve it. Eat the skin as well because it harbours most of the nutrients – iron, phosphorus, calcium, sodium, sulphur, potassium, vitamins B and C and traces of carotene. Add a tablespoon of yoghurt, sprinkle generously with fresh parsley, and you have a positive powerhouse of nourishing goodness.

100 g POTATOES – calories

Served plain	80
Mashed	119
Baked (with skin)	93
Roast	157
Chipped	257
New boiled	76
Potato crisps	533

Bubble and squeak

Admittedly this isn't the most slimming way to enjoy potatoes, but it tastes wonderful and is very nutritious, especially served with grilled tomatoes and mushrooms.

Many people make the mistake of using mashed potato for this. Don't. Just boil until they begin to disintegrate into slushiness.

1½ lb (750 g) cooked cabbage
1 large cooked onion

100 g POTATO

	With skin	Baked (with skin)	Boiled (peeled)	French-fried in cottonseed oil
Calories	96	93	65	274
Protein (g)	2.1	2.6	1.9	4.3
Carbohydrate (g)	17.1	21.2	14.5	36
Cholesterol (g)	–	0	0	0
Fat (g)	0.1	0.1	0.1	13.2
Fibre (g)	0.3	0.6	0.5	1
Minerals				
calcium (mg)	7	9	6	15
phosphorus (mg)	53	65	42	111
iron (mg)	0.6	0.7	0.5	1.3
sodium (mg)	3	4	2	6
potassium (mg)	407	503	285	853
magnesium (mg)	34	23.5	–	25
zinc (mg)	0.3	0.2	0.2	0.6
iodine (mg)	0.012	–	–	–
chlorine (mg)	155	–	–	–
sulphur (mg)	289	–	–	–
silicon (mg)	88	–	–	–
bromine (mg)	0.63	–	–	–
Vitamins				
A(IU)	tr	tr	tr	tr
B_1 (mg)	0.1	0.1	0.09	0.1
B_2 (mg)	0.04	0.04	0.03	0.08
B_3 (mg)	1.5	1.7	1.2	3.1
B_5 (mg)	0.3	0.16	0.2	0.2
B_6 (mg)	0.25	–	0.1	–
B_{12} (mcg)	0	0	0	–
folic acid (mcg)	14	8	10	10
biotin (mcg)	0.1	tr	tr	tr
C (mg)	20	20	16	21
D (mg)	0	0	0	0
E (mg)	0.1	–	–	–
Organic acids				
citric (%)	0.51	–	–	–
malic (%)	0	–	–	–
oxalic (%)	0.0057	–	–	–
Water (%)	79.8	57.5	80.5	47
Digestion time (hrs)	2	–	–	–

1½ lb (750 g) *potatoes, cooked as
above*
black pepper
salt (optional)
a little butter

Shred the cabbage and dice the
onion finely and stir them into the
disintegrating potato. Pepper very
generously, and add salt if desired.
Melt enough butter to barely coat
the bottom of a heavy frying pan –
keep it minimal. Heat the pan well.
Pile in the mixture and make a flat
cake, pressing it down with a
palette knife. Do not stir. Turn the
heat down to low and cook for
about 25 minutes, until the bottom
is very crisp and well browned.
Serve brown side up on a flat dish.

PULSES

The word 'pulse' comes from the
Latin *puls*, meaning pudding, and
in most English-speaking countries
the bean and pea members of the
legume family (*Leguminosae*) are
christened pulses. The problem is
that Americans use different
nomenclature, which can cause
confusion, and this gets worse
because botanists use names that
show their ancestry, plant breeders
use names that boast of new
creations, farmers use names that
describe habitat or use, and market
gardeners use names that suggest
their form. If in doubt hang on to
the Latin name. *Phaseolus vulgaris*
is indeed our familiar red kidney
bean, though some may call it
dwarf or French bean or simply the
Prince.

As a rough guide pulses can be
divided into: *Phaseolus*, kidney
bean group; *Glycine*, soya bean
group; and *Vicia*, broad bean
group.

Broad beans were well known in
ancient Greece and Rome and our
'beanfeasts' originate from festivals
offering thanks to Apollo for the
nourishment provided by beans.
The belief that beans contained
dead men's souls was prevalent in
Pythagoras' time but stems from
ancient Egypt. Broad beans are
obligingly hardy but the grey
leathery skins which make them so
need to be well softened in water
before use.

The beans from the *Phaseolus*
species best known in the West are
native to South America and
embrace a wide variety of climbing
beans used mainly for their pods,
such as French beans, as well as a
whole range used for their seeds,
including the navy bean, which
now commonly masquerades under
the ubiquitous guise of canned
baked beans.

Soya beans have been cultivated
for thousands of years in China and
now boast over a thousand
varieties. The United States is the
largest exporter, and soya is that
country's second biggest crop.
Soya is infinitely versatile and
can be dried, roasted, fermented,
sprouted or made into milk or
flour.

Lentils were found in ancient
Egyptian tombs and come in a wide
variety of colours – green, brown,
red or mottled. They continue to
grow where they've always grown
as one of the world's oldest crops,

in the Middle East and the Mediterranean.

Red, black or green **grams** make excellent vitamin-rich sprouters and are widely used in Indian and West Indian cookery, while **chick-peas** have surpassed even their popularity and are the main pulse used in India. They are also widely used in the Middle East, but (to add to the confusion) they are probably native to Africa.

Peas range from the delicate petits pois of France, to the big wrinkled marrowfat peas that make up mushy-pea dishes.

See also: Adzuki bean, Black-eyed pea, Broad bean, Chick-pea, Kidney bean, Lentil, Lima bean, Mung bean, Pea, Soya, Sprouted seeds.

Nutritional and medicinal properties

The problem with all pulses is the amount of intestinal disturbance they cause, embarrassingly sulphuric and anti-social without and uncomfortable within. Such flatulence is the result of two incompatible starches (stachyose and raffinose). They do not pass through the walls of the small intestine, and instead of their being converted into blood sugar intestinal bacteria go to work on them splitting them into carbon dioxide and hydrogen (an intestinal gas-bomb).

Soaking the beans goes part way towards solving this problem but it is in the cooking that the job can really be done properly. Use plenty of water to ensure soaking beans absorb all they can and throw away any that still float on the surface. Soya beans are the only group that need to be refrigerated to stop fermentation while they are soaking. A quicker method than simply soaking them is to bring the beans gently to the boil, remove them from the heat and leave them to soak for an hour.

Cooking beans generally requires three quantities of water to one of soaked beans with the exception of soya beans and chick-peas which need five to one. Apple cider vinegar added to the cooking water will tame the gas-producing activities of beans. Add it only at the very end because otherwise it will toughen the beans and lengthen the cooking time. At the beginning of the last half hour of cooking remove the saucepan from the heat, scoop out a quarter of a cup of liquid and replace it with the same quantity of apple cider vinegar. Stir the vinegar in with a wooden spoon and add whatever flavouring you want (herbs, spices, celery, carrots, onion, garlic, etc.) at this stage. Return the saucepan to the heat and simmer gently. If a bean squashes easily between thumb and forefinger it is well cooked.

Interestingly, the more often you eat beans the less intestinal gas you create. Apparently the multiplication of the intestinal bacteria responsible for breaking down stachyose and raffinose is promoted by frequent bean eating. Sprouted beans do not cause flatulence because the starch is partially converted to sugar.

Remember that long storage of

any pulses will harden them so much that no amount of soaking or boiling will tenderize them, so rotate your own stock carefully and buy in small quantities from a supplier you trust who you know has a quick turnover.

Adzuki, lentils, limas, mung beans and split peas can all be cooked in the same pot as grains, and happily all pulses are rich in lysine which is the essential amino-acid generally deficient in grains. So grains and pulse make an

100 g BEANS OR PEAS

	Fresh lima	Dried lima	Dried mung	Mung sprouts	Dried pinto beans	Fresh broad bean	Dried broad bean
Calories	123	345	340	35	349	105	338
Protein (g)	8.4	20.4	24.2	3.8	22.9	8.4	25.1
Carbohydrate (g)	22.1	64	60.3	6.6	63.7	17.8	58.2
Cholesterol (g)	–	–	–	–	–	–	–
Fat (g)	0.5	1.6	1.3	0.2	1.2	0.4	1.7
Fibre (g)	1.8	4.3	4.4	0.7	4.3	2.2	6.7
Minerals							
calcium (mg)	52	72	118	19	135	27	102
phosphorus (mg)	142	385	340	64	457	157	391
iron (mg)	2.8	7.8	7.7	1.3	6.4	2.2	7.1
sodium (mg)	2	4	6	5	10	4	–
potassium (mg)	650	1529	1028	223	984	471	–
magnesium (mg)	67	180	–	–	–	–	–
zinc (mg)	–	–	–	–	–	–	–
iodine (mg)	0.005	0.005	–	–	–	–	–
chlorine (mg)	50	4	–	–	–	–	–
sulphur (mg)	310	260	–	–	–	–	–
silicon (mg)	–	–	–	–	–	–	–
bromine (mg)	–	–	–	–	–	–	–
Vitamins							
A(IU)	290	tr	80	20	–	220	70
B_1 (mg)	0.24	0.48	0.38	0.13	0.84	0.28	0.5
B_2 (mg)	0.12	0.17	0.21	0.13	0.21	0.17	0.3
B_3 (mg)	1.4	1.9	2.6	0.8	2.2	1.6	2.5
B_5 (mg)	–	–	–	–	–	–	–
B_6 (mg)	–	0.6	–	–	–	–	–
B_{12} (mcg)	–	0	0	0	0	–	–
folic acid (mcg)	–	–	–	–	–	–	–
biotin (mcg)	–	–	–	–	–	–	–
C (mg)	29	–	–	19	–	30	–
D (mg)	–	–	–	–	–	–	–
E (mg)	–	–	–	–	–	–	–
Organic acids							
citric (%)	0.65	–	–	–	–	–	–
malic (%)	0.17	–	–	–	–	–	–
oxalic (%)	0.0043	–	–	–	–	–	–
Water (%)	67.5	10.3	10.7	88.8	8.3	72.3	11.9
Digestion time (hrs)	2½	–	–	–	–	–	–

excellent, perfectly balanced marriage as far as human nutrition is concerned; a fact the world has long unconsciously recognized with famous combinations such as beans on toast, rice and soya, beans and tortillas, and rice and dhal.

Warning Always remember that *Leguminosae* group of plants, in common with the *Solanaceae* are capable of producing nasty surprises. The seeds of laburnum and lupin (both part of the former group), can cause death if eaten in

100 g BEANS OR PEAS (continued)

	Dried chick-pea	Dried lentil	Dried peas	Fresh pigeon pea	Dried pigeon pea
Calories	360	340	340	117	342
Protein (g)	20.5	24.7	24.1	7.2	20.4
Carbohydrate (g)	61	60.1	60.3	21.3	63.7
Cholesterol (g)	–	–	–	–	–
Fat (g)	4.8	1.1	1.3	0.6	1.4
Fibre (g)	5	3.9	4.9	3.3	7
Minerals					
calcium (mg)	150	79	64	42	107
phosphorus (mg)	331	377	340	127	316
iron (mg)	6.9	6.8	5.1	1.6	8
sodium (mg)	26	30	35	5	26
potassium (mg)	797	790	1005	552	981
magnesium (mg)	–	80	180	–	121
zinc (mg)	–	–	–	–	–
iodine (mg)	–	–	0.001	–	–
chlorine (mg)	95	150	53	–	–
sulphur (mg)	110	120	103	–	–
silicon (mg)	–	–	127	–	–
bromine (mg)	–	1	0.21	–	–
Vitamins					
A(IU)	50	40	120	140	80
B_1 (mg)	0.31	0.37	0.74	0.4	0.32
B_2 (mg)	0.15	0.22	0.21	0.17	0.16
B_3 (mg)	2	2	3	2.2	3
B_5 (mg)	–	–	–	–	–
B_6 (mg)	0.6	–	–	–	–
B_{12} (mcg)	0	0	0	–	–
folic acid (mcg)	–	–	–	–	–
biotin (mcg)	–	–	–	–	–
C (mg)	–	–	–	39	–
D (mg)	–	–	–	–	–
E (mg)	–	–	–	–	–
Organic acids					
citric (%)	–	–	–	–	–
malic (%)	–	–	–	–	–
oxalic (%)	–	–	–	–	–
Water (%)	10.7	11.1	11.7	69.5	10.8
Digestion time (hrs)	–	3	$3\frac{1}{2}$	–	–

large enough quantities. Favism (a severe blood disorder) was thought to be the result of eating too many broad beans; paralysing lathyrism can result from eating too many grass peas.

More recently it has been found that a toxic factor in kidney beans called haemagglutinin can result in acute gastroenteritis if it is not completely destroyed by adequate cooking. The beans need first to be well soaked and rinsed, which will reduce the haemagglutinin to the

100 g BEANS OR PEAS (continued)

	Fresh soya beans	Dried soya beans	Fresh black-eyed peas	Dried black-eyed peas
Calories	134	403	127	343
Protein (g)	10.9	34.1	9	22.8
Carbohydrate (g)	13.2	33.5	21.8	61.7
Cholesterol (g)	–	–	–	–
Fat (g)	5.1	17.7	0.8	1.5
Fibre (g)	1.4	4.9	1.8	4.4
Minerals				
calcium (mg)	67	226	27	74
phosphorus (mg)	225	554	172	426
iron (mg)	2.8	8.4	2.3	5.8
sodium (mg)	–	5	2	35
potassium (mg)	–	1677	541	1024
magnesium (mg)	–	265	55	230
zinc (mg)	–	–	–	–
iodine (mg)	–	–	–	–
chlorine (mg)	–	40	–	60
sulphur (mg)	–	265	–	360
silicon (mg)	–	27	–	–
bromine (mg)	–	–	–	–
Vitamins				
A(IU)	690	80	370	30
B_1 (mg)	0.44	1.1	0.43	1.05
B_2 (mg)	0.16	0.31	0.13	0.21
B_3 (mg)	1.4	2.2	1.6	2.2
B_5 (mg)	–	–	–	–
B_6 (mg)	0.8	–	–	–
B_{12} (mcg)	0	–	–	0
folic acid (mcg)	–	–	–	–
biotin (mcg)	–	–	–	–
C (mg)	29	–	29	–
D (mg)	–	–	–	–
E (mg)	–	–	–	–
Organic acids				
citric (%)	–	–	–	–
malic (%)	–	–	–	–
oxalic (%)	–	–	–	–
Water (%)	69.2	10	66.8	11.9
Digestion time (hrs)	3	–	3¼	–

level found in other dried beans (soaked or unsoaked). Then boil the beans really vigorously for ten minutes. Reduce the heat and simmer them till tender. This will remove any residual danger. It is possible to use a slow cooker provided the beans are first boiled for ten minutes as instructed above. They can then be decanted into the slow cooker.

RADISH

Family: *Cruciferae*
Genus: *Raphanus*
Species: *Raphanus sativus*

This is an annual plant from the mustard family grown for its edible root. There are an enormous number of different varieties, of many different sizes, shapes and colours. They vary in shape from small and round to long and oval and may grow pointed or tapering. The colours rang from white to black, through pink, red and purple. Radishes grow throughout the year in mild climates. They have been in cultivation for so long that their origin is uncertain, but they probably originated in China, where many varieties exist today including the long-rooted winter-harvested **Chinese radish (or daikon)**, which is sometimes available in the West. **Black radish** is one of the varieties employed in medicine in the past and by homeopaths today.

Radishes are usually eaten raw in salads, as an appetizer or as a garnish, in which case they are often cut into rose shapes. The pink radish is sometimes boiled and may be served with a white or parsley sauce. The flesh of the radish is white and crisp and heavily flavoured. Sometimes the leaves of the young pink radishes are eaten raw in salads but they can also be cooked like spinach.

Nutritional and medicinal properties

Radishes contain vitamins B and C, as well as calcium, copper, iron, magnesium, phosphorus, potassium, sodium, sulphur, fibre, volatile oil, and traces of carotene.

They are excellent for relieving dyspepsia, and are used to promote salivation (hence the custom of serving them at the beginning of meals). They were once employed in the treatment of coughs and bronchitis, and may be used with other remedies to treat liver conditions, especially where bile secretion is inadequate. They are good for the teeth, gums, hair and nails. They also relieve constipation and catarrh and improve the condition of fluids flushing through the mucous membranes. They are believed to be helpful with gall-stones, and with TB. They have a mild diuretic effect and so get the kidneys to work more fully.

Radish and walnut salad

6 oranges
1 tablespoon honey
½ teaspoon cinnamon
1 lb (450 g) fresh spinach

½ cup thinly sliced onion
1 generous cup thinly sliced
  radishes
1 cup toasted walnut halves
3 tablespoons olive oil
freshly ground black pepper
celery salt

One hour in advance peel and

100 g RADISHES (raw)		
	Common	Oriental
Calories	17	19
Protein (g)	1	0.9
Carbohydrate (g)	3.6	4.2
Cholesterol (g)	0	–
Fat (g)	0.1	–
Fibre (g)	0.7	0.7
Minerals		
calcium (mg)	30	35
phosphorus (mg)	31	26
iron (mg)	1	0.6
sodium (mg)	18	–
potassium (mg)	322	180
magnesium (mg)	15	–
zinc (mg)	0.1	–
iodine (mg)	–	–
chlorine (mg)	1000	–
sulphur (mg)	715	–
silicon (mg)	100	–
bromine (mg)	0.83	–
Vitamins		
A(IU)	10	10
B_1 (mg)	0.03	0.03
B_2 (mg)	0.03	0.02
B_3 (mg)	0.3	0.4
B_5 (mg)	0.18	–
B_6 (mg)	0.1	–
B_{12} (mcg)	0	–
folic acid (mcg)	10	–
biotin (mcg)	–	–
C (mg)	26	32
D (mg)	0	–
E (mg)	0	–
Organic acids		
citric (%)	–	–
malic (%)	–	–
oxalic (%)	–	–
Water (%)	94.5	94.1
Digestion time (hrs)	3¼	–

section the oranges with a knife, catching the juice. Pour the honey, and sprinkle the cinnamon, over them and leave to stand for one hour.

Wash the spinach leaves carefully and shred by hand into fairly large pieces. Combine them with the onions, radishes and nuts. Toss, dress and season. Add the oranges and all their liquid. Toss again and serve immediately.

RICE

Family: *Gramineae*
Genus: *Oryza*
Species: *Oryza sativa*

Half the world eats rice but usually in its 'polished' refined form, polishing being a process which removes the outer husk (or rice bran) and some of the germ of the grain which contains vitamins and polyunsaturated oils. Afte being denuded it is then polished with glucose to improve the colour, and dusted with talc.

Happily there is still plenty of unprocessed rice available. Indeed it is growing in popularity. Brown rice is basically any sort of rice which has had the husk removed but not the bran, and its characteristics are the same as white polished rice except that it is more nutritious, better for the digestion and takes longer to cook as the bran forms a cellophane-like skin which does not allow the water to penetrate it quickly. It is best to boil it vigorously at first, then let it simmer for 30–40 minutes without stirring or peeping. Then remove it from the heat and leave it covered in the pot for 10 minutes before serving. Use one part of rice to two of water and allow ½ cup uncooked rice per portion.

Rice was first recorded over 5000 years ago, and cultivated rice was used in India in 3000 BC. In 2800 BC the Chinese emperor proclaimed a ceremony to be performed for the planting of rice. Alexander the Great was familiar with rice when he invaded India, and the Moors introduced it to Spain in 700 AD, from where it was taken to Italy and then on to South America.

Today there are over 7000 varieties grown worldwide but it can all basically be divided into **long-grain**, which is thin and spindly (like Patna rice) and cooks up light, dry and fluffy with easily separated grains; **medium grain**, which is shorter and plumper but retains a little 'bite' once cooked (like risotto rice); **short (or round) grain**, which as its name implies is even shorter and plumper, and is used as pudding rice as it cooks up massed and creamy; and **glutinous rice** which is especially favoured by Asians as it cooks up sticky and cohesive (and so is easily picked up by chop sticks), while remaining nicely chewy.

There is also **parboiled** rice, which is treated by steam pressure before the outer bran is removed, a process which forces vitamins into the grain from the outer coat thereby increasing its nutritional value and making it tougher and so more resistant to overcooking.

Instant precooked rice is fully cooked and then dehydrated, and only needs the addition of boiling water to make it edible. **Boil-in-the-bag rice** comes in a perforated bag and although foolproof to cook is doubly expensive. **Ready cooked rice** comes in cans and has added oil, emulsifier and citric acid which increases its calorie content and quadruples its price. **Puffed rice** is heated under pressure so it explodes to several times its original size and can then be presented in cereals or biscuits. Such processing destroys all the vitamins so they have to be added back after processing. **Converted rice** has the vitamins forced into the centre of the grain by steam treatment and can then be milled without losing too many nutrients. **Rice polish** is the bran left behind when the rice is milled and is high in the B vitamins.

Wild rice (*Zizania aquatica*) is unrelated to ordinary rice, although it is also grown in water. It is 12 feet tall which makes it difficult to harvest and very expensive (currently £10 for a pound). Originally harvested by American Indians in their flat-bottomed boats in the Minnesota lakes. They gleaned it by bending the seed heads over the deck and beating them till the seeds fell off. Wild rice is now big business and its yield has been increased by modern farming methods. Harvested by combines it may taste the same but somehow the romance has gone out of it.

See also: Flours, Grains.

Nutritional and medicinal properties

Excessive milling removes all the vitamin-rich scutellum of the grain, particularly B$_1$, which is not crucial if the diet is varied but which can result in beriberi – a disease marked by swelling of the body and paralysis – if it is not. Commercial milling (as opposed to the old-fashioned pestle-and-mortar method) is particularly culpable. In the Menam Delta in Thailand

100 g RICE (raw)	Brown	White	Rice bran	Wild
Calories	360	363	276	353
Protein (g)	7.5	6.7	13.3	14.1
Carbohydrate (g)	77.4	80.4	50.8	75.3
Cholesterol (g)		–	–	
Fat (g)	1.9	0.4	15.8	0.7
Fibre (g)	0.9	0.3	11.5	1
Minerals				
calcium (mg)	32	24	76	19
phosphorus (mg)	221	94	1386	339
iron (mg)	1.6	0.8	19.4	4.2
sodium (mg)	9	5	tr	7
potassium (mg)	214	92	1495	220
magnesium (mg)	88	28	–	129
zinc (mg)	–	1.3	–	–
iodine (mg)	0.002	–	–	–
chlorine (mg)	2	1	–	–
sulphur (mg)	10	3	12	–
silicon (mg)	40	11	885	–
bromine (mg)	–	–	–	–
Vitamins				
A(IU)	0	0	0	0
B$_1$ (mg)	0.34	0.07	2.26	0.45
B$_2$ (mg)	0.05	0.03	0.25	0.63
B$_3$ (mg)	4.7	1.6	29.8	6.2
B$_5$ (mg)	–	0.6	–	–
B$_6$ (mg)	–	0.3	–	–
B$_{12}$ (mcg)	–	0	–	–
folic acid (mcg)	–	29	–	–
biotin (mcg)	–	3	–	–
C (mg)	0	0	0	0
D (mg)	–	0	–	–
E (mg)	–	0	–	–
Organic acids				
citric (%)	–	–	–	–
malic (%)	–	–	–	–
oxalic (%)	–	–	–	–
Water (%)	12	12	9.7	8.5
Digestion time (hrs)	2	2½	–	–

beriberi was rife until the government impregnated specially treated rice grains with vitamins, sealing them to protect against loss in washing and cooking and then distributing them through the rest of the commercial rice.

Washing rice also leaches out B_1, and in the East such water is usually saved for soups. Mulligatawny soup was originally based on rice water. During the colonial wars in Madras the British officers besieged at Trichinopoly were served rice by their faithful sepoys while the sepoys themselves subsisted on the water in which it was cooked. The sepoys stayed healthy while the officers got beriberi!

Brown rice is easily digested and provides all the essential nutrients for the body, so it is a complete food in itself. It also contains B_6 and vitamin K and is altogether richer in nutrients than its white cousin, which has to have B_1, niacin and iron added back into it after processing. It is bulky, satisfying, low in calories (123 per 100 grams when cooked), rich in minerals and so body building. Unpolished rice contains no purines whatsoever. (Purines are substances found in food which may be toxic and cannot be utilized but must be eliminated, which puts additional strain on the eliminative organs.)

Rice or rice water is excellent for stopping diarrhoea, for flatulence, and for ulcers, and is helpful for chronic nephritis, anaemia, high blood pressure (I have brought dangerously high blood pressure down to normal in a week by putting patients on a supervised brown-rice fast). It is also useful for dressing wounds, and being gluten free is valuable for coeliacs.

Spicy brown rice salad

This recipe was passed on to me by Stephen Matthews, who used to be a chef in the army, and imaginatively and ingeniously adapted to a wholefood vegetarian diet as part of his medical treatment.

6 oz (175 g) brown rice
1 tablespoon sesame seed oil
1 red pepper, finely diced
1 green pepper, finely diced
1 onion, finely chopped
2 chillies, very finely chopped
2 tomatoes, diced
4 oz (100 g) mushrooms, sliced
1 oz (25 g) almonds, chopped
1 oz (25 g) sunflower seeds
½ teaspoon freshly ground black pepper
1 teaspoon chilli powder
1 tablespoon tomato purée
3 tablespoons mayonnaise
a few lettuce leaves
1 teaspoon chopped parsley

Boil the rice, covered, for 25 minutes or until tender. Drain and cool. Stir-fry the vegetables in the sesame oil, being careful not to brown. Leave to cool, then mix with the rice, and add the nuts, seeds and black pepper. Mix the chilli powder, tomato purée and mayonnaise together and fold this mixture carefully into the rice and vegetables. Serve on a bed of lettuce and sprinkle with chopped parsley.

ROSEMARY

Family: *Labiatae*
Genus: *Rosmarinus*
Species: *Rosmarinus officinalis*

This is an evergreen perennial shrub belonging to the mint family. A native to the Mediterranean, where it can commonly be seen growing in wild profusion on dry hillsides, it is also found in Asia Minor, and grows cultivated and wild in parts of northern Europe and North America. It also enjoys the climate of southern England, liking poor, calcareous soil, but here it is not as aromatic because of the lack of sun. It can be grown from cuttings or roots.

Rosemary has lustrous, dark-green, needle-like pointed leaves and tiny pale blue or mauve flowers. Its name comes from the Latin words *ros* (dew) and *marinus* (sea), presumably because a field of rosemary resembles hazy blue mist, like the sea dew. It flowers late in the spring and sometimes again in the summer. It is very aromatic, being rich in camphor, and the scent is reminiscent of pine needles drying in hot sun.

Rosemary has long been a symbol of friendship, everlasting love and remembrance and was said to bring luck and prevent witchcraft. It is important in literature and folklore and legend suggests that the flowers were white until the Virgin Mary dried her blue cloak over them. Drying clothes spread over aromatic bushes, particularly rosemary, thyme and lavender, on a hot summer day is a wonderful idea but do inspect for various bits of insect life afterwards.

Rosemary was valued by the ancients for its aromatic qualities and medicinal uses. Ever since Elizabethan times, it has been used to aid nervous depression. Traditionally rosemary is woven into bridal garlands and a little is supposed to be included in wedding and Christmas cakes. It was often burned in sickrooms to purify the air. It was used in churches in place of frankincense. The oil was first extracted by distillation in 1330 by Raymundus Lullus and it is still extensively used in perfumery. One of the most famous items containing the herb was Queen of Hungary's Water. The Romans used rosemary in a wide variety of preparations, including tinctures, conserves, syrups, spirits and unguents.

In my opinion, rosemary has a rather violent taste and is often used in cooking to excess, particularly in Italian recipes. The most I can stand is dipping a frond of rosemary in olive oil and basting grilled food with it. Sometimes I will add a sprig to a vegetable stew or soup and then remove it when the taste is sufficiently strong. The infused leaves make a bitter, rather strong, but by no means unpleasant tea.

Nutritional and medicinal properties

Rosemary leaves contain about 5 per cent protein, 15 per cent fat, 64 per cent carbohydrates, minerals (including calcium, iron and magnesium), vitamins (including A and C), and 0.5 per cent volatile oil, increasing to 2 per cent in very hot climates. They also contain saponoside, heterosides and tannin. Rosemary oil kills various types of bacteria but it is also toxic to humans and can be fatal if taken in large doses. On a minor level, it can cause skin problems and contact dermatitis, as well as eye irritations to certain individuals, but on a much more serious level, it can cause abortion, convulsions and even death. So, if the oil is to be used internally, it should always be taken under the close supervision of a qualified consultant medical herbalist.

Rosemary is tonic, stimulant and carminative in treating indigestion, stomach pains, headaches, head colds and nervous tension. Externally, it is useful for rheumatism, eczema, bruises and wounds. An infusion will help to prevent baldness, dry scaly skin and dandruff. Rosemary is excellent for vasoconstrictory types of headaches and migraines, meaning those that improve if a heated pad is laid on the forehead or the neck. It is also useful for palpitations and other signs of nervous tension affecting the circulation. It is useful for malfunctioning livers and any condition where poor circulation and poor liver function are combined. It is an excellent memory specific helping to get blood circulating into the brain and easing depression and debility linked with nervous tension.

The rich fragrance of rosemary will also control cabbage moths, bean beetles, carrot flies, and mosquitoes.

Rosemary cider

A combination of rosemary and cider as the basis for a fruit salad may sound extraordinary but it really works, particularly if the fruit salad is one majoring on pineapple, bananas and oranges. Add a tablespoon to the juice in every bowl and, if they are in season, scatter a few of the blue rosemary flowers from rosemary over the fruit.

2 tablespoons finely chopped fresh rosemary leaves (dried won't work)
1 pint (600 ml) dry cider

Macerate the rosemary in the cider in a sealed jar for a week. Strain and bottle.

RUNNER BEAN

Family: *Leguminosae*
Genus: *Phaseolus*
Species: *Phaseolus coccineus*

The runner bean is a climbing plant which can grow to over 12 feet in height. However, the tops are usually pinched out at about 6 feet to encourage the plant to grow out rather than up. They are often called scarlet runners because of their bright red flowers, although there are varieties with white, or red and white flowers.

The runner bean was first grown in America and was brought to England in 1683. At first it was grown for its decorative flowers only, and not used as a food. However, by the eighteenth century it was eaten regularly and is now one of the most popular vegetables in Britain, grown by most amateur gardeners with a vegetable plot.

Runner beans have a coarse skin and should be eaten when young and tender so that they are not 'stringy'. The beans can be dried and stored in an airtight container, or blanched and frozen. These two methods are particularly useful if you grow your own and have a large surplus supply.

Nutritional and medicinal properties

Runner beans contain a variety of vitamins and minerals, including vitamins A and C, iron, potassium and calcium.

Runner bean salad

The simplicity of this summer salad belies the subtle contrast between the different textures of each vegetable.

12 oz (325 g) runner beans,
　preferably young
12 oz (325 g) tomatoes
1 cucumber
French dressing made with olive
　oil, lemon juice, grainy
　mustard, and black pepper

Top and tail the beans, and if necessary pull off the strings. Tie in a bundle and cook in boiling water until barely tender (about 20 minutes). Drain, refresh in cold water and drain again thoroughly. Skin and quarter the tomatoes,

and remove the seeds. Peel the cucumber and quarter lengthways, then cut into small chunks.

Prepare the dressing. Dress each of the three vegetables separately, and arrange in a large dish, with the beans in the centre and the tomatoes and cucumber on either side.

RYE

Family:　*Gramineae*
Genus:　*Secale*
Species:　*Secale cereale*

Rye is a particularly tolerant plant and will thrive in the most inhospitable climate with little rainfall and on the poorest acid soil, so it is still widely cultivated in Eastern Europe, Russia and the French Massif Central. It probably began as a weed from wheat and it was the Romans who first tamed it and began to cultivate it seriously. By the Middle Ages rye was so widespread that it was Europe's staple grain and early Dutch settlers in America began to grow it so successfully that it later became the basis of rye-whisky distilling (rye whisky is now a major American export).

Rye groats are whole grains which can be pre-soaked and cooked like rice, for an hour (1 ounce will swell to about 3½ ounces). They can then be used as a breakfast cereal with dried fruit. To accelerate cooking time the grains can be cracked with a rolling pin. Rye grains also sprout well. The tall stems of rye are used for thatching, and summer-planted rye can be used initially for animal grazing in November and then harvested as a grain crop the following summer.

A poisonous fungus called ergot destroys rye grains by replacing them with a horn-shaped purplish-black parasite several times longer than normal grains. The affected grain is poisonous to humans and livestock, and it is thought that certain plagues in the Middle Ages were due to ergotism. The virus attacks the central nervous system, causing convulsions and epilepsy, and people literally shook to death. Many were accused of witchcraft, because of their 'visions' and trances. The other form of ergot poisoning showed as gangrene, mummification, atrophy and loss of extremities, and the disease was christened 'St Anthony's Fire' because a sensation of burning in the feet and hands was characteristic. The most notorious recent attacks of ergotism occurred in France and Belgium in 1953 and in the Ukraine and Ireland in 1929.

European midwives have long known that ergot could help in cases of difficult childbirth and now chemicals isolated from ergot are still used as official drugs to induce contraction of involuntary muscles in stubborn childbirth; for the control of certain types of migraine; and to stop bleeding, because of the vasoconstricting properties of the plant.

See also: Flours, Grains.

Nutritional and medicinal properties

Rye has long been valued for its blood-cleansing properties as it helps stimulate the circulation and prevents hardening of the arteries. It is also good for regulating glandular activity and stopping

100 g RYE (raw)	
Calories	334
Protein (g)	12.1
Carbohydrate (g)	73.4
Cholesterol (g)	–
Fat (g)	1.7
Fibre (g)	2
Minerals	
calcium (mg)	38
phosphorus (mg)	376
iron (mg)	3.7
sodium (mg)	1
potassium (mg)	467
magnesium (mg)	115
zinc (mg)	–
iodine (mg)	0.001
chlorine (mg)	1
sulphur (mg)	28
silicon (mg)	30
bromine (mg)	0.37
Vitamins	
A(IU)	0
B_1 (mg)	0.43
B_2 (mg)	0.22
B_3 (mg)	1.6
B_5 (mg)	–
B_6 (mg)	–
B_{12} (mcg)	–
folic acid (mcg)	–
biotin (mcg)	–
C (mg)	0
D (mg)	–
E (mg)	–
Organic acids	
citric (%)	–
malic (%)	–
oxalic (%)	–
Water (%)	11
Digestion time (hrs)	$3\frac{1}{2}$

constipation. It is rich in iron and B-complex vitamins and so is helpful in cases of anaemia. It is high in fluorine, which encourages the formation of tooth enamel. It has the highest sodium, potassium, calcium and iodine content of all the cereals.

Creamed rye

This may sound like baby food – and indeed it is excellent nourishment for babies – but I find it wonderfully soothing adult food, at either end of the day, in a nervous world.

2 cups water
1 cup wholemeal rye flour
½ teaspoon sea salt
knob of unsalted butter
1 tablespoon honey

Heat the water and then pour in the flour, stirring vigorously otherwise lumps will form. Add the salt and simmer for 15 minutes stirring well the whole time. Serve hot with a knob of butter and dribbles of honey.

SAGE

Family: *Labiatae*
Genus: *Salvia*
Species: *Salvia officinalis*

Sage is a pungent, aromatic perennial plant of the mint family and grows abundantly in temperate climates. It is a large group of plants which include over 750 species, widely distributed throughout the world. Some are used in cooking, others in medicine and there is at least one Central American species which is a powerful hallucinogenic traditionally employed in villages and magical ceremonies. The most important, and certainly the best known, is *Salvia officinalis*. The word *salvia* is from the Latin *salvere*, meaning to be in good health.

Red, or common or garden sage, has grey-green leaves which are slightly downy and rounded at the tips, elongated and oval in shape. They grow in pairs on a white woody stem and produce blue, white or purple flowers on spikes, in June and July. The plant grows 2–3 feet high, is a hardy perennial, and enjoys sun and rich soil. Sage tends to get rather woody after four or five years and then needs to be propagated from two-year-old cuttings.

Sage is native to the northern Mediterranean and grows wild in southern Europe and round the whole of the Mediterranean coast. It is particularly common in the hills of Dalmatia and dried wild sage and sage honey are important exports of Yugoslavia.

Sage was used medicinally by the Romans who seldom employed it in their cooking. The original quotation 'Why should a man die who has sage growing in his garden?' comes from the Latin. The Romans learnt their medicinal uses of sage from the Greeks whose knowledge of its uses was published by Dioscorides.

The flavour of sage is extremely powerful, to my mind it tastes rather like dried blood. It contains overtones of camphor, and I always feel needs to be used, certainly for cooking, very discreetly.

Nutritional and medicinal properties

Sage contains a hydrocarbon known as salvina, as well as other essential oils, such as boneol, pinene, cineol and thujone. It is also rich in oestrogenic substances and contains flavonoids, saponins, tannin and resin as well as various minerals. It is astringent, healing and antiseptic on mucosal surfaces.

It is a peripheral vasodilator and stops perspiration, and in this respect it is particularly useful for night sweats, and also for excessive salivation and lactation. It regulates hormonal problems in the menopause. I have treated patients particularly successfully for night sweats during the menopause by administering three drops of sage oil three times a day in honey water. It acts as an excellent mouthwash and gargle for infections of the throat and it restores digestive and circulatory function during convalescence. The tea is useful in liver disease and in nervous conditions like anxiety and depression. It may be used as a douche in leucorrhoea and in baths to treat skin problems. It has also been used traditionally to treat female infertility because of its high oestrogen content. It is reputed to retard ageing and enhance the memory, to prevent hand trembling and eyes dimming.

Warning This is a very powerful herb and particularly when used in its oil form should be taken under the close supervision of a qualified consultant medical herbalist. I normally will not administer sage for more than three weeks at a time without a break and it is to be avoided altogether during pregnancy. Use the infusion, which has a strong, distinct, bitter flavour on a one-week-on three-off basis, unless under the supervision of a medicinal herbalist.

Sage rarebit

This is a fast snack for one
½oz (12 g) butter
½oz (12 g) flour
½ cup milk
3 tablespoons grated Cheddar or Cheshire cheese
1 teaspoon fresh chopped sage
English mustard, to taste
salt
freshly ground black pepper
1 slice wholemeal toast

Melt the butter. Add the flour and cook, then add the milk, making a thick roux. Stir in the cheese, sage, mustard and seasoning and simmer. Pour the topping over the toast and grill for a few minutes until brown.

SALT

This is the most fundamental of all tastes in food. It is one of the minerals essential to animal life. It occurs in all body fluids, including blood, sweat and tears; 0.9 per cent of the body and blood cells are salt. It is used in food as a condiment or preservative and has antiseptic properties.

The first salt was probably collected from scooped-out shallow holes along the seashore, and later it was taken from mines and sea-water. In the ancient world salt may not have been known to inland peoples and certainly explorers from Europe took salt to some parts of America and India. Some traditional diets of milk and animal flesh, raw or roasted, are not inadequate in salt, but once cereals and vegetables start to feature in the diet, with boiled meat, it seems that salt becomes necessary as a supplement.

Today salt is collected by evaporation from the ocean, is mined underground (this requires purification), or is taken from brine springs. Salt-water is heated until it evaporates to obtain salt and the higher the temperature the whiter and finer the salt. Quite recently the state of Oregon made the term **sea salt** illegal, charging that the implied superiority is groundless. Indeed, if there were such a thing available as unrefined sea salt, it would be grey in colour, consisting of approximately 58 per cent chloride, 33 per cent sodium, 4 per cent magnesium, 3 per cent sulphur, 1 per cent calcium, 1 per cent potassium, and traces of all other known minerals. (The concentration of minerals in salt-water is not standard throughout the oceans and seas.) Sea-salt production involves large-scale facilities (thousands of acres of collection ponds, huge kilns, long packaging lines, large storage facilities, railway sidings) – the sort of endeavour done massively or not done at all. Any company that wants to sell something that it can legally call sea salt has to buy it from companies that actually evaporate sea-water to obtain salt. The usual additives to salt are potassium iodide, dextrose, sodium bicarbonate (to keep the iodine from turning the salt purple) and sodium silico-aluminate, rice powder or calcium carbonate (to keep the salt free-flowing). In recent years the leading producers of salt have included the United States, Britain, the USSR, China, India, France and West Germany.

Nutritional and medicinal properties

Salt (sodium chloride) keeps the body fluids in balance. In the body there is a fine balance of sodium and potassium and these act together to maintain the osmotic pressure in a state of equilibrium inside and outside the cells and ensure the proper functioning of the neuro-muscular system. The concentration of sodium salts in the body is vital. The kidneys act as the basic regulator, excreting water and salt as necessary. However, an imbalance of the sodium and potassium due to the intake of excess sodium can lead to high blood pressure, arthritis, water retention, hormone imbalance and other problems.

A deficiency of sodium causes muscular shrinkage and weakness, nausea, loss of appetite, and flatulence. No matter where the salt is from, sodium and chlorine are vital minerals for the body. Deficiency of chlorine causes hair and tooth loss, weak muscles and poor digestion. Chlorine regulates our acid–alkaline balance, it enhances osmosis, stimulates production of hydrochloric acid and helps maintain healthy joints and tendons. The two minerals are bound, as sodium chloride, in a variety of foods including sea vegetables, carrots, celery, beets, lentils, olives, cheese, pickles and soya sauce. Sea vegetables are a particularly good source of natural sodium chloride because the salt is accompanied by the abundant trace minerals, including iodine, held in solution in sea-water.

Because sodium and chloride are so widely distributed in natural foods, it is almost never nutritionally essential to add salt to food. Salt with food is an acquired not an inborn taste. The only circumstance in which it is necessary to add salt to your diet in when you do long strenuous exercise in extremely hot weather to which you have not had a chance to acclimatize. Remember that nearly 90 per cent of the salt you eat is actually hidden in food. The amount of salt needed daily by an adult in a temperate climate is 4 grams, and this can always be obtained from natural foods. Most people add so much salt to their diet that their intake can be as much as 20 grams a day. Canned and processed foods invariably have added salt, and the additives in them, including monosodium glutamate, sodium bicarbonate, sodium nitrite, sodium benzoate, sodium propionate and sodium citrate, also contain salt. Foods containing salt include some surprising examples like hard cheeses, dried, evaporatorated or condensed milk, baking powder and breakfast cereals. It is important to realize that all salt, whether it be rock or plain table salt, has virtually the same chemical composition and sodium content; so there is no point in just switching to another kind because it sounds healthier.

There are various **salt substitutes** on the market, some of which contain mostly potassium chloride, and others of which are mostly a mixture of potassium chloride and ordinary salt. Check with your doctor before using these if you are diabetic or have heart or kidney disease. Unfortunately it is often not very clear from the label whether a product is very-low-sodium (mostly potassium chloride) or merely sodium-reduced (a mixture with ordinary salt).

If cooking with these substitutes you can replace salt in exactly the same quantities although some manufacturers recommend that those which contain mostly potassium chloride should be added towards the end of the cooking time as prolonged heating can accentuate a bitter aftertaste. Because it is not yet established whether the substitutes have the same preservative properties as salt, it is probably best not to use them in foods like pickles. Used in bread, where salt normally helps to control the development of yeast and strengthen the gluten, all give good results with little effect of texture or appearance.

Our taste for salt seems to be largely acquired so in theory it should be possible to unlearn it and cut down progressively without too much difficulty. It is worth experimenting with herbs and spices as flavouring instead and of course with children it is better to discourage the taste for salt and salty foods at a very early age. A good salt substitute is two parts kelp powder mixed with one part parsley, one part marjoram, one part garlic powder and one part cayenne pepper.

100 g TABLE SALT

Calories	0
Protein (g)	0
Carbohydrate (g)	0
Cholesterol (g)	0
Fat (g)	0
Fibre (g)	0
Minerals	
calcium (mg)	253
phosphorus (mg)	tr
iron (mg)	0.1
sodium (mg)	38758
potassium (mg)	4
magnesium (mg)	119
zinc (mg)	–
iodine (mg)	–
chlorine (mg)	–
sulphur (mg)	–
silicon (mg)	–
bromine (mg)	–
Vitamins	
A(IU)	0
B$_1$ (mg)	0
B$_2$ (mg)	0
B$_3$ (mg)	0
B$_5$ (mg)	–
B$_6$ (mg)	0
B$_{12}$ (mcg)	0
folic acid (mcg)	0
biotin (mcg)	0
C (mg)	–
D (mg)	0
E (mg)	0
Organic acids	
citric (%)	–
malic (%)	–
oxalic (%)	–
Water (%)	0.2
Digestion time (hrs)	–

Sesame salt

The Japanese call this *gomosio*. It stretches the saltiness of salt, and the usual ratio is eight parts sesame meal to one of salt, although you can go as high as 14 to 1.

Stir some sesame meal constantly in a heavy-bottomed frying pan until thoroughly heated through and toasted. Decant and now heat up the salt and return the toasted sesame, stirring the mixture until well amalgamated. Decant again. Cool and store in a covered container.

SAVORY

Family: *Labiatae*
Genus: *Satureja*
Species: *Satureja hortensis* (summer savory); *Satureja montana* (winter savory)

There are several varieties of savory, including winter savory (*Satureja montana*), yerba buena (*Satureja douglasii*), bean herb and Bohnenkraut. Almost all varieties are believed to come from the Mediterranean area and are native to southern Europe and North Africa. But it is possible to grow savory in temperate climates. The savories have been employed in food flavouring for over 2000 years, probably even longer than sage.

The Roman poet Virgil praised both winter and summer savory and recommended growing it around hives for bees. The fragrance attracts bees and it can also be rubbed on bee stings. The Latin name *Satureia* was first used by Pliny and savory was believed to be a favourite of satyrs because of its peppery taste. The herb possesses effective stimulant properties which led to its former use as an aphrodisiac, hence the belief in its popularity amongst satyrs. The American settlers took savories with them to the New World, and today market gardeners plant summer savory between rows of bean crops to ward off black fly.

Summer savory is a bushy plant with a hairy stem which divides above the ground into wide, half-inch-long leaves and supports light blue to violet flowers in bunches. It needs light, with rich soil and full sun. It has a biting flavour, rather like thyme but somewhat more bitter and very distinctive. Like thyme, it dries well and retains its flavour without becoming hay-like. It is an interesting addition to a bouquet garni and is used to flavour bean and pea dishes.

Winter savory is a hardy, low-growing shrub with woodier and more bristly stems. It flowers earlier than summer savory, and the blossoms are white or pale lavender. It enjoys poor soil but lots of sun. It has a fractionally inferior flavour to summer savory.

Nutritional and medicinal properties

Summer savory contains essential oils (carvacrol and cymene), as well as phenolic substances, resins, tannins and mucilage.

It is antiseptic, expectorant, carminative, stomachic, stimulant and diuretic and protects against worms. Its main use is in gastric complaints to help the digestion and to stimulate the appetite. It is an excellent antiseptic gargle. Its old reputation as an aphrodisiac was probably due only to its stimulating effect. Winter savory contains almost the same constituents as summer savory and medicinally is used in much the same way.

Tomato sauce with summer savory

The beauty of this sauce is that it only takes a matter of moments to make, tastes so fresh and peppery and goes with or in almost anything – baked potatoes, brown rice, pasta, omelette, etc.

1 lb (450 g) tomatoes
2 teaspoons butter
2 teaspoons olive oil
2 teaspoons finely chopped fresh
  summer savory
a little salt

Skin and chop the tomatoes, then sweat them gently in the butter, oil and herbs for a few minutes. Stir. Add salt and taste.

SESAME

Family:　*Pedaliaceae*
Genus:　*Sesamum*
Species:　*Sesamum indicum*

Sesame is a native of Africa and is one of the world's most important oil seeds. It has been cultivated in the East for thousands of years. China and India still grow most of the world's crop.

The seeds may be red, brown or black but more usually they are creamy white, depending on the variety. Modern strains contain nearly 60 per cent oil. Pure **sesame** oil is almost without taste or smell and does not go rancid very easily, which is one of the reasons for its popularity, particularly in hot climates. It has been used in cooking in Africa and the Far East for many centuries. The oil contains about 40 per cent linoleic acid and 50 per cent oleic acid together with a generous dose of lecithin.

The beautiful nutty taste of **sesame seeds**, particularly after roasting, makes them popular as toppings on bread and cake. Halva, made from ground sesame, has a characteristic rich, nutty taste. The paste known as tahini is cream or cream-grey in colour and has the texture, though not the taste, of runny peanut butter. Sesame seeds are made into margarine and cooking and salad oils. In some countries they are known as gingelly, til or beniseed.

Sesame sprouts are ready to eat within one or two days and if grown longer than 48 hours become very bitter to taste. Eat them when the length of the shoot becomes as long as the seed.

See also: Oils, Sprouted seeds.

Nutritional and medicinal properties

The meal remaining after oil extraction is a rich source of protein, especially the amino-acid methionine as well as calcium, phosphorus and niacin. Sesame seeds contain little carbohydrate. The lecithin content lowers blood cholesterol levels and the seeds have mucilaginous (soothing) properties.

100 g SESAME SEEDS

	Whole	Hulled
Calories	563	582
Protein (g)	18.6	18.2
Carbohydrate (g)	21.6	17.6
Cholesterol (g)	–	–
Fat (g)	49.1	53.4
Fibre (g)	6.3	2.4
Minerals		
calcium (mg)	1160	110
phosphorus (mg)	616	592
iron (mg)	10.5	2.4
sodium (mg)	60	–
potassium (mg)	725	–
magnesium (mg)	181	–
zinc (mg)	–	–
iodine (mg)	–	–
chlorine (mg)	–	–
sulphur (mg)	–	–
silicon (mg)	–	–
bromine (mg)	–	–
Vitamins		
A(IU)	30	–
B_1 (mg)	0.98	0.18
B_2 (mg)	0.24	0.13
B_3 (mg)	5.4	5.4
B_5 (mg)	–	–
B_6 (mg)	–	–
B_{12} (mcg)	0	0
folic acid (mcg)	–	–
biotin (mcg)	–	–
C (mg)	0	0
D (mg)	–	–
E (mg)	–	–
Organic acids		
citric (%)	–	–
malic (%)	–	–
oxalic (%)	–	–
Water (%)	5.4	5.5
Digestion time (hrs)	–	–

Tahini

This is very easy to make in a blender. In the Middle East it is used as the basis of various salad dressings and to flavour hummus.

Put 1 cup sesame seeds in a blender and grind to a fine powder. Add

1–2 teaspoons of sesame oil and continue blending until the mixture forms a paste.

SORGHUM

Family: *Gramineae*
Genus: *Sorghum*
Species: *Sorghum vulgare*

A native of Africa, sorghum is used there as a thick porridge, for cakes, as a fermented beer and for animal fodder. It survives drought particularly well and has spread abroad to the US, China, Manchuria, India, Pakistan and the West Indies, going under the guise of many local names.

It is quite close to maize in composition but is lower in fat and higher in protein and ranks third after wheat and rice in world importance as a cereal.

Kafir, from South Africa, varies in colour from white to pink to red. **Milo**, commonly found in East Africa, is pink and has larger seeds. **Feteritas** has even larger white seeds and grows in the Sudan. **Shallu** from India looks similar to feteritas, with slightly smaller white seeds. **Sweet sorghum** has a juicy sugar-rich stem which is crushed to make syrup and animal feed, as well as beer. **Grassy sorghum** is used as pasture.

See also: Flours, Grains.

Nutritional and medicinal properties

Sorghum has good body-building properties and is easily digested,

100 g SORGHUM	
Calories	332
Protein (g)	11
Carbohydrate (g)	73
Cholesterol (g)	–
Fat (g)	3.3
Fibre (g)	1.7
Minerals	
calcium (mg)	28
phosphorus (mg)	287
iron (mg)	4.4
sodium (mg)	–
potassium (mg)	350
magnesium (mg)	–
zinc (mg)	–
iodine (mg)	–
chlorine (mg)	25
sulphur (mg)	12
silicon (mg)	–
bromine (mg)	–
Vitamins	
A(IU)	0
B_1 (mg)	0.38
B_2 (mg)	0.15
B_3 (mg)	3.9
B_5 (mg)	–
B_6 (mg)	–
B_{12} (mcg)	–
folic acid (mcg)	–
biotin (mcg)	–
C (mg)	0
D (mg)	–
E (mg)	–
Organic acids	
citric (%)	–
malic (%)	–
oxalic (%)	–
Water (%)	11
Digestion time (hrs)	–

but unfortunately is not very easy to find.

Sorghum with beans

The broad beans are an interesting foil for the somewhat bland sorghum.

4 cups water
8 oz (225 g) sorghum
sea salt
1 onion chopped
2 tablespoons oil
2 cloves garlic, peeled and
    chopped
½ teaspoon ground coriander
8 oz (225 g) shelled broad beans
10 fl oz (300 ml) water
freshly ground black pepper

Cover the sorghum with the water and quickly bring to the boil. Add a pinch of salt, turn down the heat, cover closely and simmer for an hour, checking halfway through (sorghum tends to absorb a lot of water) and replenishing the water as necessary. When the grains are well separated and slightly chewy it is ready.

Meanwhile fry the onion in the oil, and just as it begins to brown add the garlic and coriander, stirring well. When the garlic browns add the beans and water, season and simmer till tender. Stir in the cooked sorghum. Test for seasoning and serve piping hot as a vegetable-and-grain side-dish.

SOYA BEAN

Family: *Leguminosae*
Genus: *Glycine*
Species: *Glycine max*

The soya bean is a native of South East Asia and was cultivated in China over 4000 years ago but it was quite unknown in Europe until the end of the seventeenth century and even then remained a curiosity until the nineteenth century. The enormous interest in the West in the soya bean has been due mainly to American research which has proved the unusual nutritional value of soya. It is undoubtedly the world's most important legume being used not only as a food but as a raw material in industry, for paint manufacture, brewing, cosmetics and drugs.

Soya can be eaten as a fresh bean (it does not like frost), as a dried bean and as a bean flour and is a good source of cooking oil. In the East it is fermented to make various kinds of curd (**tofu** is one) and bean cheese and soya milk is made from it. **Soya sauce** is perhaps the product westerners are most familiar with. There are many types of soya sauce and the methods used for making it vary according to place. In general it is made by fermenting a salted mixture of cooked soya beans in wheat or barley flour and then extracting the liquid. The result is a thin sauce with a salty flavour somewhat reminiscent of meat. It is usually dark brown in colour though it can vary from black to pale straw. **Tempeh**, which is a sort of cheese made from fermented soya beans, is rich in its own natural antibiotics – the result of the fermentation process.

Soya-bean oil is one of the most widely used in the world and in fact most blended cooking oils are soya-based. It is rich in linoleic acid and polyunsaturates. These make it difficult to store well because they can oxidize and the oil develops a rank flavour, but from the health point of view soya-bean oil is probably the best of all cooking oils.

See also: Oils, Pulses, Sprouted seeds.

Nutritional and medicinal properties

As a food the soya bean is extremely rich in both protein and oil, in the form of unsaturated fat. It contains

100g SOYA

	Dried beans (raw)	Fresh beans (cooked)	Ground beans (cooked)	Grits (dry)	Grits (cooked)	Raw sprouts
Calories	403	130	185	403	157	46
Protein (g)	34.1	11.1	15.6	33.9	13.5	6.2
Carbohydrate (g)	33.5	10.6	10.1	33.3	12.9	5.7
Cholesterol (g)	–	–	–	–	–	–
Fat (g)	17.7	5.6	8	17.6	6.7	1.4
Fibre (g)	4.8	1.6	2.3	4.9	1.9	0.76
Minerals						
calcium (mg)	226	72.2	102	229	88	47.6
phosphorus (mg)	554	178	253	556	218	66.7
iron (mg)	8.4	2.7	3.8	8.5	3.3	1.05
sodium (mg)	5.0	2.2	2.7	5.3	2.6	–
potassium (mg)	1677	539	756	169	674	–
magnesium (mg)	–	–	–	–	–	–
zinc (mg)	–	–	–	–	–	–
iodine (mg)	–	–	–	–	–	–
chlorine (mg)	–	–	–	–	–	–
sulphur (mg)	–	–	–	–	–	–
silicon (mg)	–	–	–	–	–	–
bromine (mg)	–	–	–	–	–	–
Vitamins						
A(IU)	80	27.8	44.4	78.4	36.3	76.2
B_1 (mg)	1.1	0.2	0.3	1.05	0.25	0.2
B_2 (mg)	0.31	0.08	0.13	0.3	0.1	0.2
B_3 (mg)	2.2	0.6	0.8	2.2	0.72	0.76
B_5 (mg)	–	–	–	–	–	–
B_6 (mg)	–	–	–	0.78	–	–
B_{12} (mcg)	0	0	0	0	0	0
folic acid (mcg)	–	–	–	–	–	–
biotin (mcg)	–	–	–	–	–	–
C (mg)	–	0	0	–	–	13.3
D (mg)	–	–	–	–	–	–
E (mg)	–	–	–	–	–	–
Organic acids						
citric (%)	–	–	–	–	–	–
malic (%)	–	–	–	–	–	–
oxalic (%)	–	–	–	–	–	–
Water (%)	10	71	73.8	–	–	86.3
Digestion time (hrs)	–	3	–	–	–	–

as much protein as steak, and is rich in lecithin and all the essential amino-acids, plus iron, calcium and phosphorus.

Soya beans are a valuable food for diabetics and the high lecithin content is excellent as protection against cholesterol deposits and to fight fatigue. Soya is believed to prevent pellagra, skin eruptions and nervous diseases.

100 g SOYA (continued)

	Cooked sprouts	Fermented with cereal (miso)	Curd	Unfortified milk	Fully fortified milk	Full-fat flour
Calories	38.4	171	72	33	64.6	421
Protein (g)	5.3	10.6	7.8	3.4	3.2	37.1
Carbohydrate (g)	4	23.3	2.5	2.3	7.1	30
Cholesterol (g)	–	–	–	–	–	–
Fat (g)	1.44	4.7	4.2	1.5	3.5	20
Fibre (g)	0.8	2.4	0.08	0	0	2.4
Minerals						
calcium (mg)	43.2	71	125	20.9	146	200
phosphorus (mg)	50	312	125	50	45.8	557
iron (mg)	0.72	1.8	1.9	0.82	0.8	8.4
sodium (mg)	–	2941	6.7	–	–	1.4
potassium (mg)	–	335	42	–	–	1714
magnesium (mg)	–	–	–	–	–	–
zinc (mg)	–	–	–	–	–	–
iodine (mg)	–	–	–	–	–	–
chlorine (mg)	–	–	–	–	–	–
sulphur (mg)	–	–	–	–	–	–
silicon (mg)	–	–	–	–	–	–
bromine (mg)	–	–	–	–	–	–
Vitamins						
A(IU)	80	58.8	0	40.9	37.5	114
B$_1$ (mg)	0.2	0.06	0.06	0.08	0.08	0.9
B$_2$ (mg)	0.15	0.1	0.03	0.03	0.03	0.31
B$_3$ (mg)	0.72	0.6	0.08	0.18	0.2	2.1
B$_5$ (mg)	–	–	–	–	–	–
B$_6$ (mg)	–	–	–	–	–	0.6
B$_{12}$ (mcg)	0	0	0	0	1.7	0
folic acid (mcg)	–	–	–	–	–	–
biotin (mcg)	–	–	–	–	–	–
C (mg)	4	0	0	0	–	0
D (mg)	–	–	–	–	–	–
E (mg)	–	–	–	–	–	–
Organic acids						
citric (%)	–	–	–	–	–	–
malic (%)	–	–	–	–	–	–
oxalic (%)	–	–	–	–	–	–
Water (%)	89	53	84.8	92.4	–	8
Digestion time (hrs)	–	–	–	–	–	–

Warning Soya beans and soya flour must never be eaten uncooked. Raw soya beans contain a trypsine inhibiter which prevents the assimilation of the amino-acid methionine by the body.

Tofu lemon mayonnaise

This tastes quite acceptable and has far less fat than ordinary egg mayonnaise.

6 oz (175 g) tofu

100 g SOYA (continued)

	Low-fat flour	Defatted flour	Powder	Protein	Sauce
Calories	356	326	350	321	67
Protein (g)	43.2	47	42.9	75	5.6
Carbohydrate (g)	36	38	21.4	14.3	11
Cholesterol (g)	–	–	–	–	–
Fat (g)	6.7	0.8	26.4	tr	1.1
Fibre (g)	2.5	2.3	–	0.36	0
Minerals					
calcium (mg)	261	260	182	121	83
phosphorus (mg)	636	660	96.4	679	106
iron (mg)	9.1	11	9.3	–	5
sodium (mg)	1.1	1	3.6	211	7222
potassium (mg)	1818	1800	–	179	367
magnesium (mg)	–	–	–	–	–
zinc (mg)	–	–	–	–	–
iodine (mg)	–	–	–	–	–
chlorine (mg)	–	–	–	–	–
sulphur (mg)	–	–	–	–	–
silicon (mg)	–	–	–	–	–
bromine (mg)	–	–	–	–	–
Vitamins					
A(IU)	79.5	40	–	–	0
B_1 (mg)	0.8	1.1	0.78	–	tr
B_2 (mg)	0.36	0.34	0.29	–	0.3
B_3 (mg)	2.6	2.6	4.3	–	0.6
B_5 (mg)	–	–	–	–	–
B_6 (mg)	0.68	0.72	–	–	–
B_{12} (mcg)	0	0	0	0	0
folic acid (mcg)	–	–	–	–	–
biotin (mcg)	–	–	–	–	–
C (mg)	0	0	–	0	0
D (mg)	–	–	–	–	–
E (mg)	–	–	–	–	–
Organic acids					
citric (%)	–	–	–	–	–
malic (%)	–	–	–	–	–
oxalic (%)	–	–	–	–	–
Water (%)	8	8	–	–	–
Digestion time (hrs)	–	–	–	–	–

2 tablespoons unsweetened,
   unsalted soya milk
2 tablespoons fresh lemon juice
1 tablespoon sesame oil
freshly ground white pepper to
   taste

Liquidize all the ingredients together, and adjust the seasoning to taste.

SPINACH

Family: *Chenopodiaceae*
Genus: *Spinacia*
Species: *Spinacia oleracea*

Spinach is a relative of beet, Swiss chard and lamb's quarters, producing a cluster of wide, succulent, dark or pale green leaves which are equally delicious raw or cooked. A native of Persia, where it was used for medicine, spinach was brought to England by the Crusaders and has been cultivated in Europe since the Middle Ages. In Renaissance cookery it was used to marble pale dishes and originally it was treated more like a herb than a vegetable. By the time spinach has been adopted in English cottage gardens the days of pottage were over and it was served as a vegetable in its own right, cooked in honey, sugar and spices.

Summer spinach is delicate, with rounded soft green leaves and a lighter flavour. **Prickly seeded winter spinach** is coarser both in texture and in flavour and it is usually better to discard its stalks. Other varieties of spinach include **spinach-beet** (or perpetual spinach), **Swiss chard** (or sea-kale beet) and **orache**, which is wild spinach and sometimes sports red leaves.

Fresh spinach is available from May to July, and September to November, and forced spinach covers the rest of the year.

In the United States, France, Italy and Turkey spinach is often eaten raw as a salad. Remember when cooking spinach that it shrinks alarmingly so allow at least 8 oz (225 g) per person. Wash it really well. Shake it dryish and start to cook it with just a little butter over a very low heat until the leaves start to sweat, at which time you can turn up the heat and stir with a wooden spoon until they are well heated through, which will only take a couple of minutes.

Spinach goes well with cream, cream cheese and eggs and adds a pretty touch of colour to delicate cold sauces intended for fish or eggs.

Nutritional and medicinal properties

Spinach has long been considered extremely healthy although the iron content has been overrated (perhaps because of Popeye's avid promotion of it). It contains plenty of vitamins C, A and B and some vitamin K, as well as potassium, calcium, magnesium, iron, iodine and phosphorus, and it is low in calories. Drained canned spinach has more calcium and salt and less vitamin C than fresh spinach, and defrosted and cooked leaf spinach has approximately the same nutrients as when fresh and cooked, though if it is finely chopped it loses some of its vitamins C and A.

Warning Cooked spinach yields up oxalic acid that binds up the trace minerals in it just as phytic acid does in grain – with the result that the high calcium and iron content cannot be properly utilized. So it is not a good idea for pregnant women or the elderly to eat copious quantities of it. Its oxalic acid can be partially neutralized by cooking in milk, but it's best to eat it raw.

Spinach is recommended for constipation (it has noticeable laxative properties), for anaemia and for all sorts of nerve deficiencies, for hypertension, bronchitis and dyspepsia and the vitamin K in it makes it useful in promoting blood clotting.

100 g SPINACH

	Boiled	Raw
Calories	23	26
Protein (g)	3	3.2
Carbohydrate (g)	3.6	4.3
Cholesterol (g)	0	0
Fat (g)	0.3	0.3
Fibre (g)	0.6	0.6
Minerals		
calcium (mg)	93	93
phosphorus (mg)	38	51
iron (mg)	2.2	3.1
sodium (mg)	50	71
potassium (mg)	324	470
magnesium (mg)	–	88
zinc (mg)	0.4	–
iodine (mg)	–	0.036
chlorine (mg)	–	1130
sulphur (mg)	–	1245
silicon (mg)	–	810
bromine (mg)	–	–
Vitamins		
A(IU)	8100	8100
B_1 (mg)	0.07	0.1
B_2 (mg)	0.14	0.2
B_3 (mg)	0.5	0.6
B_5 (mg)	0.21	–
B_6 (mg)	0.18	–
B_{12} (mcg)	–	–
folic acid (mcg)	140	–
biotin (mcg)	0.1	–
C (mg)	28	51
D (mg)	–	–
E (mg)	–	–
Organic acids		
citric (%)	–	–
malic (%)	–	–
oxalic (%)	–	–
Water (%)	92	90.7
Digestion time (hrs)	–	–

Wilted spinach and banana salad

This is the most delicious combination of three flavours I ever tasted.

2 bananas, thinly sliced
3 tablespoons olive oil
2 lb (1 kg) summer spinach, washed and torn into mouth-sized pieces
1 cup toasted hazelnuts, lightly broken up

Fry the bananas in the oil for a couple of minutes, stirring well all the time. Pour piping hot on to the spinach and toss. Scatter the hazelnuts.

SPROUTED SEEDS

If the thought of eating seeds rather than planting them seems rather novel, don't let this put you off. After all the seed, like the nut, is a powerhouse of food to the germinating plant and so makes a valuable food for us as well.

Sprouted seeds have a history as old as civilized man's use of seed. I cannot sing the praises of freshly sprouted seeds highly enough. They contain an unequalled balance of amino-acids, fatty acids and natural sugars, together with an extremely high level of minerals, and they are capable of sustaining life on their own, provided several kinds are eaten together. They are also the cheapest form of food available – and the most organic, because they can be grown without any artificial aids whatsoever on your own kitchen window-sill.

It is possible to sprout any seeds, though undoubtedly some will co-operate more easily than others. I find mung, alfalfa, adzuki, soya, lentil and fenugreek the easiest to sprout, but all the grains and beans will also grow.

How to grow your own sprouts

Growing sprouts is the simplest form of indoor gardening you will ever encounter. You can use a plastic bowl, a polythene bag, a wide-mouthed glass jar, or an inexpensive, special sprouting salad kit available from most health-food stores. Personally I find the latter gives me guaranteed perfection, so I prefer it, but I know that many of my patients use wide-necked glass jars with consistent success.

First remove stones and any other unwanted material by putting the seeds in a large sieve and rinsing them well under the tap, picking out the unwanted bits with your fingers. Then put the seeds into a jar and cover them with a few inches of pure mineral water or water which has been filtered through a purifier. This is important because water out of the kitchen tap which contains chlorine tends to inhibit germination. Leave the seeds to soak all night in a warm place (I use the top of my coal-fired boiler). Next morning pour off the water.

Now rinse the seeds, either by transferring them to a sieve and pouring water through them, or by covering the top of the jar with cheesecloth, securing it to the neck of the jar with a rubber band, and then pouring water through the cheesecloth, swilling it round in the jar and finally draining it away. Remember to drain very thoroughly, whatever method you use, because a common cause for failure in sprouting any seed is excess of water, which causes them to rot. Leaving the seeds as dry as you can, tilt the jar on its side and leave it in a warm place. Repeate this rinsing ritual at least twice a day.

The ideal sprouting temperature is 70°F (21°C), and some people prefer to keep the seeds in a dark place at this stage. After 2–5 days you will notice that the seeds have split and begun to grow tiny stalks and leaves. At this point, if you haven't done so already, put them in a sunny window-sill. Keep them moist with a plant spray.

Optimum vitamin content occurs 48–98 hours after germination. Seeds can now be rinsed and eaten straight away or stored in an air-tight container or sealed polythene bag in the refrigerator. You can eat the complete seeds, hulls and all, although some people prefer to remove the hulls – but remember that they provide an excellent source of fibre.

If you become as passionate about sprouting as I am, I can recommend no better book on the subject than *Sprout for the Love of Everybody* by Viktoras Kulvinskas (Omangod Press, PO Box 64, Woodstock Valley, CT 06282).

Nutritional and medicinal properties

Seeds are high in protein, containing about 35 per cent, but like other vegetable proteins they need to be combined with foods higher in amino-acids, in which they are low. Seeds are best complemented by nuts and dairy produce. Add them to pulse dishes, cheese and vegetable casseroles, sauces, and grain dishes or, to make more protein available, add them to bread, soups and salads.

Seeds seal in their goodness, so the rich level of B vitamins keeps longer than B vitamins in vegetables, which decrease soon after harvesting. Seeds are also a good source of vitamins E and A, phosphorus and magnesium, and contain some iron and zinc.

All seeds store energy in the form of starch. When they begin to sprout, enzymes which hitherto have lain dormant, become active and begin to break down the stored starch into simple sugars and to split long-chain proteins into free amino-acids, as well as converting saturated fats into free fatty acids. In fact this enzymic activity is so intense at this early stage of sprouting that it stimulates the body's own enzymes into greater activity and so accelerates the body's innate healing activity. Sprouts are in effect predigested and so have many times the nutritional efficiency of the seeds from which they grew. Ounce for ounce they provide more nutrients than any other natural food known, and when I teach my patients how to grow them, as I always insist on doing as part of their healing programme, I lovingly refer to them as Mother Nature's mega-multi-vitamin-and-mineral pill

Within a few hours of germination vitamin C develops and continues increasing for some days. The vitamin C in soya beans, for example, multiplies five times in three days of germination. Most importantly, as far as vegans are concerned, vitamin B_{12} is found in most sprouted seeds and can provide the body's daily requirement in one large helping.

The body can only assimilate minerals properly if they are part of organic molecules. Unhappily the calcium, zinc and iron in peas and beans and some grains are bound to phytic acid, making them unavailable for absorption. Phytin is an important ingredient of many seeds and in certain varieties it accounts for up to 80 per cent of the phosphorus they contain. However, sprouting greatly reduces the phytin content of seeds, so liberating the minerals bound to phytin for use. Simultaneously it increases their level of desirable phosphorus compounds like lecithin (necessary for healthy nerves and brain function). Lecithin also helps to break up and transport fats and fatty acids round the body and encourages the transportation of nutrients through cell walls, stimulating the secretion of hormones at the same time.

Stir-fried sprouted lentils

This dish has a nice crunchy texture and a lightly sweet taste, and I've found it a diplomatic way to introduce sceptical carnivores to the beauty and versatility of sprouted seeds.

3 tablespoons oil (olive and soya
   mixed)
4 leafy sticks celery, finely diced
1 large onion, chopped
2 oz (50 g) parsnip, diced
12 oz (325 g) sprouted green lentils
2 cloves garlic, finely sliced
4 tablespoons soya sauce
¼ teaspoon sea salt
extra olive oil for sprinkling

Heat the oil in a deep heavy-bottomed frying pan or a stainless steel wok (no aluminium, please!). Add the celery, onion and parsnip, and fry until barely tender. Add the sprouted lentils, garlic and soya sauce, turn up the heat and fry briskly, stirring continuously, for 3–4 minutes. Add the salt, turn down the heat to minimum, cover the pan and steam gently for 10 minutes until barely tender. This dish is best if it still retains a slight crunchiness, so keep checking by tasting.

Serve very hot with a little extra oil drizzled over the top, with wholewheat bread and green salad.

SUGAR

The term 'sugar' was originally applied to a sweet crystalline substance, sucrose, pressed from a sugar-cane plant; however, its meaning has been broadened to cover many organic compounds of similar construction. There are many sugars that occur in nature not only from plants but also in animals. The most important sugars are glucose or dextrose (grape sugar), fructose or levulose (fruit sugar), sucrose (cane sugar), maltose (malt sugar), and lactose (milk sugar).

The product we think of as ordinary sugar is sucrose, for which the alternative name is cane sugar – whatever its source. In fact the sucrose we buy is usually obtained from cane or beet.

Sugars vary in their melting point, solubility in water and above all in their sweetness. Assuming cane sugar is listed at 150 for sweetness the comparison would be as follows:

Fruit sugar (fructose)	259
Cane sugar (sucrose)	150
Grape sugar (glucose)	111
Malt sugar (maltose)	48
Milk sugar (lactose)	24

So fruit sugar is ten times sweeter than milk sugar.

Almost all plants manufacture sugar. Usually this is sucrose in the leaves and stems. Sucrose also occurs in many fruits, especially strawberries and pineapples, and in many root vegetables, such as carrots and beetroot. It is also in the nectar of flowers, although in honey it has been converted to simpler sugars by an enzyme in the bees' saliva.

Although sugar did not become a major carbohydrate food source until the nineteenth century, even neolithic man enjoyed its sweet taste. The main source of sugar, sugar cane, originated in the South Pacific or Asia and was cultivated in India and China from early times. Although sugar was known in Europe from the Middle Ages its refining made it expensive. Columbus took sugar-cane cuttings to the West Indies on his second voyage to Santo Domingo, and the first intensive sugar cultivation was established there in 1508. Cortes took sugar cane to Mexico from where it spread to Brazil, Peru and Argentina. By the mid 1600s tropical America had become the world's biggest producer of sugar cane.

It was not until 1794 that Andreas Marggrat, a German scientist, took sugar from beets, an idea which then spread around the world. The plant had been known as a sweet vegetable since the Middle Ages, but from the eighteenth century it assumed a new importance.

During the eighteenth century, the amount of spice in recipes declined and the level of sugar began to climb in proportion. In the following centuries the trend continued and the displacement is now almost total.

Nutritional and medicinal properties

The health implication of sugar that everybody knows about is its drastic effect on the teeth. Statistically dental disease is the number one health problem in America and Britain and sugar is the universally recognized culprit where dental decay is concerned. Sugar reacts with saliva to form acids that dissolve the enamel of the teeth, forming an ideal environment for the bacteria that cause decay.

Sugar in its refined state is only 'empty calories'; it is 99.96 per cent sucrose and totally devoid of vitamins, minerals and enzymes. John Yudkin had every reason to call it 'pure, white and deadly'. Vitamins, minerals and enzymes are essential for the digestion, assimilation and utilization of sugar, but analysis of molasses, the by-product of sugar-refining, shows six B vitamins and eight minerals which have been detached from the sugar, and these are just a portion of the nutrients your system must somehow provide to metabolize the sugar. The missing elements must be stolen from the 'real food' in a diet, from nutrients in your blood that are intended for other functions, even from the reserves stored in your very bones. Only in this way can a simple carbohydrate (such as refined sugar) imitate a complex one and act like a real food.

By contrast, a complex carbohydrate which is a real food has its sugars accompanied by fibre, vitamins, minerals, enzymes, protein and fat – in other words everything necessary to complete the metabolic activities that will be fired by sugar. Complex carbohydrates supply the body with a slow, steady, stream of blood sugar and none of the essential companions are missing. This is natural sugar metabolism. Eating refined sugar

100 g SUGAR (beet or cane)	White sugar (granulated and loaf)	Demerara	Liquid glucose BP	Blackstrap molasses (third extraction)
Calories	394	394	318	213
Protein (g)	tr	0.5	tr	0
Carbohydrate (g)	105	104.5	84.7	55
Cholesterol (g)	–	–	–	0
Fat (g)	0	0	0	0
Fibre (g)	0	0	0	0
Minerals				
calcium (mg)	2	53	8	684
phosphorus (mg)	tr	20	11	84
iron (mg)	tr	0.9	0.5	16.1
sodium (mg)	tr	6	150	96
potassium (mg)	2	89	3	2927
magnesium (mg)	tr	15	–	–
zinc (mg)	–	–	–	–
iodine (mg)	–	–	–	–
chlorine (mg)	tr	14	–	–
sulphur (mg)	–	–	–	–
silicon (mg)	–	–	–	–
bromine (mg)	tr	35	190	–
Vitamins				
A(IU)	0	–	–	0
B$_1$ (mg)	tr	tr	0	0.11
B$_2$ (mg)	tr	tr	0	0.19
B$_3$ (mg)	–	–	–	0.2
B$_5$ (mg)	0	tr	0	–
B$_6$ (mg)	0	0	0	–
B$_{12}$ (mcg)	–	–	–	–
folic acid (mcg)	0	tr	0	–
biotin (mcg)	0	tr	0	–
C (mg)	0	0	0	–
D (mg)	0	0	0	–
E (mg)	0	0	0	–
Organic acids				
citric (%)	–	–	–	–
malic (%)	–	–	–	–
oxalic (%)	–	–	–	–
Water (%)	tr	tr	20.4	24
Digestion time (hrs)	–	–	–	–

causes the blood sugar level to leap and plunge dramatically.

Sugar also inhibits the ability of the white blood cells to destroy bacteria. Tests show that a couple of teaspoons of sugar can undermine the strength of white blood cells by 25 per cent. Sugar can reduce your resistance to everything from colds to cancer.

Many members of the medical establishment fail to recognize the relationship between sugar consumption and adult-onset diabetes. It seems they are waiting for proof positive; eventually they will get it, if only because what goes up always comes down and as the sugar consumption comes down among the enlightened in the western world, so will the incidence of diabetes.

Bearing all of this in mind, for those who suffer from hunger pains between meals, or from the symptoms of hypoglycemia (low blood sugar) it is far better to eat small amounts of proteins between meals (a few spoonfuls of yoghurt or a small handful of sunflower seeds) than to seek a boost from sugar, which — because of the wild swings in blood sugar level it induces — will only entrench the condition.

John Yudkin has no difficulty in seeing the sugar–diabetes link and observes that sugar is linked to gout and duodenal ulcers and that people suffering from diabetes, gout and duodenal ulcers are also predisposed to coronary disease. He lists various advantages for those who eliminate or curtail sugar consumption including reduction of dental decay, particularly in children, helping weight control (an indirect link to coronary disease), improvement of digestion and the improvement or correction of various blood abnormalities involving fats, uric acid, glucose, the stickiness of blood platelets and the concentration of insulin and cortisol.

All this can be summarized as follows. If you want to improve your diet, your life expectancy and your overall physical and mental health, don't eat sugar. This means don't eat any sugar at all — just become accustomed to doing without it.

If you are unable to give up sugar then I would suggest that you stick to very small quantities of the **black sugar** that comes from Barbados, Guyana or Mauritius, which is clearly labelled with the country of origin. The darker in colour the higher the proportion of health-protecting elements and structural information it contains. Bear in mind, though, that brown sugars generally contain added colouring. For a sugar to be a true unrefined sugar it must still contain a thin film of molasses surrounding the sucrose crystal which contains some 200 organic nutrients which are useful in themselves and also essential for the correct break down of sugar in the body. Bearing all this in mind it is far preferable that you use a small amount of **honey** or **black strap molasses** as sweetening. The following sweeteners do not depend on sucrose for their sweetening power.

Sweetener	Kind of sugar	Sweetening power % (sucrose = 100)
rice syrup	maltose	20
barley malt syrup	maltose fructose	40
date sugar	glucose and	100
honey	fructose	140

Of the above only **date sugar** is solid and it is the only one that is a whole food. It consists of dates that have been pitted, dried and ground. It is suitable for sprinkling on foods but does not mix well or dissolve easily and therefore can be a problem if used for baking and cooking. The liquids are easier to work with in baking and cooking, but all recipes that are being converted from solid-form sucrose need to have their liquid content appropriately adjusted to compensate for the liquid of the syrup and/or honey. Use ¾ cup honey to replace 1 cup sugar and at the same time decrease the amount of liquid in the recipe by up to ¼ cup of each ¾ cup honey used. Note the more delicate the flavour of the recipe, the lighter the honey should be. The darker the honey the higher the mineral content and the stronger the flavour. Honey can also be mixed half and half with **molasses** or **malt syrup** but this should only be done where the molasses or malt flavour is compatible with the other ingredients in the recipe.

Warning – artificial sweeteners
All artificial sweeteners have to be approved for safety by the Food Advisory Committee before they can be used by the food industry or sold over the counter. The Committee on Toxicity of Chemicals in Food, Consumer Products and the Environment reports to the FAC, and the government is advised if there is a need to withdraw a product on grounds of uncertainty as to its safety, as happened with cyclamates in 1969. At one time saccharine was thought to induce bladder cancer in rats, but no such link has been shown in humans. Although aspartame was recently the subject of investigation about its effect on blood pressure and behaviour, the Food Advisory Committee remains satisfied as to its safety. I feel that these types of sugars are as suspect as any other artificial additives and therefore would not advise their use. Note also that substances like thaumatin, acesulsame K, mannitol, xylitol, hydrogenated glucose syrup, isomolt and sorbitol are increasingly being added to manufactured foods instead of ordinary sugar.

SUNFLOWER

Family: *Compositae*
Genus: *Helianthus*
Species: *Helianthus annuus* (common annual); *Helianthus orgyalis* and *Helianthus decapetalus* (perennial)

Probably sunflowers came originally from Peru, but they have been cultivated for so long that their origin is now lost in the mists of time. They are grown as a crop in Russia, Bulgaria, Hungary, Romania, Argentina and Africa. North American Indians appreciated them for their medicinal value, and may well have appreciated the importance of the highly unsaturated **sunflower oil** from the seeds well before we in Europe did. The linoleic-acid content is second only to that of safflower and altogether half the seed is made up of molecules of oil. It also contains oleic and palmitic acids.

Sunflower oil is also rich in vitamin E and contains good amounts of vitamins A and D. The oil is fine, almost tasteless and very pale yellow. It is excellent as cooking oil and for use in salad dressing. The seeds take 1–2 days to sprout and **sunflower sprouts** should be eaten when the sprout has reached the same length as the seed. The buds of sunflowers may be used in salads.

Beware of shelled sunflower seeds which are tinged with patches of yellow or tan. This indicates that the high oil content in them has turned rancid. High-quality shelled sunflower seeds are a uniform grey in colour.

See also: Oils, Sprouted seeds.

Nutritional and medicinal properties

Sunflower seeds are remarkably rich in the B-complex vitamins and are an excellent source of phosphorus, magnesium, iron, calcium, potassium, protein and vitamin E. I have found them a very useful aid to help some of my patients stop smoking. I gather this is because sunflower seeds contain

100 g SUNFLOWER SEEDS	
Calories	560
Protein (g)	24
Carbohydrate (g)	19.9
Cholesterol (g)	–
Fat (g)	47.3
Fibre (g)	3.8
Minerals	
calcium (mg)	120
phosphorus (mg)	837
iron (mg)	7.1
sodium (mg)	30
potassium (mg)	920
magnesium (mg)	38
zinc (mg)	–
iodine (mg)	–
chlorine (mg)	90
sulphur (mg)	87
silicon (mg)	554
bromine (mg)	–
Vitamins	
A(IU)	50
B_1 (mg)	1.96
B_2 (mg)	0.23
B_3 (mg)	5.4
B_5 (mg)	–
B_6 (mg)	1.2
B_{12} (mcg)	0
folic acid (mcg)	–
biotin (mcg)	–
C (mg)	–
D (mg)	–
E (mg)	–
Organic acids	
citric (%)	–
malic (%)	–
oxalic (%)	–
Water (%)	4.8
Digestion time (hrs)	–

ingredients which mimic some of the effects of nicotine. To this extent they give smokers some of the gratification they seek from nicotine. They are easy to carry around and I encourage my hypoglycemic patients to eat a teaspoon or so every couple of hours.

A combination of equal quantities of pumpkin seeds, sunflower seeds and sesame seeds is a perfectly balanced protein – and the three seeds combined sprinkled over cereals taste delicious.

Sunflower seed sweets
(makes 20–30)

Even very young children can make these (though you will have to supervise the mincing and liquidizing) and there is something very satisfying about making your own sweets, or so my three-year-old god-daughter tells me.

4 oz (100 g) dried apricots
4 oz (100 g) raisins
4 oz (100 g) figs
4 oz (100 g) sunflower seeds
2 oz (50 g) rolled porridge oats
juice and grated rind of ½ an
*   orange*
1 teaspoon vanilla essence
4 tablespoons water
desiccated coconut

Mince the dried fruit, and pulverize the seeds and oats in a liquidizer with the juice and rind, the essence and the water. Stir in the minced fruit. Drop a teaspoon at a time into desiccated coconut, and roll into balls. Chill.

SWEDE (OR RUTABAGA)

Family: *Cruciferae*
Genus: *Brassica*
Species: *Brassica   napus*   var.
        rapobrassica

We tend to eat swedes with more relish than the French do who relegate them to cattle fodder. In the US swede is called rutabaga. Originally it was called the 'Swedish turnip'. It is similar to kohlrabi in that the edible part is an underground swelling of the stem rather than an actual root. It closely resembles the turnip in shape but is larger and has purplish-brown skin grooved deeply round the base of the stem. The flesh is yellow and the core tends to be woody.

Swedes flourish all over Europe but are late-comers. No records of their cultivation can be found earlier than the seventeenth century. Their season runs from October to April.

Nutritional and medicinal properties

Swedes are rich in calcium, vitamin C and niacin. The tall, soft sprouts of the swede that grow after it has been lifted and stored can be boiled and served with butter like asparagus and are very rich in vitamins A, B and C.

Baked marrow and swede

This is a far cry from swede as it is usually served – boiled, sloppy and

100 g SWEDE

	Raw	Boiled
Calories	46	36
Protein (g)	1.1	0.9
Carbohydrate (g)	11	8.2
Cholesterol (g)	–	–
Fat (g)	0.1	0.1
Fibre (g)	1.1	1.1
Minerals		
calcium (mg)	66	59
phosphorus (mg)	39	31
iron (mg)	0.4	0.3
sodium (mg)	5	4
potassium (mg)	239	167
magnesium (mg)	15	–
zinc (mg)	–	–
iodine (mg)	0.02	–
chlorine (mg)	100	–
sulphur (mg)	530	–
silicon (mcg)	–	–
bromine (mg)	–	–
Vitamins		
A(IU)	580	550
B_1 (mg)	0.07	0.06
B_2 (mg)	0.07	0.06
B_3 (mg)	1.1	0.8
B_5 (mg)	0.11	0.07
B_6 (mg)	0.2	0.12
B_{12} (mcg)	0	0
folic acid (mcg)	27	21
biotin (mcg)	0.1	tr
C (mg)	43	26
D (mg)	–	–
E (mg)	–	–
Organic acids		
citric (%)	–	–
malic (%)	–	–
oxalic (%)	–	–
Water (%)	87	–
Digestion time (hrs)	3¼	–

flavourless – and baking preserves the nutritional content of both vegetables.

1 medium-sized marrow
1 teaspoon sesame oil
2 medium-sized turnips
¼ teaspoon salt
freshly ground black pepper to
*   taste*
2 bay leaves

Preheat oven to 350°F (180°C, gas mark 4). Peel the marrow, take out the seeds and cut into 2 in (5 cm) chunks. Heat the oil in a large ovenproof casserole pot and sauté the marrow for 2 or 3 minutes. Peel and cut the swede into 1 in (2.5 cm) cubes and add to the marrow, sautéing while stirring for a further minute. Add the remaining ingredients. Remove from the heat. Cover and place in the oven. Bake for 30 to 40 minutes, till tender.

TARRAGON

Family: *Compositae*
Genus: *Artemisia*
Species: *Artemisia dracunculus*

Tarragon is one of the great culinary herbs related to wormwood, southernwood and mugwort. It is a bushy perennial about 3 feet high with narrow leaves and small grey-green flowers. It does not like wet soil, preferring sun or partial shade. In winter, it needs to be cut down and covered with straw to protect it against frost. Alternatively, lift it in the autumn and keep it in a cold frame to protect it. This will also ensure a winter supply. Beds should be renewed every three or four years. This is crucial, otherwise the flavour tends to go off.

True French tarragon rarely if ever sets viable seeds, so it has to be grown from cuttings or by root division and good strains are rarer than gold-dust. Seed is always from the very inferior Russian tarragon (*Artemisia dracunculoides*) which has paler leaves and has a very different taste, more pungent and with little of the delicate and special flavour for which French tarragon is desired. It is commonly used in Iran as a salad plant.

Tarragon needs to be carefully dried otherwise it tends to taste inferior. Tarragon vinegar is easily made. Gather the fresh herb just before it flowers, and stuff it into a bottle, filling the bottle up with white wine vinegar. After two months, it is ready for decanting but leaving the herb in the bottle looks attractive and also produces a better flavour. This makes an excellent vinegar for mixed mustards, salad dressings and mayonnaise.

Nutritional and medicinal properties

Tarragon produces a volatile oil, estragon, which is used as a flavouring in liqueurs and in perfumery. Chemically the oil is the same as anise oil. This promotes digestion, and stimulates the appetite, heart and liver. Indeed the ancient herbalists used to call tarragon 'a friend to head, heart and liver'. It was formerly used for toothache and to promote appetite.

Tarragon eggs

This is an interesting way to combine the flavours of tarragon and eggs.

4 eggs
fresh tarragon leaves

Wrap each egg (in its shell) round with strands of tarragon leaves, covering in cling film and then in foil. Store in the refrigerator for 24 hours, then remove the wraps and soft-boil.

TEA

Family: *Ternstroemiaceae*
Genus: *Thea*
Species: *Thea sinensis*

Next to water tea is the most popular drink in the world. There are two basic types of tea, green and black (which is classified as red in China). They are produced by different curing processes. **Green teas** are produced without fermentation and **black teas** are produced with fermentation. In green-tea production, once the leaf buds and leaves have been collected they are treated by steam or dry heat to kill the enzymes, then rolled, dried and finally sorted into different grades. In black-tea production the plant pickings are allowed to wither for a day or so until they are soft enough for rolling. They are then rolled and spread out to ferment, during which process the enzymes go to work converting proteins, amino-acids, fatty acids, phenols and other compounds into new compounds that give black tea a different colour and flavour.

Tea is mentioned in early Chinese writings as 'the gift of heaven' and features in Buddhist legends. It spread to Japan and the Far East but it was not cultivated in India until 1832 when the British introduced it. Not long afterwards it became popular in England and the USA. When it was first introduced in Britain early in the seventeenth century, it was called 'cha' or 'tcha' after the Mandarin and Cantonese dialects spoken in Macao from where it was imported, and some people still speak of 'a cup of char'.

Tea has long been established in the Middle East, first appearing among the conquering Arab armies in the ninth century, and at the time was frowned on by the ruling elite, but the Iranian people and the Mongolian Turks regarded it as their national drink and still do. The Russians like the Iranians have created a whole school of tea-drinking filled with mystique and centred round the samovar. Indeed one of the most delightful experiences of my life was sipping tea in a *Chaihana*, an oasis of green tranquillity in the concrete lack of imagination that was Tashkent in Central Asia.

Nutritional and medicinal properties

Chinese green-tea brews do not contain the same deleterious sprays (like salts of copper) found in the usual imported varieties which cause our imported tea's bad effects, and in China this green tea is valued for its digestive properties, its ability to assist the circulation and regulate body temperature. I visited China at the height of summer when the temperature soared to a sticky 95°F (35°C) and everywhere I went I was offered tall, covered mugs of weak green tea. Sipping it kept me wonderfully cool and left me feeling very refreshed.

100 g TEA

	Leaves (Indian)	Infusion* (Indian)
Calories	108	1
Protein (g)	19.6	0.1
Carbohydrate (g)	3	tr
Cholesterol (g)	–	–
Fat (g)	2	tr
Fibre (g)	–	–
Minerals		
calcium (mg)	430	0.3
phosphorus (mg)	630	1
iron (mg)	15.2	tr
sodium (mg)	45	0.4
potassium (mg)	2160	17
magnesium (mg)	250	1.1
zinc (mg)	3	tr
iodine (mg)	–	–
chlorine (mg)	52	tr
sulphur (mg)	180	–
silicon (mg)	–	–
bromine (mg)	–	–
Vitamins		
A(IU)	0	0
B$_1$ (mg)	0.14	tr
B$_2$ (mg)	1.2	0.01
B$_3$ (mg)	–	6
B$_5$ (mg)	1.3	tr
B$_6$ (mg)	–	–
B$_{12}$ (mcg)	0	0
folic acid (mcg)	–	–
biotin (mcg)	–	–
C (mg)	tr	tr
D (mg)	0	0
E (mg)	–	–
Organic acids		
citric (%)	–	–
malic (%)	–	–
oxalic (%)	–	–
Water (%)	9.3	–
Digestion time (hrs)	–	–

* 10 g tea leaves infused with 100 ml boiling water for 2–10 minutes, then strained.

Black tea contains twice the amount of caffeine (2–4 per cent) in coffee and apparently coffee got its bogus name of caffeine poisoner because people tended to brew it very strongly and so imbibe more caffeine. The theine in tea, like caffeine, makes it a very strong stimulant which excites the nervous system and can cause palpitations and the oversecretion of gastric juices. The tannin in black tea inhibits the proper absorption of iron and can result in indigestion and lack of energy.

Chay-bi-nana (mint tea)

This is drunk all along the coast of North Africa and in the Middle East, where it is sipped with a teaspoon, never from the actual cup which would be considered impolite.

3 teaspoons green tea leaves
1 tablespoon dried mint or better still, *a handful of fresh whole mint leaves*
sugar to taste (optional)

Warm the pot with a little hot water and pour out. Add the tea leaves and pour a little more hot water into the pot. Swirl round again and pour out the water but not the leaves. Add the mint, slightly crushed, and the sugar if desired. Add 1½ pints (900 ml) boiling water and steep for 5 minutes, no more. Taste and serve. If any mint surfaces remove it.

This tea is considered beneficial for upset stomachs, colds and flu.

THYME

Family: *Labiatae*
Genus: *Thymus*
Species: *Thymus vulgaris* (common or garden thyme)

Thyme belongs to the mint family and is closely related to pot marjoram and sweet marjoram. It enjoys dry soils and grows wild all over the low hills of the Mediterranean, Asia Minor and Greece. There are very many varieties of thyme. Garden thyme is an aromatic perennial shrub with somewhat gnarled woody stems, which grows about a foot tall producing grey-green leaves, and lilac to white flowers. It dries extremely well and is in fact very nearly desiccated even when living. The drier the soil, the better thyme thrives. It can also be successfully quick-frozen.

Garden thyme comes originally from southern Europe and the Mediterranean. It was introduced to the rest of Europe some time before the sixteenth century. It exudes a spicy incense-like perfume which is highly attractive to bees, and the word thyme may come from the Greek word for fumigate. Other authorities suggest that the word thyme comes from the Greek *thymbra*, meaning courage. The Greeks almost certainly used not this species but *Thymus capitatus*. Virgil extolled the virtues of thyme honey from Mount Hymettus and anyone who has ever tasted the real thing would certainly endorse his praise. Thyme is believed to have been among the herbs in the manger when Christ was born. In the days of chivalry, ladies would embroider thyme and a honey bee on their scarves, which they would then give as favours to the bravest knights. In the ancient world, thyme was praised for its antiseptic qualities and was used for purification both as a fumigation and taken internally.

In general, when cooking with thyme it should be used sparingly because it is so pungent and warm tasting. It complements peppers, courgettes and aubergines beautifully.

Thyme tea has a strongly bitter-sweet flavour, and is pleasant on its own or with a bit of cinnamon stick.

Nutritional and medicinal properties

Garden thyme contains 1 per cent of volatile oil that is composed mainly of thymol and carvacrol, along with minor amounts of many other aroma chemical compounds. Its other chemical constituents include tannins, flavonoids, phenolic acids such as caffeic acid and chlorogenic acid and triterpene acids. Much of the cultivated garden thyme both in Europe and in the United States is used in the production of thyme oil. This oil is used as a flavouring agent in processed foods, as well as in pharmaceutical and cosmetic products. It is also used as an antiseptic, anti-spasmodic, carminative and counter-irritant or rubefacient, and in commercial products like cough drops, ear drops, mouthwashes and some feminine hygiene products.

The biological effect of garden thyme is due to thymol and/or carvacrol. Both of these have anti-bacterial and anti-fungal properties, as well as anti-spasmodic, carminative and expectorant properties, thymol being the most dominant. They also have anti-parasitic effects particularly against hookworms. Both are irritant to the skin and when ingested by accident can cause nausea, vomiting, stomach ache, headache, dizziness and even convulsions and coma if taken in large quantity, as well as subsequent cardiac and respiratory collapse.

In China, wild thyme has been used for treating arthritis and rheumatoid arthritis with some success. In the West, it is used to treat asthma, and children's respiratory conditions as well as bed-wetting and diarrhoea. It is also recommended for chronic gastric inflammations and is an excellent mouthwash for periodonthritis as well as a superb gargle for throat infections. It can also be used externally for itchy eczema as long as the skin is not broken. Occasionally, a wild thyme wine is used for treating traumatic injuries that make the whole body ache. It is taken internally. The wine is easily made by soaking 62 grams of dried thyme in 1 pint of white wine for 24 hours and then straining.

Bouquet garni

A bouquet garni adds a unique flavour to vegetable stock, and to certain of the more robust vegetable soups.

Tie together two whole bay leaves, two sprigs of thyme dried on the stalk, a few sprigs of fresh parsley, a strip of orange or lemon peel and a piece of celery. Leave a long string on the bunch, so that it can be easily extracted from the pot when the cooking is finished.

TOMATO

Family: *Solanaceae*
Genus: *Lycopersicum*
Species: *Lycopersicum esculentum*

The wild species of tomato probably originated in Peru or Ecuador but long before Columbus discovered America it had reached Mexico and been domesticated. It is thought to have reached Europe from Mexico in 1555. It was usually regarded as a curiosity and was not used for food until the mid 1700s. There is no record of the tomato in the United States until Thomas Jefferson grew it in 1781 but it was not popular until after the Civil War and until this century many people believed it to be poisonous. Certainly it is a member of the *Solanaceae* family, some members of which are extremely poisonous.

Botanically, the tomato is a fruit although its inclusion in the main course of meals makes it seem like a vegetable. For this reason, the US Supreme Court in 1893 classified it as a vegetable for the purpose of trade, a classification which still holds true in the United States today.

The plant is herbaceous, a fast-growing tender perennial which is usually cultivated as an annual in warm and temperate climates of the world. Today it is grown in practically every country in the world in both tropical and temperate climates. But there is an enormous number of varieties and the flavour varies considerably, as does the water content.

Tomatoes which look good are by no means the best ones to buy. The oddly shaped wrinkled ones, which one can often stumble across in Mediterranean countries, have an incomparable taste. Particular varieties of tomato are suitable for particular purposes – for example the plum-shaped one grown in Italy (although of British origin) is good for canning, or conversion into tomato purée. In Mediterranean countries tomatoes are halved and spread out in the sun to dry and then preserved in olive oil. These dried tomatoes develop a very special flavour beside which fresh tomatoes pale. During the winter, the market stalls of some Mediterranean countries sell a very rough tomato purée which has a delightful smoky flavour which permeates the local food quite distinctly. Canned tomatoes are very popular in Italian cookery while commercial tomato purée has a very different flavour, so it is very important in following Mediterranean recipes to use the correct tomato ingredient.

Nutritional and medicinal properties

Tomatoes are an excellent source of vitamins A and C, have a high sugar and water content, and are also high in fibre, potassium and folic acid. The citric, malic and oxalic acids in them will stir up the activity of silicon in the body, loosening stiff joints and so eventually relieving chronic arthritis. Tomatoes are often picked green and ripened during transportation – these are less nutritious than vine-ripened tomatoes. The green parts of the plant contain poisonous alkaloids and should not be eaten.

The tomato is believed to be a natural antiseptic and protects against infection. Copious consumption of tomatoes would help the skin by purifying the blood, and help with gout, rheumatism, TB, hypertension and sinus troubles. There are also indications that tomato is good for cases of congestion of the liver, for dissolving gall-stones, for relieving gas in the stomach, and for colds and obesity. A poultice applied to a troubled skin externally is also helpful. The nicotinic acid in tomatoes is believed to reduce cholesterol in the blood, and the vitamin K is an anti-haemorrhagic.

Summer tomatoes have more vitamin C than winter ones and those staked high are especially rich in this vitamin. Green, unripe tomatoes have slightly more calories, carbohydrate and vitamin A than ripe tomatoes. Boiled tomatoes are nutritionally similar to ripe tomatoes but have a fractionally higher vitamin A content (1000 IU for 100 g compared to 900 IU for the same fresh weight). Canned tomatoes are similar to fresh tomatoes but have less calcium, more sodium and less potassium. Diet canned tomatoes have a very low sodium content. Canned or bottled tomato juice is nutritionally similar to canned tomatoes, but has less fibre, less vitamin A and slightly fewer calories. Tomato purée has more calories, carbohydrate, sodium and vitamins than ripe tomatoes.

100 g TOMATO

	Red ripe	Green
Calories	22	24
Protein (g)	1.1	1.2
Carbohydrate (g)	4.7	5.1
Cholesterol (g)	0	–
Fat (g)	0.2	0.2
Fibre (g)	0.5	0.5
Minerals		
calcium (mg)	13	13
phosphorus (mg)	0.27	27
iron (mg)	0.5	0.5
sodium (mg)	3	3
potassium (mg)	244	244
magnesium (mg)	14	–
zinc (mg)	0.2	–
iodine (mg)	0.01	–
chlorine (mg)	1800	–
sulphur (mg)	500	–
silicon (mg)	175	–
bromine (mg)	2	–
Vitamins		
A(IU)	900	270
B_1 (mg)	0.06	0.06
B_2 (mg)	0.04	0.04
B_3 (mg)	0.7	0.5
B_5 (mg)	0.33	–
B_6 (mg)	0.1	–
B_{12} (mcg)	0	–
folic acid (mcg)	6.4	–
biotin (mcg)	1.5	–
C (mg)	23	20
D (mg)	0	–
E (mg)	0.04	–
Organic acids		
citric (%)	0.38	–
malic (%)	0.12	–
oxalic (%)	0.0075	–
Water (%)	93.5	93
Digestion time (hrs)	2	–

Gazpacho andaluz
(*serves 6*)

This is simplicity itself to make if you have a liquidizer and my husband chides me roundly if he isn't served it on a regular basis throughout the summer – it's a firm favourite of his. I suspect he enjoys ladling in the crisp colourful garnishes just as much as he loves the taste of the soup.

1½ lb (750 g) tomatoes
4 large, thick slices wholemeal bread
3 cloves garlic, crushed
2 dessertspoons apple cider vinegar
about 3 tablespoons olive oil
¾ pint (400 ml) tinned tomato juice
2 tinned red peppers, chopped
1 large Spanish onion, diced
1 small cucumber, diced
black pepper, freshly ground
¾ pint (400 ml) iced water
homemade mayonnaise (optional)

garnish
black olives
hardboiled eggs
1 red and 1 green pepper
1 small cucumber
grated Parmesan cheese (optional)

Remove the skin from the tomatoes, immersing them briefly in boiling water before peeling it off. Remove the seeds and chop the flesh. (If you are hard-pressed, you can get away with tinned tomatoes.) Remove the crust from the bread and use the grinder attachment of the liquidizer to make breadcrumbs with it. Add the garlic to the crumbs, then stir in the vinegar and just as much olive oil as the crumbs will absorb.

In the liquidizer blend the tomato juice and flesh well and gradually add the red peppers, onion and cucumber so that it all becomes smooth. Now add the breadcrumb mixture and liquidize again. Season to taste. Dilute with the water until it is the consistency of thin cream; it can be made creamier by adding a couple of tablespoons mayonnaise. Chill and serve with an ice cube floating in each bowl.

Offer the diced garnishes in separate little bowls. These should be selected according to taste and stirred in until the soup is nearly solid. Hot garlic bread served on the side is an inspired embellishment.

TURNIP

Family: *Cruciferae*
Genus: *Brassica*
Species: *Brassica rapa*

Turnips are part of the mustard branch of the swede family. They are believed to be one of the first vegetables cultivated by man. The Greeks and Romans used them but they later became popular in France and frequently feature in dishes with a high fat content, like duck and mutton dishes, because they have such an affinity to fat. Extensive cultivation of turnips in England began in 1724 when it was first grown as a forage crop.

Main-crop turnips are best eaten in season, in the autumn and winter, though summer supplies are available from harvestings from July to October.

The two main varieties are **globe-shaped turnips** with creamy white skin and pale white flesh, best eaten when they are only 2 inches across and about six weeks old, and **flat-rooted turnips**, with white and scarlet-to-purple tinged skin and pale white flesh.

Turnip tops, which make a delightful dish in their own right, should not be ignored. Choose young sprouting leaves, boil them briefly for 8 minutes and drain. Chop them and return them to the saucepan to dry out, adding seasoning and a knob of butter. These are particularly high in vitamins A, B and C and replete with fibre. A hundred grams provide more than the minimum recommended daily allowance of vitamins A and C.

Nutritional and medicinal properties

Turnips are 90 per cent water so they have little nutrition in them, but their redeeming virtues are their taste and paucity of calories. They do have traces of vitamins and minerals but if you want nutrition eat the young tops. Because of their high water content cook with care, as they tend to quickly degenerate into a water mass.

Raw young turnips, which taste deliciously sweet and crisp and make excellent crudités, are good for cleaning the teeth and strengthening the gums. In the old days turnip water was used to treat coughs, hoarseness and asthma.

Turnips with garlic

The only two things I distinctly recall about my first visit to Italy are having my bottom pinched all the

100 g TURNIP	Raw	Greens (raw)	Boiled	Greens (boiled)
Calories	30	28	23	20
Protein (g)	1	3	0.8	2.2
Carbohydrate (g)	6.6	5	4.9	3.3
Cholesterol (g)	–	–	0	–
Fat (g)	0.2	0.3	0.2	0.2
Fibre (g)	0.9	0.8	0.9	0.7
Minerals				
calcium (mg)	39	246	35	184
phosphorus (mg)	30	58	24	37
iron (mg)	0.5	1.8	0.4	1
sodium (mg)	49	–	34	–
potassium (mg)	268	–	188	–
magnesium (mg)	20	58	20	–
zinc (mg)	–	–	–	0.4
iodine (mg)	0.025	0.076	–	–
chlorine (mg)	830	–	–	–
sulphur (mg)	1210	438	–	–
silicon (mg)	140	–	–	–
bromine (mg)	1.2	4.25	–	–
Vitamins				
A(IU)	tr	7600	tr	6300
B_1 (mg)	0.04	0.21	0.04	0.15
B_2 (mg)	0.07	0.39	0.05	0.24
B_3 (mg)	0.6	0.8	0.3	0.6
B_5 (mg)	0.20	–	0.14	0.3
B_6 (mg)	0.11	–	0.06	0.16
B_{12} (mcg)	0	–	0	0
folic acid (mcg)	20	–	10	110
biotin (mcg)	0.1	–	tr	0.4
C (mg)	36	139	22	69
D (mg)	–	–	–	–
E (mg)	–	–	–	–
Organic acids				
citric (%)	0	–	–	–
malic (%)	0.23	–	–	–
oxalic (%)	0.0018	0.0146	–	–
Water (%)	91.5	90.3	–	–
Digestion time (hrs)	4	3¼	–	–

way up the Appian Way and this recipe. I much preferred the latter. It is an Italian recipe which originates in Genoa.

Halve and clean 1 lb (450 g) baby turnips and blanch them in boiling, slightly salted water for 3 minutes. Drain them, then sweat them gently in a heavy-bottomed pan with lots of olive oil and a suggestion of salt.

Pound two cloves of garlic with a pestle to a creamy paste and add a touch of white-wine vinegar. When the turnips are cooked stir this mix in thoroughly with them. Add some finely chopped parsley. Serve very hot.

VINEGAR

Vinegar is one of the most ancient natural fermentations known to man. In all likelihood it was invented when our ancient ancestors let their beer go sour and started to use the resulting liquid. They probably then found as the result of experience that it could preserve anything from herbs to hides, made tough meat tender and killed germs. It was Louis Pasteur who showed, in 1864, that bacteria present in vinegar were directly responsible for converting alcohol to acetic acid.

The manufacture of vinegar takes place in two stages. First the sugar in the liquid is converted to alcohol by yeast, and then the alcohol is converted to acetic acid by bacteria. So vinegar can be produced by any liquid capable of first being changed to alcohol. The most widely used materials are apples and grapes, which produce cider and wine vinegar respectively, and malted barley and oats.

Industrial alcohol is used in white distilled vinegar.

Vinegar can be made by the slow, natural process where fermented liquid is simply kept in open barrels pierced with enough holes to permit proper air circulation. The alcohol is lighter than the rest of the liquid and rises to the top of the barrel. As it changes to acetic acid in contact with the air it becomes heavier and sinks. The process, which takes anything from one to three years, goes on continually until the whole barrel contains only vinegar.

The quick modern method of making vinegar uses large oak generators. Lukewarm strong, fermented liquid is continually circulated through porous material such as corn cob or wood shavings and then sprayed in fine droplets through the air, a process which converts it to vinegar. The rate of production of vinegar is directly proportional to the amount of surface exposed to the air.

Commercial **wine vinegar** is made by dripping wine through open casks loosely filled with wood shavings to provide plenty of surface. It is on this surface that wine and bacteria are exposed to oxygen in the air. During the process by which the bacteria turn the alcohol to acetic acid, heat is produced. The faster the reaction the more heat there is, and it dries off the volatile aromas – so inferior vinegars are made quickly at the expense of flavour.

Wine vinegar may be red or white, depending on the wine used. Superior varieties are produced by the Orléans and the Boerhaave slow processes. **Malt vinegar**, which has a very strong flavour based on beer, is traditionally made in England and other northern European countries. **Cider vinegar** is made from cider, is particularly popular in America, and is recommended for its health-giving properties. **Distilled vinegar** – natural vinegar distilled in a vacuum – is popular in the North of England and in Scotland. This is a good pickling vinegar. **Spirit vinegar** is made by distilling before all the alcohol is converted to vinegar, giving a very strong-flavoured brew. Other vinegars are made from mead, fruit wine or fermented liquors. Flavoured vinegar, using flavours such as tarragon, thyme or chillies, may be bought or made at home. The flavour permeates through the vinegar as it matures. Synthetic vinegar is made from synthetic acetic acid diluted with water and coloured with caramel. This produces a poor flavour and generally contains harmful chemicals.

Nutritional and medicinal properties

All vinegars except apple cider vinegar increases the acidity of the blood.

Apple cider vinegar is rich in potassium and phosphorus and contains traces of iron, chlorine, sodium, magnesium, sulphur, fluoride, silicon and other trace minerals. Good brands contain 120 milligrams of potassium in each 100 millilitres.

Doctor D. C. Jarvis' famous book *Folk Medicine* describes in detail how he used apple cider vinegar to treat patients suffering from a whole range of ailments from arthritis through to skin complaints, obesity, dizziness and food poisoning. Certainly I advise all my patients suffering from acid diseases to take apple cider vinegar and honey on a regular basis. The dosage is 2 teaspoons of organic apple cider vinegar in one glass of water, and this may be sweetened with honey and drunk hot or cold. I generally encourage them to take a glass with every meal. I also recommend apple cider vinegar as a gargle for sore throats and, in diluted form, to help troubled skin. For the face it can be used in proportions of one part apple cider vinegar to one part of water and for the body it can be added to the bath in proportions of one part apple cider vinegar to ten parts of water.

Pickled cucumbers

This originally appeared in the *Habitat Cooks' Diary* (1980). Normally I give pickles a wide berth, but this is so good it makes me wish I was Jewish. The alum helps keep the pickles crisp, and is available from chemists. Personally, knowing what alum does to your insides, I leave it out. The pickle gets eaten far too quickly to go soggy anyway.

18 sprigs fresh dill
18 cloves garlic
6 mild chilli peppers
36 black peppercorns

1 tablespoon mixed pickling spice
1½ teaspoons alum (optional)
6 lb (3 kg) pickling cucumbers,
   about 3 in (8 cm) long,
   scrubbed

15 pints (8.5 litres) water
12 oz (325 g) coarse salt
8 tablespoons apple cider vinegar
6 vine leaves (optional)

100 g VINEGAR	Distilled vinegar (per 2 tbspns, 28.5 g/ 1 oz)	Vinegar (per 100 g)	Cider vinegar (per 2 tbspns, 28.5 g/ 1 oz)
Calories	1	4	4
Protein (g)	0.1	0.4	tr
Carbohydrate (g)	0.2	0.6	1.7
Cholesterol (g)	0	0	0
Fat (g)	0	0	0
Fibre (g)	0	0	0
Minerals			
calcium (mg)	4	15	1.7
phosphorus (mg)	9	32	2.5
iron (mg)	0.13	0.5	0.17
sodium (mg)	6	20	0.3
potassium (mg)	25	89	29
magnesium (mg)	6	22	–
zinc (mg)	–	–	–
iodine (mg)	–	0	–
chlorine (mg)	–	47	–
sulphur (mg)	–	19	–
silicon (mg)	–	–	–
bromine (mg)	–	–	–
Vitamins			
A(IU)	–	0	–
B_1 (mg)	–	0	–
B_2 (mg)	–	0	–
B_3 (mg)	–	0	–
B_5 (mg)	–	0	–
B_6 (mg)	–	0	–
B_{12} (mcg)	–	0	–
folic acid (mcg)	–	0	–
biotin (mcg)	–	0	–
C (mg)	–	0	–
D (mg)	–	0	–
E (mg)	–	0	–
Organic acids			
citric (%)	–	–	–
malic (%)	–	–	–
oxalic (%)	–	–	–
Water (%)	–	–	–
Digestion time (hrs)	95	–	93.8

Into each of six sterilized jars, put three sprigs of dill, three cloves of garlic, one chilli, six peppercorns, a pinch of pickling spice and the alum if you must. Tightly pack the cucumbers into the jars.

Make the brine by boiling the water with the salt and vinegar and pouring this, while still hot, over the cucumbers. Set aside any brine left over. Cover each jar with a vine leaf, and seal. After two or three days, bubbles will appear, indicating fermentation. Top the jars up with the reserved brine, brought to the boil, and seal the jars once again.

When the brine clears it means the fermentation has stopped. You can eat the pickle four or five days after this. In any case, eat it all within a few months.

pickled for use in chutneys. The ripe dried walnut, which the Greeks called *karyon* (meaning head) because it resembled the human brain, is usually eaten. The shells are thin with a faint sheen, and crack neatly in half, revealing the twisted, curly shaped nut. Walnuts which are barely ripe have a very delicate flavour. Mature nuts are a common flavouring in cakes but are also used in stuffings. Careful selection of walnuts is important because there are many varieties to choose from, and because stale walnuts taste decidedly rancid.

Walnut oil is very expensive but has a wonderful flavour and can be stretched with good results by mixing it half and half with peanut oil or sunflower oil. It is rich in polyunsaturates and is highly recommended for extra special salad dressings.

See also: Nuts, Oils.

Nutritional and medicinal properties

Walnuts are very nutritious and are recommended for liver ailments. Ripe walnuts contain traces of vitamin C, but unripe walnuts contain a substantial quantity. They are said to be good for constipation as they have a definite laxative effect. The leaves of the walnut tree, used both internally and externally, are of benefit in a wide range of eruptive skin conditions, and I prescribe a tincture for this sort of problem with a great deal of success. Poultices soaked in this tincture act as an anti-inflammatory. A tea

WALNUT

Family: *Juglandaceae*
Genus: *Juglans*
Species: *Juglans regia* (English walnut); *Juglans nigra* (black walnut); *Juglans cinerea* (white or butter-nut walnut)

Juglans regia bears the name *regia*, meaning royal, both because of its attractive appearance and because of its historical importance as a source of timber and food. The European walnut is one of the many species found over the northern hemisphere, often in mountainous country. The black walnut and white walnut (or butter-nut walnut) are native to the eastern United States. Walnuts are thought to have originated from Iran or China and were cultivated throughout Europe by the Romans. There are seventeen species throughout the world.

The unripe fruit is known as green walnut and in Britain is

made from the leaves is weakly hypoglycemic.

Walnut oil dressing

I first discovered walnut oil in the Dordogne. Mixed with red wine vinegar, it makes an excellent salad dressing.

6 tablespoons walnut oil
2 tablespoons red wine vinegar
½ teaspoon honey
1 teaspoon grainy mustard
freshly ground black pepper
1 teaspoon finely chopped fresh
*   tarragon*

Swish all the ingredients together in a lidded jam jar and pour over the salad just before serving.

WATER

Water is made up of hydrogen and oxygen in the proportions expressed by the chemical formula H_2O. In its purest form it is a colourless, tasteless, odourless liquid. The human body is 70 per cent water and its replenishment is vital for the digestion and transportation of food within the body, as it is continually lost through these metabolic processes.

Ninety-seven per cent of the world's water occurs in the oceans but this is too salty to drink and very little of it is used in farming or manufacturing. Of the other 3 per cent most comes originally from glaciers and ice-caps. Snow is the most natural form of water, followed by rain. However, the latter nowadays probably contains gases from the air, including carbon dioxide, chlorides, sulphates, nitrates, ammonia, and organic and inorganic dust.

Nutritional and medicinal properties

Our water supply is purified and filtered by the addition of many chemicals, including chlorine and fluorine – the latter in an attempt to reduce tooth decay in children. Chlorine certainly kills germs but significant research has linked chlorine to high blood pressure, anaemia and diabetes and it has even been indicated as a contributor to heart disease. Even in minute quantities, chlorine can undermine the body's defences against atherosclerosis. This is because chlorine creates electrically charged molecules – free radicals – which can combine with alpha-tocopherol, one of the fractions of vitamin E, and eliminate it from the body. Additionally, free radicals can damage the lining of blood vessels and so create an ideal environment for the formation of plaque.

The addition of fluoride to our water has caused a storm of controversy. On the plus side it has been established that when it is taken before the formation of permanent teeth by children fluoride protects against tooth decay. Although it cannot be proved, it appears to provide similar protection for adults. It may also help protect them against osteoporosis and heart attacks. However, it must be remembered that fluoride is one of the trace minerals and therefore needs to be used in really minute quantities. Too much is poison. Fluoride is the most powerful of a group of compounds called halogens which inhibit enzymes by binding up the metal ions they need in order to function properly. Fluoride has been proved to be both mutagenic and carcinogenic.

It would be wise for us to remember that the fluoridization of water is a massive medical experiment that is already banned in ten European countries. Dr George Waldbott, one of medicine's first allergy specialists, has uncovered a condition he calls 'chronic fluoride toxicity syndrome'. Symptoms include chronic fatigue, headaches, excessive water consumption, frequent urination, arthritic-like pains in muscles and bones, gastrointestinal upsets and depressions. He believes that such a wide range of side-effects is due to the fact that fluoride interferes with enzyme functions and mineral balances, and enzymes in particular are the catalysts we need for all our bodily processes.

Wherever the hardness of **hard water** is due to calcium and magnesium, its drinkers have a significantly lower rate of death from heart disease. Calcium is used by the heart muscles for contraction, and magnesium is used to produce the relaxation of the heart muscles between beats. Magnesium can actually act as a preventative – rather than a cause – of kidney stones.

Soft water is generally pro-portionately higher in sodium, which can upset the balance between sodium and potassium, interfering with the electrical impulse responsible for a regular heart-beat. It is therefore wise for soft-water drinkers to supplement their diets with calcium and magnesium. If you can't tell whether your water is soft or hard, make ice-cubes from it. Hard water will make clear cubes with a small white spot in the centre where the minerals concentrate, while soft water will make consistently cloudy ice-cubes.

Distilled water does not exist in nature. It is really dead water which lacks not only the minerals which have been extracted from it, but the electromagnetism. The one thing that can be said in its favour is that it is absolutely pure and, contrary to popular belief, will not leach minerals out of the bones and blood.

As far as nutritional value goes, some bottled **mineral waters** contain certain minerals, but seldom in significant amounts. These do affect the flavour, and waters with a high mineral content taste quite distinctive. For making tea and coffee, bottled still water is favoured by the purists who dislike the taste of tap water or object to the surface scum produced by hard water. Over two-thirds of the bottled water sold in Britain is sparkling – either artificially carbonated or naturally sparkling as the result of carbon dioxide given off by rocks over which the water flows. Still waters occur naturally but some are produced by removing carbon dioxide from sparkling water. All British sparkling waters are artificially carbonated. Since February 1986 bottled waters have been subject to strict regulations regarding composition, purity and labelling.

Some pipes have an effect on the water. Hypertension, nervous and immune disorders and cancer have all been linked to contaminants leached from pipes made with materials such as galvanized iron, plastic, copper, lead, zinc and asbestos-containing cement. The effects tend to be more drastic when the water is soft, because soft water is more acidic than hard. In Britain there is concern about the lead levels in some areas. A nationwide lead survey has been completed in those areas where the level is judged too high and the water will be treated. In a few cases lead plumbing will need to be replaced. Unfortunately, the programme will not be completed until 1989.

Nitrates are seldom present in our drinking water in really significant amounts but in some areas the supply contains more than the maximum 50 milligrams per litre recommended by the EEC guidelines. Water with over 100 milligrams per litre is withdrawn from public consumption and the Department of Environment is currently considering whether or not to lower the acceptable limit to 50 milligrams per litre to bring the UK more in line with the rest of Europe. Water filters, which work out more cheaply than buying bottled mineral water, do not, however, filter out added fluoride

from the water. Most water filters will remove up to 90 per cent of the chlorine, 70–98 per cent of the lead, 95–98 of the mercury, and 50–90 per cent of the cadmium. Check the carton for the filtering agent. One successful and safe filter is finely divided carbon, in the form of charcoal which absorbs and attracts the pollutants.

WATERCRESS

Family: *Cruciferae*
Genus: *Nasturtium*
Species: *Nasturtium officinale*

Watercress is an aquatic plant of the mustard family, and is native to Europe and Asia. It is now widely naturalized in the United States and Canada, is common in the UK and has been introduced to the West Indies and South America.

The plant is a creeping perennial with green rounded leaves and freely rooting succulent stems. It needs a constant supply of fresh, clear, cold, running water, whether it is growing wild or being cultivated.

Watercress is so common that its valuable medicinal and dietetic properties are often forgotten, even though it was once highly regarded as a medicine.

Although cress was cultivated around streams in Britain for many hundreds of years, it was not until 1808 that Mr William Bradbury created the first man-made beds, at Springhead in Kent. In the nineteenth century freshly cut cress was often sold at town markets as a breakfast food for industrial workers. Today in Britain, watercress cultivation is often based around freshwater springs at the base of chalk uplands, in areas like Dorset, Hampshire and Lincolnshire. The main season runs from October to May with two months break during mid-winter due to the severity of the frosts. Watercress is often sold on the same day as being cut and is therefore superbly nutritious. It should never be picked wild, unless you can guarantee the purity of the water in which it has grown.

Watercress has a deliciously spicy, peppery flavour and a pleasingly crisp texture, which makes it ideal for salads and as a garnish for soups and sauces. Even when cooked, it retains its peppery taste.

Nutritional and medicinal properties

Watercress is rich in vitamins A, B_2, C, D and E and contains nicotinamide, as well as various trace minerals, including manganese, iron, phosphorus, iodine, calcium, potassium, sodium and lots of sulphur. Its numerous medicinal attributes from countries all over the world include its use as an aphrodisiac, purgative and asthma remedy. I have found it an excellent cough remedy when mixed with honeycomb. It is also used for eye disorders, bleeding gums, arthritis and rheumatism, hardening of the arteries, kidney and liver cleansing and dropsy. It has antibiotic properties similar to those of the onion family and so makes useful preventive medicine against chronic congestive illnesses. It is also highly alkaline.

Watercress and orange salad

This is one of my favourite salads – a perfect marriage of colour,

100 g WATERCRESS	
Calories	19
Protein (g)	2.2
Carbohydrate (g)	3
Cholesterol (g)	–
Fat (g)	0.3
Fibre (g)	0.7
Minerals	
calcium (mg)	151
phosphorus (mg)	54
iron (mg)	1.7
sodium (mg)	52
potassium (mg)	282
magnesium (mg)	20
zinc (mg)	0.2
iodine (mg)	–
chlorine (mg)	775
sulphur (mg)	5390
silicon (mg)	–
bromine (mg)	–
Vitamins	
A(IU)	4900
B_1 (mg)	0.08
B_2 (mg)	0.16
B_3 (mg)	0.9
B_5 (mg)	0.1
B_6 (mg)	0.13
B_{12} (mcg)	0
folic acid (mcg)	–
biotin (mcg)	0.4
C (mg)	79
D (mg)	0
E (mg)	1
Organic acids	
citric (%)	–
malic (%)	–
oxalic (%)	–
Water (%)	93.3
Digestion time (hrs)	3¼

texture and taste. I haven't given exact quantities, because it depends what flavours you want to emphasize.

2 oranges
little green lettuce hearts or
   shredded iceberg lettuce
1 bunch watercress
a few walnuts, broken

vinaigrette
lemon juice
honey
grainy mustard
freshly ground black pepper
walnut oil
vinegar

Peel the oranges, remove the pith and cut them into segments. Lay these on a bed of well-washed lettuce hearts or shredded lettuce. Cover with well-picked-over sprigs of watercress. Scatter the walnuts on top and dress it all with vinaigrette. Serve immediately.

To make the vinaigrette, mix the seasonings with the lemon juice and honey first, then beat in the oil, and then the vinegar. The proportion of oil to vinegar is usually 3 to 1. Any left-over vinaigrette will keep quite happily in a jar in the cupboard.

WHEAT

Family: *Gramineae*
Genus: *Triticum*
Species: *Tricticum   durum*
         (durum wheat); *Tricticum vulgare* (common wheat for bread)

Wheat is the greatest of the cereals in area and tonnage of cultivation, and in versatility. It originated some 10,000 years ago in the eastern Mediterranean and the most primitive species, emmer wheat, much favoured in the Iron Age, is still grown in inhospitable areas like the highlands of the Middle East. Rivet (or cone) wheat was once the principal wheat of southern England, but is now rarely cultivated and is used only for animal feed. It was introduced into Britain by the Romans, who got most of their grain from Egypt. Wheat was grown in China before the birth of Christ. Columbus took it to the West Indies in 1493, and Cortes took it to Mexico in 1519. Missionaries took wheat to Arizona and California, and English colonists introduced it to Australia.

Until the twentieth century most favoured wheats were over 4 feet tall and the trend has been to improve grain yield with fertilization. The problem is that this produces a heavier head and a longer stalk which tends to fall over and so cannot be easily harvested, so breeders in Japan and Mexico (with the help of research in Cambridge) have now produced varieties which are only waist or knee high. The young plant looks like grass and is bright green, turning golden brown when ripe.

There are about 30,000 varieties of wheat of which only 300 are grown commercially, in the moist, cool temperatures that suits it best; although it can be grown in Arctic to near tropical conditions. At the moment wheat contributes only about a quarter of the average Briton's daily protein.

Commercially popular species of wheat include durum wheats, white wheat, hard red winter wheat and soft winter wheat. **Durum wheats** are ultra-hard and grow mainly in warm dry climates, producing flour for pasta. The grains are amber coloured. Pasta is available as wholemeal, white or coloured with various ingredients. You can buy a quick-cooking variety, and pasta is produced in an infinite variety of shapes. It is easy to make your own and the tasty results are well worth the effort. **White wheat** is low in protein and very starchy. It is used for making breakfast cereals and pastry. **Hard red winter wheat**, is a very quick-growing wheat from Canada. It is ready to harvest within three months and is widely used for bread-baking. **Soft winter wheat** is high in protein and lower in gluten than its hard sister and makes a heavier, different but rather tasty bread. Maris Dove is the most popular British variety.

Most wheat is milled into flour but the wheat grains (or berries, as they are sometimes called) can be used in many interesting dishes. **Wholemeal grain** is cooked like rice in boiling water but it takes a lot longer – about 1½ hours – and emerges chewier; 1 ounce cooks up to 3 ounces. Pre-soaking and pressure-cooking shortens the cooking time. Cook the grains the night before and serve as a breakfast cereal with cold milk and honey. An alternative for breakfast is to reheat it, cooking it into a porridge. Or put some in the bottom of a wide-necked vacuum flask, cover with boiling water, seal securely and leave overnight. Decant and drain. Reheat in fresh hot water. Better still, cook overnight in a crock-pot on low heat using 1 cup of wheat to 4 cups of hot water. Drain and serve with cinnamon and maple syrup.

Cracked wheat is whole wheat grains cracked by pressure machinery which splits the hard outer casing, enabling the grains to cook faster without robbing them of their nutritional value. **Kibbled wheat** is whole wheat grains broken into small pieces in a 'kibbler' instead of being milled. It used for bread-making and breakfast cereals. **Sprouted wheat** is whole wheat grains soaked in water for 8 hours, then placed in a seed-sprouter and rinsed twice daily till the seeds reach the desired size. They have a sweet flavour and are a good source of vitamins B and E.

There are still a few mills in northern England which turn whole wheat grains into **pearled wheat** for frumenty by polishing it in a special drum so that the outer skin layer comes away, and then nipping off the ends of the berry so that each grain, as it cooks, swells into a soft little ball suspended in a creamy jelly, but protected with enough of the skin to make it chewy. Served plain it makes a chewy porridge, and unsweetened will replace rice or potatoes, but it is most delicious of all sweetened with honey and dried fruits, cooked in milk and laced with spices. At a pinch, kibbled or cracked wheat can be used for frumenty but they are not as good as pearled wheat.

See also: Bread, Flours, Grains, Wheatgerm.

100 g WHEAT

	Hard spring	Hard winter	Soft winter	Durum	Wheat bran	White
Calories	330	330	326	332	213	335
Protein (g)	14	12.3	10.2	12.7	16	9.4
Carbohydrate (g)	69.1	71.7	72.1	70.1	61.9	75.4
Cholesterol (g)	–	–	–	–	–	–
Fat (g)	2.2	1.8	2.0	2.5	4.6	2
Fibre (g)	2.3	2.3	2.3	1.8	9.1	1.9
Minerals						
calcium (mg)	36	46	42	37	119	36
phosphorus (mg)	383	354	400	386	1276	394
iron (mg)	3.1	3.4	3.5	4.3	14.9	3
sodium (mg)	3	3	3	3	9	3
potassium (mg)	370	370	376	435	1121	390
magnesium (mg)	160	160	160	160	490	160
zinc (mg)	–	–	–	–	–	–
iodine (mg)	0.001	–	–	–	–	–
chlorine (mg)	7	–	–	–	–	–
sulphur (mg)	9	–	–	–	13	–
silicon (mg)	46	–	–	–	50	–
bromine (mg)	0.15	–	–	–	–	–
Vitamins						
A(IU)	0	0	0	0	0	0
B_1 (mg)	0.57	0.52	0.43	0.66	0.72	0.53
B_2 (mg)	0.12	0.12	0.11	0.12	0.35	0.12
B_3 (mg)	4.3	4.3	3.6	4.4	21	5.3
B_5 (mg)	–	–	–	–	–	–
B_6 (mg)	–	–	–	–	–	–
B_{12} (mcg)	–	–	–	–	–	–
folic acid (mcg)	–	–	–	–	–	–
biotin (mcg)	–	–	–	–	–	–
C (mg)	0	0	0	0	0	0
D (mg)	–	–	–	–	–	–
E (mg)	–	–	–	–	–	–
Organic acids						
citric (%)	–	–	–	–	–	–
malic (%)	–	–	–	–	–	–
oxalic (%)	–	–	–	–	–	–
Water (%)	13	12.5	14	13	11.52	11.5
Digestion time (hrs)	3¾	3¾	3¾	–	2¾	–

Home-made wholemeal noodles

If you enjoy bread baking you'll enjoy this, and home-made noodles, though they may break on cooking, are much tastier than their tame shop-bought cousins.

4 cups stoneground wholemeal flour
1 cup rice flour
generous pinch of sea salt
½ teaspoon mixed dried herbs
4 tablespoons sunflower oil
4 tablespoons cold water

Sift the flours, salt and herbs together through a coarse-meshed sieve. Rub in the oil and then add the water slowly while mixing until you have a really stiff dough. Knead for 10 minutes until the dough feels really tough and stretchy. Roll out very thinly and cut into ½ inch (1 centimetre) strips, each about 4 inches (10 centimetres) long. Leave to rest for 10 minutes. Boil in vegetable broth for 7–8 minutes. Serve immediately.

WHEATGERM

Wheatgerm is the part of the wheat seed that contains material from which new wheat plants grow. The wheat kernel itself contains a small lemon yellow area at its base. This is the wheatgerm or heart of the wheat. Originally, wheat was ground between two flat stones and this method is still found today, although the majority of wheat is milled by steel rollers, which generate heat and can cause the wheatgerm oil to become rancid. The wheatgerm was separated from the wheat and fed to animals until it was discovered to be a very valuable food. It is no coincidence that from the beginning of the century, once the steel-roller process became widespread, there was a rapid increase in the growth of degenerative diseases, particularly heart disease. Prior to the removal of wheatgerm from flour, there were no recorded cases of coronary thrombosis in the USA. Now it is one of the major killer diseases. Some eminent doctors believe that heart disease is directly linked with the amount of vitamin E in the diet, of which wheatgerm is an excellent source.

Natural wheatgerm should be refrigerated as it is perishable and should be bought from shops which store it in a cool place. Rancid wheatgerm has a characteristic sour smell. **Stabilized wheatgerm** is treated to overcome problems of rancidity, but this process destroys much of the goodness so always check the label for the constituents, some of which you may not want to eat.

Wheatgerm oil can be taken as a dietary supplement. It should be refrigerated immediately after purchase and should never be heated. It is very expensive so is generally only used medicinally.

Nutritional and medicinal properties

Using wheatgerm as a supplemental food, you will have an extraordinarily concentrated source of vitamin E. Taking the oil from the germ you have an even greater concentration since all the E is in the oil. You could concentrate it even further by isolating the E from the oil. Of course the further you go in steps of concentration, the more you leave behind in variety and balance.

Wheatgerm oil is also a good source of vitamin F. It is an excellent source of B vitamins and protein.

Great care must be taken to obtain the best quality wheatgerm otherwise what should be good for you will instead be bad. In the case of wheatgerm much of what is available is rancid. Rancidity occurs because most wheatgerm is rolled into flakes, which breaks the sac containing the wheatgerm oil. Exposed to air, oxygen begins to work on the oil and make it rancid. You can be almost certain that if the wheatgerm flakes are not vacuum packed within the day they are rolled, they will be rancid. So never buy wheatgerm flakes that have not been vacuum packed. They should have a sweet smell; if rancid they have an acrid odour. After opening, store them in the refrigerator. The best way of all to guarantee wheatgerm oil will not be rancid is not to buy it in the flake form at all, but unrolled. Unrolled wheatgerm is variously known as embryo, chunk or unflaked wheatgerm. This is, however, harder to find than ordinary wheatgerm.

Octacosanol is the active ingredient in wheatgerm responsible for its proven ability to increase vigour, stamina and endurance. It may also quicken reflexes, increase fertility, prevent miscarriages, lessen the severity of muscular dystrophy and multiple sclerosis, cure pregnancy toxaemia, and strengthen the heart muscles.

100 g WHEATGERM	
Calories	363
Protein (g)	26.6
Carbohydrate (g)	46.7
Cholesterol (g)	0
Fat (g)	10.9
Fibre (g)	2.5
Minerals	
calcium (mg)	72
phosphorus (mg)	1118
iron (mg)	9.4
sodium (mg)	3
potassium (mg)	827
magnesium (mg)	336
zinc (mg)	–
iodine (mg)	–
chlorine (mg)	–
sulphur (mg)	–
silicon (mg)	–
bromine (mg)	–
Vitamins	
A(IU)	0
B_1 (mg)	2.01
B_2 (mg)	0.68
B_3 (mg)	4.2
B_5 (mg)	–
B_6 (mg)	–
B_{12} (mcg)	–
folic acid (mcg)	–
biotin (mcg)	–
C (mg)	0
D (mg)	–
E (mg)	15.8
Organic acids	
citric (%)	0.34
malic (%)	–
oxalic (%)	–
Water (%)	11.5
Digestion time (hrs)	3

Wheatgerm pancakes

Wheatgerm is very versatile and can be added to almost any food. These pancakes are a particularly delicious way to get a lot down you all at once and are very quick to make.

6 eggs
5 tablespoons cottage cheese
⅔ cup wheatgerm
¼ teaspoon vanilla essence

1 tablespoon unsalted butter
maple syrup

Liquidize the eggs, cheese, wheatgerm and vanilla for 30 seconds. Melt the butter in a 10 in (25 cm) heavy-bottomed frying pan. Pour in all the egg mixture and cook over a medium heat till browned on the bottom. Turn and brown on the other side. Serve immediately with maple syrup.

YEAST

This is a fungus consisting of minute single-celled plants which exist in soil and fruit. It is used both as a raising agent and as an agent of fermentation, so it is deliberately cultivated for baking bread and for wine-making. The yeast plant can change sugar into carbon dioxide and alcohol.

Most people are familiar with baker's yeast, which looks rather like a cheese and smells of beer. It is actually composed of millions of yeast plants, which multiply by budding when grown in a suitable warm, sugary medium, such as fruit juice. In bread-making, to activate the yeast into growth it is necessary to add the carbohydrate, sugar, liquid and warmth. Excess sugar, cold, fat or salt will retard the growth of the yeast, while excessive heat will kill the plant. As the yeast grows, a ferment is produced which breaks down the carbohydrate and produces alcohol and bubbles of carbon dioxide which cause the dough to rise and appear porous.

When the bread is baked the alcohol is evaporated and the yeast plant destroyed. If left to rise too long, the fermentation forms acid.

Fresh compressed yeast is moist and crumbly and preferred by some to dried yeast. It is obtainable from specialist food stores and bakeries and will keep, if well wrapped, in a refrigerator for 2–3 days. If correctly wrapped, it can be frozen for several months. **Dried yeast** is a concentrated dormant form of yeast, available from most shops in tins and packets. If stored in air-tight conditions, it will keep up to six months. When substituting dried yeast in a recipe for fresh, use half the quantity and follow the packet directions.

Brewer's yeast is a weak semi-liquid yeast used for beer and ale making. **Wine yeasts** are naturally present on the grape and their flavour is superior for wine-making.

When fresh brewer's yeast is mixed with salt it is broken down by its own enzymes. The soluble residue is evaporated under pressure to give a sticky brown substance called **yeast extract** (the best-known proprietary name for this in the UK is Marmite). Be wary of the yeast extracts, as they can be appallingly high in added salt (1 oz often contains 1300 mg salt), though there are low-salt varieties available.

Nutritional and medicinal properties

Brewer's yeast contains an extremely rich concentration of nutrients. It comes closer than anything else to being a 'super food'. It contains sixteen of the twenty amino-acids and the complete B-complex range; it is especially rich in B_1 and B_2, but also contains niacinamide, pantothenic acid, biotin, cholin, pyridoxine, folic acid, vitamin B_{12} and inositol. It also has large amounts of phosphorus, iron and calcium and two of the vital trace elements, chromium and selenium, Yeast varies according to the medium on which it is grown and not all

100 g YEAST	Compressed baker's	Dried	Marmite
Calories	53	169	179
Protein (g)	11.4	35.6	39.7
Carbohydrate (g)	1.1	3.5	1.8
Cholesterol (g)	–	–	–
Fat (g)	0.4	1.5	0.7
Fibre (g)	6.9	21.9	–
Minerals			
calcium (mg)	25	80	95
phosphorus (mg)	390	1290	1700
iron (mg)	5	20	3.7
sodium (mg)	16	50	4500
potassium (mg)	610	2000	2600
magnesium (mg)	59	230	180
zinc (mg)	2.6	8	2.1
iodine (mg)	–	–	–
chlorine (mg)	–	–	6600
sulphur (mg)	–	–	–
silicon (mg)	–	–	–
bromine (mg)	–	–	–
Vitamins			
A(IU)	–	–	–
B_1 (mg)	0.71	2.33	3.1
B_2 (mg)	1.7	4	11
B_3 (mg)	–	–	–
B_5 (mg)	3.5	11	–
B_6 (mg)	0.6	2	1.3
B_{12} (mcg)	tr	tr	0.5
folic acid (mcg)	1250	4000	1010
biotin (mcg)	60	200	–
C (mg)	tr	tr	0
D (mg)	0	0	0
E (mg)	tr	tr	–
Organic acids			
citric (%)	–	–	–
malic (%)	–	–	–
oxalic (%)	–	–	–
Water (%)	70	5	25.4
Digestion time (hrs)	–	–	–

brewer's yeast contains B$_{12}$. The torula (nutritional or 'candida') yeast was developed with a de-bittered taste. It is usually grown on waste sulphite liquor from wood pulp.

If you are not accustomed to it, nutritional yeast can cause flatulence due to the high concentration of B vitamins. To prevent this, begin with small portions and increase gradually. In my view, the best way to start is with ¼ teaspoon for several days, then increasing every third or fourth day by a further ¼ teaspoon until a level 1–2 teaspoons a day is reached. If you have followed the gradual approach but flatulence still persists into the second month it may be because there is insufficient stomach acid to handle the protein. This can be corrected by taking hydrochloric-acid tablets or by sipping two teaspoons of apple cider vinegar in some water before taking the brewer's yeast — this activates the production of hydrochloric acid in the stomach.

Warning Never take baker's yeast or any other live yeast as a food supplement. The live yeast goes on working in the gut and actually eats up the vitamin B in the body. This includes yeast used for brewing. If you are a home brewer and you want to make use of spent yeast you should rinse it in fresh water, dry it and then de-activate the yeast by heating it to 95°F (35°C) in the oven for 30 minutes.

Also note that torula yeasts can upset some people, but this tends to be true only if it is grown in waste sulphite liquor. If in doubt write to the manufacturer and ask for the source.

Pineapple and carrot pick-up

If you prefer your brewer's yeast sweetly disguised, try this.

2 cups unsweetened pineapple juice
½ cup diced really fresh carrot
1 tablespoon orange juice
1 tablespoon brewer's yeast
a touch of honey.

Liquidize vigorously. Serve.

YOGHURT

This is a semi-solid dairy product produced by fermenting milk with a culture of bacteria. During the fermentation process the lactose (milk sugar) is converted to lactic acid, which causes the milk to clot. The name yoghurt comes from Turkey and yoghurt has been eaten for centuries in the Balkans, Armenia and Iran. Poor sanitation causes milk to become contaminated, but fermentation acts as a preservative so that yoghurt can be eaten safely even when other dairy products cannot. Yoghurts in different parts of the world will vary from a smooth, creamy, set curd to a fermenting one which smells beery and is full of bubbles. Sheep's milk undoubtedly makes the finest yoghurt but cow's milk is more digestible, and tiny babies get on best with goat's milk yoghurt.

Yoghurt can be successfully made at home, although most is now commercially made. Our modern taste demands a yoghurt which is less acidic and often fruit sugar and preservatives are added so that the culture is killed off. Commercial yoghurt has various forms of gelatine and vegetable gums added for thickness, all of which denature the yoghurt, whether they be gelatine, agar-agar or guar gum. Supermarket shelves are increasingly packed with fruited yoghurts whose sugar, artificial flavours and colouring make what should be a superior food into a totally worthless one. A common ruse with fruited yoghurt is the phrase 'no sugar added', which disguises the fact that the fruit preserves bought by the yoghurt manufacturer to flavour the yoghurt *already* have the sugar and corn syrup added by the fruit-preserve manufacturer.

The list of non-yoghurt ingredients found lurking in frozen yoghurt would not embarrass a chemical factory and include sugar, corn syrup, sodium citrate, polysorbate 80, vegetable gum, gelatine, carboxymethyl cellulose, mono- and diglycerides, artificial flavours and artificial colouring. Commercial frozen yoghurt, especially the thickest and creamiest, may not have any live yoghurt culture added to it at all.

The problem with most commercially made yoghurts is that they are made by the 'flash' method, taking about 3 hours. Your own home-made yoghurt will undoubtedly be superior and take some 6–7 hours, time for the full development of the health-giving yoghurt micro-organisms, *Lactobacillus vularis* and *Streptococcus lactis*. Properly developed in the ideal temperature range, home-made yoghurt will have a firm custard-like consistency. Making your own also eliminates sugar, as well as artificial colourings and flavourings – commercially flavoured yoghurt has almost as many calories as ice-cream.

Nutritional and medicinal properties

Yoghurt has the same food value as milk except that it has a lower sugar level and is more acidic. It is a good source of protein and calcium and contains as few as 15 calories per ounce, so it is good for dieters (but beware of the commercially flavoured yoghurts). It is an excellent whole protein in itself and contains significant amounts of carbohydrate and vitamins B_2 and B_3. Many manufacturers also add vitamins A, C and D.

In 1904 Ilya Metchnikoff of the Pasteur Institute of Paris began to research into the properties of yoghurt. He published his findings in *The Prolongation of Life* in 1908 and his research gave rise to a burgeoning interest in yoghurt throughout the world. His own interest was first sparked by the longevity of Bulgarian peasants who ate large amounts of milk soured with *Lactobacillus bulgaricus* – a food now commonly known as yoghurt.

Modern research has since confirmed his findings. *Lactobacil-*

lus does indeed create an environment hostile to harmful bacteria. The yoghurt breaks down milk to lactic acid and the bacteria which cause putrefaction in the form of gas cannot live in this lactic acid. Yoghurt bacteria are also capable of manufacturing the entire range of B-complex vitamins in the intestine. This is very important because many modern drugs kill intestinal flora.

Another advantage of yoghurt is that people who are allergic to milk can generally eat it safely. The bacterial culturing agent consumes most of the lactose, which is one of the main reasons for intolerance to milk, particularly in adults. The bacteria also acts on the milk protein so that it becomes in effect pre-digested. The changes to the lactose and protein of milk in yoghurt render it easily digestible, even by chronic invalids.

Home-made yoghurt

Yoghurt-making is an extremely simple process which requires a minimum of special equipment. If you're a beginner you will need a dairy thermometer.

2 pints (1.25 litres) milk (whole milk will make creamier yoghurt, skimmed milk will have fewer calories)
½ cup non-fat dried milk powder (if desired – see below)
yoghurt culture or 2 tablespoons plain yoghurt.

If the yoghurt you use for a starter fails to work, it probably means the yoghurt is wcakly cultured. Use the yoghurt failure in stock for cooking and try again. The success or failure of a commercial yoghurt as a starter for home-made yoghurt will tell you a lot about the commercial yoghurt's quality.

Milk powder will thicken the yoghurt. Too much will make it chalky. Personally I like my yoghurt thin so I omit the milk powder. Adding more culture will thicken the yoghurt up to a point, then it won't go any thicker. Too much culture will make it very tart. Too little will make it lumpy. The absolutely vital ingredient is a good culture.

1. Heat the milk to scalding (170°F/77°C kills the bacteria that interfere with the yoghurt process, and remember that most dairy animals are heavily injected with antibiotics in their feed). Milk tends to scorch if heated too quickly, even if it is stirred frequently, so take your time and heat it over a low heat. Allow to boil for 5 seconds.
2. Cool the milk down to 120°F/49°C. Whisk the milk powder with some of the heated milk in a separate bowl (or liquidize it). Stir this into the rest of the milk.
3. Cool to 115°F/46°C. At this temperature you should be able to put your finger into the milk and feel it is very hot but not too hot to keep your finger in it. Add the culture (or plain yoghurt) to the milk and stir well.
4. Pour the milk into an immaculately clean container, cover with a clean cloth, insulate

and leave to thicken, which will take between 3 and 8 hours depending on the culture or yoghurt used.

5. To test for readiness bury a chopstick upright in the centre of the yoghurt. If it stands by itself, the yoghurt is ready. Incubated

too long it will become too tart.

6. Refrigerate until well chilled.

Suggestions for insulation
★ A wide-necked thermos.
★ A Kilner jar (or other glass preserving jar) wrapped up in towels.

100 g YOGHURT

	Natural	Flavoured	Fruit	Hazelnut
Calories	52	81	95	106
Protein (g)	5	5	4.8	5.2
Carbohydrate (g)	6.2	14	17.9	16.5
Cholesterol (g)	0	–	–	–
Fat (g)	1	0.9	1	2.6
Fibre (g)	0	–	–	–
Minerals				
calcium (mg)	180	170	160	180
phosphorus (mg)	140	140	140	140
iron (mg)	0.09	0.16	0.24	0.23
sodium (mg)	76	64	64	70
potassium (mg)	240	220	220	240
magnesium (mg).	17	17	17	20
zinc (mg)	0.6	0.64	0.63	0.69
iodine (mg)	–	–	–	–
chlorine (mg)	180	160	150	160
sulphur (mg)	–	–	–	–
silicon (mg)	–	–	–	–
bromine (mg)	–	–	–	–
Vitamins				
A(IU)	70	–	–	–
B_1 (mg)	0.05	0.05	0.05	0.06
B_2 (mg)	0.26	0.25	0.23	0.27
B_3 (mg)	0.1	–	–	–
B_5 (mg)	–	–	–	–
B_6 (mg)	0.04	0.04	0.04	0.04
B_{12} (mcg)	tr	tr	tr	tr
folic acid (mcg)	2	8	3	5
biotin (mcg)	–	–	–	–
C (mg)	0.4	0.4	1.8	0.4
D (mg)	tr	tr	tr	tr
E (mg)	0.03	0.04	0.07	0.58
Organic acids				
citric (%)	–	–	–	–
malic (%)	–	–	–	–
oxalic (%)	–	–	–	–
Water (%)	85.7	79	74.9	73.4
Digestion time	–	–	–	–

* Leave the jar on top of a heating pad, set low.
* Leave the jar (wrapped) in a warm airing cupboard.
* Put in a gas oven heated by the pilot light.
* In the summer put the jar outside, sheltered from the wind.

Personally I prefer the undisturbed insulation method to the electrical type of yoghurt maker. I think it produces a better tasting yoghurt. Perhaps this is because the very gradual drop in temperature of some 15°F allows the full range of biological activities to take place whereas this is impossible in a machine that maintains a constant temperature.

Yoghurt culture

In the Middle East and Eastern Europe it is still common to pass strains of yoghurt from one generation to the next. While at university I once helped to keep a yoghurt culture alive for nearly a year.

Most commercial yoghurt cultures are made with specific proportions of different freeze-dried bacteria. During succeeding batches of yoghurt various alterations of composition can, and with most cultures usually do, occur. One type of bacteria begins to dominate the others and harmless airborne bacteria join the yoghurt and multiply. Consequently the acidity level changes and with it the taste and consistency. At this point it is time to buy another envelope of starter. On average this will take about two months if you're making yoghurt every week.

A lot depends on the kind of milk you use. Skimmed milk, soya milk, goat's milk, cream and sterilized milk can all be successfully used. Cow's milk yoghurt is inclined to curdle when heated but this can be prevented by a little flour or other stabilizer.

BIBLIOGRAPHY

An exhaustive list of all my sources would be tedious rather than helpful. Apart from the books mentioned in the text these are all books that have been of special help and interest to me.

Ehret, Arnold, *Mucusless Diet Healing System* (Ehret Literature Publishing Co., Cody, Wyoming, 1953)

Ballentine, Rudolph, *Diet and Nutrition* (Himalayan International Institute, Honesdale, Pennsylvania, 1982)

Bircher, Ruth, *Eating Your Way to Health* (Faber & Faber, London, 1961)

Walker, Caroline & Cannon, Geoffrey, *The Food Scandal* (Century, London, 1984)

Trum Hunter, Beatrice, *The Great Nutrition Robbery* (Charles Scribner's Sons, New York, 1978)

Hall, Dorothy, *The Natural Health Book* (Angus & Robertson, London, 1976)

Roden, Claudia, *A Book of Middle Eastern Food* (Penguin, London, 1968)

Hartley, Dorothy, *Food In England* (Macdonald, London, 1954)

David, Elizabeth, *French Country Cooking* (Penguin, London, 1958)

Van der Seder, Elzra & Gevaert, Annette, *Cooking for a Healthier Life* Volume I (Luna Publication 9830, Latem, Belgium)

Hutchens, Alma, *Indian Herbology of North America* (Ontario, 1982)

Stobart, Tom, *Herbs, Spices and Flavouring* (Penguin, London, 1977)

Colbin, Anne-Marie, *The Book of Whole Meals* (Ballantine Books, New York, 1983)

Peterson, Vicki, *The Natural Food Catalog* (Avco Publishing Company Inc., New York, 1978)